Leon Trotsky Speaks

Leon Trotsky in 1940.

Leon Trotsky Speaks

Pathfinder Press, Inc.
New York

ACKNOWLEDGMENTS

Permission has been granted by the publishers to reprint material from the following:

Documents of Russian History, 1914-1917, edited by Frank A. Golder. The Century Company, New York, 1927, reprinted by permission of Appleton-Century-Crofts, Educational Division, Meredith Corporation.

Soviet Documents on Foreign Policy (Volume I), edited by Jane Degras, published by Oxford University Press under the auspices of the Royal Institute of International Affairs.

The Prophet Armed by Isaac Deutscher, Copyright 1954. *The Prophet Outcast* by Isaac Deutscher, Copyright 1963. Oxford University Press.

The Russian Revolution by Marcel Liebman. Copyright 1967 by Les Editions Gerard & Co. Translation Copyright 1970 by Jonathan Cape Limited. Published in the United States by Random House, Inc.

To the Finland Station by Edmund Wilson. Doubleday & Co., Inc. Permission by Edmund Wilson.

Trotsky's Diary in Exile, 1935 by Leon Trotsky. Cambridge, Mass.: Harvard University Press, Copyright 1958, by the President and Fellows of Harvard College.

First Edition, 1972

Edited by Sarah Lovell

Pathfinder Press, Inc.
410 West Street
New York, N.Y. 10014

CONTENTS

PREFACE

The growing number of books by Leon Trotsky in print or in preparation now attests to a growing interest in his life, ideas, and personality. In an age of revolution this is understandable as Trotsky was above all a revolutionary, probably the greatest of the century next to his contemporary Lenin. The present collection, unlike other Trotsky anthologies which are based primarily on his books, pamphlets, and other written works, is focused on his speeches.

Along with his other talents — theoretician, writer, military commander, organizer, historian, social and cultural critic — Trotsky had great oratorical powers, of which there is testimony from those who heard him and from those who studied his work.

Anatoly V. Lunacharsky, commissar of education in the first Soviet government and a notable speaker himself, gave an evaluation of Trotsky as a speaker which appeared in a small book, *Silhouettes,* written in 1923 when he had known Trotsky for almost two decades:

"The chief external endowments of Trotsky are his oratorical gift and his talent as a writer. I consider Trotsky probably the greatest orator of our times. I have heard in my day all the great parliamentary and popular orators of socialism, and very many of the famous orators of the bourgeois world, and I should have difficulty in naming any of them, except Jaures, whom I might place beside Trotsky.

"Effective presence, beautiful broad gesture, mighty rhythm of speech, loud, absolutely tireless voice, wonderful compactness, literariness of phrase, wealth of imagery, scorching irony, flowing pathos, and an absolutely extraordinary logic, really steel-like in its clarity — those are the qualities of Trotsky's speech. He can speak epigrammatically, shoot a few remarkably well-aimed arrows, and he can pronounce such majestic political discourses as I have heard elsewhere only from Jaures. I have seen Trotsky talk for two and a half to three hours to an absolutely silent audience, standing on their feet, and listening as though bewitched to an enormous political treatise."

Similar estimates are made by writers who did not know and hear Trotsky personally. Isaac Deutscher, the biographer of Trotsky, studied his speeches in the Russian and investigated the opinions of people who had heard Trotsky speak. In *The Prophet Armed,* finished in 1952 as book one of his trilogy, Deutscher wrote of the twenty-three-year-old Trotsky after his first escape from Siberia in 1902:

"No sooner had he arrived in London than Lenin and Martov pitted him in debate against venerable old Narodnik and anarchist emigres in Whitechapel. The novice was pleasantly surprised at the ease with which he swept the floor with his gray-bearded opponents. After that he toured the Russian colonies in western Europe. Contemporaries have described the first sudden and irresistible impact of his oratory, the elan, the passion, the wit, and the thunderous metallic voice, with which he roused audiences and bore down upon opponents. This appears all the more remarkable as only a few years before he could only stammer in blushing perplexity before a tiny, homely audience and as he had spent most of the time since in the solitude of prison and exile. His oratory was quite untutored: he had hardly yet heard a single speaker worthy of imitation. This is one of those instances of latent unsuspected talent, bursting forth in exuberant vitality to delight and amaze all who witness it."

The literary critic Edmund Wilson, in his 1940 study of the Russian Revolution *To the Finland Station,* drew the following picture of Trotsky in the 1905 revolution:

"He had developed, through much lecturing in exile, into an extraordinary public speaker—it was the opinion of Lunacharsky that he even surpassed Jaures—a master of both delivery and argument, who, whatever the imperfections of his relationships with people as individuals, had the genius for compelling them in the mass. He could handle the grim Marxist logic with a freer and more sweeping hand so as to make it an instrument for persuasion and wield the knife of the Marxist irony for purposes of public exhibition, when he would flay the officials alive and, turning their skins inside out, display the ignominious carcasses concealed by their assurances and promises; he could dip down and raise a laugh from the peasant at the core of every Russian proletarian by hitting off something with a proverb or fable from that Ukrainian countryside of his youth; he could point epigrams with a swiftness and a cleanness that woke the wonder of the cleverest intellectuals; and he could throw wide the horizons of the mind to a vision of that dignity and liberty that every man among them there should enjoy."

In a more recent study completed in 1967, *The Russian Revolution,* Marcel Liebman saw Trotsky as "the poet" of the 1917 revolution:

"It was he who at meeting after meeting, in proclamation after proclamation, gave voice to the enthusiasm and fury of the people; he who had his finger on the people's pulse; he who made it beat faster; he who showed the entire nation that their actions had a scope far beyond the narrow confines of Russia.

"Life had fully prepared him for his double role of organizer and poet of the revolution. To begin with he was an outstandingly talented writer and speaker; he had the temperament of an artist and the brain of a mathematician. As a writer he scaled the heights; as an orator he was peerless."

Trotsky himself left accounts of his speaking during the turbulent events of 1917. In his autobiography written in 1929, *My Life,* he recalled:

"Life was a whirl of mass meetings. When I arrived in Petrograd, I found all the revolutionary orators either hoarse or voiceless. The revolution of 1905 had taught me to guard my voice with care, and thanks to this, I was hardly ever out of the ranks. Meetings were held in plants, schools, and colleges, in theaters, circuses, streets, and squares. I usually reached home exhausted after midnight; half-asleep I would discover the best arguments against my opponents, and about seven in the morning, or sometimes even earlier, I would be pulled painfully from my bed by the hateful, intolerable knocking on the door, calling me to a meeting in Peterhof, or to go to Kronstadt on a tug sent for me by the navy boys there. Each time it would seem to me as if I could never get through this new meeting, but some hidden reserve of nervous energy would come to the surface, and I would speak for an hour, sometimes two, while delegations from other plants or districts, surrounding me in a close ring, would tell me that thousands of workers in three or perhaps five different places had been waiting for me for hours on end. How patiently that awakening mass was waiting for the new word in those days!

"The mass meetings in the Modern Circus were for me quite special. My opponents likewise considered them so, but in a different light. They regarded the Circus as my particular fortress, and never even attempted to speak in it. But whenever I attacked the conciliationists in the Soviet, I was interrupted by bitter shouts: 'This is not your Modern Circus.' It became quite a refrain.

"I usually spoke in the Circus in the evening, sometimes quite late at night. My audience was composed of workers, soldiers, hard-working mothers, street urchins — the oppressed underdogs of the capital. Every square inch was filled, every human body compressed to its limit. Young boys sat on their fathers' shoulders; infants were at their mothers' breasts. No one smoked. The balconies threatened to fall under the excessive weight of human bodies. I made my way to the platform through a narrow human trench, sometimes I was borne overhead. The air, intense with breathing and waiting, fairly exploded with shouts and with the passionate yells peculiar to the Modern Circus. Above and around me was a press of elbows, chests, and heads. I spoke from out of a warm cavern of human bodies; whenever I stretched out my hands I would touch someone, and a grateful movement in response would give me to understand that I was not to worry about it, not to break off my speech, but keep on."

Few of Trotsky's speeches were transcribed before 1917; he was able to make few after 1929, when he was exiled from the Soviet Union.

One of the latter was made at Trotsky's home in Coyoacan, Mexico, on November 7, 1937, at a celebration of the Russian Revolution and of Trotsky's birthday, which dates coincide. This was described by Joseph Hansen, Trotsky's secretary and guard, in his introduction to the 1970 edition of *My Life*:

"During the day the patio and house filled with people coming for the fiesta. They were mostly very poor people, members of the unions in which Trotsky's Mexican followers were active.
. . .

"Trotsky, of course, was called on to make a speech. I noticed that he seemed hesitant. No doubt he would have preferred to avoid it. After all, he had arrived in Mexico only the previous January and the speech had to be given in Spanish. Despite his reluctance, there was no escape.

"He appeared to brace himself, as if he were taking a deep breath. He stepped forward to the balustrade; and he was transformed. He took complete possession and spoke out as if this were completely natural and something he did every day. He pitched his voice so that it soared somewhat and could be heard with complete ease.

"It was a simple speech of thanks and appreciation. A few words about the October Revolution and its meaning. An expression of gratitude for the hospitality of Mexico and the warmth of the Mexican people.

"Trotsky spoke only a few minutes but it gave me a glimpse of him as a speaker. It was quite clear that he had studied the art and had practiced it until it had become virtually effortless for him. He was decidedly not of the school that speaks at an audience or reads it a lecture, glass of water in one hand, hanging on to the podium with the other.

"The audience responded with emotion and acclaim."

Trotsky also made a striking impression when he spoke informally with visitors, journalists, and his comrades. Jean van Heijenoort, who served as Trotsky's secretary and guard in all four countries of his last exile, remembered in a 1941 essay, "Lev Davidovich" (reprinted in *Leon Trotsky, The Man and His Work,* 1969):

"In conversations with Lev Davidovich what visitors were struck by chiefly was his capacity to find his bearings in a novel situation. He was able to integrate it in his general perspective, and at the same time always give immediate and concrete advice. During his third emigration he often had the opportunity of conversing with visitors from countries he was not acquainted with directly, perhaps from the Balkans or Latin America. He did not always know the language, did not follow their press, and had never had any particular interest in their specific problems. First of all he would allow his interrogator to speak, occasionally jotting down a few brief notes on a slip of paper in front of him, sometimes asking for a few details: 'How many members has this party?' 'Isn't this politician a lawyer?'

"Then he would speak, and the mass of information that had been given him would be organized. Soon one could distinguish the movements of different classes and of different layers within these classes, and then, bound up with these movements, there would be revealed the play of parties, groups, and organizations, and then the place and the activities of various political figures, down to their profession and personal traits, would be logically fitted into the picture."

When Trotsky spoke " . . . what attracted attention was his mouth. Whether he spoke in Russian or a foreign language his lips constrained themselves to shape words distinctly. He was irritated at hearing confused and precipitate speech from others, and always compelled himself to enunciate with complete distinctness. It was only in addressing Natalia Ivanovna in Russian that on occasion his enunciation became more hurried and less articulate, descending sometimes into a whisper. In conversations with visitors in his study his hands, resting on the edge of his worktable at first, would soon begin moving with large, firm gestures, as though aiding his lips in molding the expression of his thought."

Many of Trotsky's speeches were never transcribed; others were transcribed but remain locked in the files of the Soviet secret police; still others remain to be translated. The aim of the present volume is to provide a selection of Trotsky's speeches representative of his style and content in the three periods into which we have divided his political career. To better serve as an introduction to Trotsky, the speeches are preceded by background historical and biographical information and are followed by notes about persons, groups, and events cited by Trotsky with which the reader of today may not be familiar. While the majority of this volume consists of actual speeches, we have not hesitated to include items whose contents added something substantial.

None of the material printed here has been abridged by us; the texts are either complete or were abridged before their first appearance in print. With few exceptions, we have avoided using speeches readily available in other Trotsky books and pamphlets. Some translations were made especially for this book; with the others, we have taken the liberty of revising spellings, punctuation, etc., in order to achieve greater stylistic uniformity. Credit to the translators, when known, and data about sources are given in the prefatory information to each chapter.

Sarah Lovell
January 1972

PART ONE

Preparing the Revolution

begins in 1906 when the twenty-six-year-old leader of the St. Petersburg Soviet stands in a czarist courtroom and answers charges of trying to overthrow the Russian government in the 1905 revolution; follows him through his escape to Europe and a ten-year exile during which World War I begins and he writes the manifesto of the first wartime international conference against the war; finds him in New York when Russian czarism is overthrown; takes him back to Russia where he becomes president of the Soviet and organizer of the insurrection; and concludes with a speech he is making on the day the Soviets have established a revolutionary government at the end of 1917.

Trotsky at the age of eighteen.

1

On Trial for Insurrection

Although Leon Trotsky (born Lev Davidovich Bronstein on November 7, 1879) was not quite twenty-seven years old when he went on trial for insurrection in 1906, he was a veteran of revolutionary politics. His initiation began when he was seventeen, a high-school student at Nikolayev in the Ukraine. Arrested two years later for helping to build an underground organization of students and workers, he was held in prison for two and a half years and then sentenced without trial to four years' deportation in Siberia. He and Alexandra Lvovna Sokolovskaya, another leader of the Nikolayev group, were legally married so that they could live together in Siberia; two daughters were born there.

In the prisons and the Siberian camps of czarist Russia and in the exile colonies of Europe the future leaders of Russia were developing revolutionary theory and organization. Deportation broadened Trotsky's outlook and deepened his education. He had already declared his support of Marxism, one of the tendencies competing for the allegiance of the prisoners and exiles. Now he had a chance to study, debate, and grow politically. He joined the Social Democratic Siberian Union and became a supporter of the paper Iskra *[Spark], published abroad by Lenin, Plekhanov, and other leaders of the Russian Social Democracy.*

Siberia now became too confining. With Alexandra Lvovna's help, he escaped and went abroad to what he felt was the center of the Russian political struggle, the Iskra *group. Arriving in London at the age of twenty-three, he was welcomed by Lenin and drawn into the work of writing and debating the anti-Marxist emigres. But his collaboration with Lenin was cut short the following year when the Russian Social Democratic Workers' Party, section of the Second International, held its second congress in 1903, and the party split into two parts— the Bolsheviks (majority), led by Lenin, and the Mensheviks (minority), led by Martov. The basic cause of this rupture was conflicting opinion about the organizational character of the revolutionary party.*

Lenin by this time had definite ideas on the kind of party

required to lead a revolution. His conception, which he soon
would term "democratic centralism," demanded that the revolutionary party, while democratic in decision-making, be
highly centralized and disciplined in action.

Trotsky opposed Lenin's arguments as elitist and aligned
himself with the Mensheviks. Soon after, however, he left the
Mensheviks over political differences. For the next decade he
remained independent of both factions and tried to reunite the
party.

In the midst of the 1917 revolution, Trotsky saw the need
for Lenin's kind of party and joined the Bolsheviks, an independent party since 1912. He viewed his 1903 break with
Lenin on this question as the major error of his political career, and defended Lenin's organizational theory and practice
for the rest of his life. From 1917 on, Lenin said later, there
was "no better Bolshevik."

Trotsky's major difference with the Mensheviks in 1904 concerned their attitude to the coming Russian revolution. The Mensheviks looked to the liberal capitalists as the leaders in the
overthrow of the monarchy; Trotsky to the workers. This
was to be the keystone of his thinking on the character of the
revolution, the theory of permanent revolution, which was
about to receive its first test in the stormy events that began
in Russia in 1905.

Trotsky got back into Russia in February, one of the first
exiles to return. Returning also was Natalia Ivanovna Sedova,
a student rebel emigre whom he had met in Paris and lived
with abroad, beginning a lifetime relationship; two sons were
born of this marriage.

At first Trotsky had to stay underground, writing articles
and leaflets. It was not until October that he made his first
public speech at a mass demonstration in St. Petersburg, where
the leadership of the struggle against the monarchy had passed
into the hands of the workers. The workers not only staged
a general strike but also formed a new kind of organization,
the St. Petersburg Soviet of Workers' Deputies. The soviet,
Russian word for council, was a workers' representative body
whose delegates were elected from the shops and political parties. It arose in 1905, for the first time, out of the need to
coordinate and lead the workers' struggles, which began with
economic demands for shorter hours and higher pay and soon
advanced to political demands. Trotsky played a leading role
in this new organization, becoming its acting president in its
last days.

The St. Petersburg Soviet lasted only fifty days before it
was crushed and its leaders arrested in December 1905. The

main charge against fifty-two of its leaders, when they were brought to trial in September 1906, was that they had been "preparing an armed uprising" against the then existing "form of government." In My Life, Trotsky gave the following description of the trial:

"The yard of the court building and the adjoining streets were turned into a military camp. All the police of St. Petersburg were mobilized. But the trial itself was carried on with a certain amount of freedom: the reactionary government was out to disgrace [Count Sergei] Witte [semiliberal prime minister who had persuaded Czar Nicholas II to issue the Manifesto of October 17] by exposing his 'liberalism,' his weakness in dealing with the revolution. About four hundred witnesses were called; and more than two hundred witnesses came and offered evidence. Workers, manufacturers, members of the secret police, engineers, servants, citizens, journalists, post-office officials, police chiefs, students, municipal councillors, janitors, senators, hooligans, deputies, professors, soldiers, all passed in file during the month of the trial, and, under the cross-fire of the judges' bench, of the prosecution, of the attorneys for the defense, and of the defendants—especially the latter—reconstructed, line by line, and stroke by stroke, the activity of the workers' Soviet."

The trial was utilized as a political platform against czarism by the defendants and, as president of the Soviet, Trotsky was assigned to answer the main charge. This he did on October 4, in the speech that follows. It should be read as more than a defense of the Soviet against the czarist prosecutor; Trotsky here was also defending his concept of the revolution against his critics inside and around the revolutionary camp.

By this time Trotsky had made hundreds of speeches, but this was the first to be transcribed and preserved. The first translation into English, made by John G. Wright, is taken from Fourth International, March 1942.

The dates in this chapter in connection with the revolution in 1905 are from the old Russian calendar, which was thirteen days behind the prevailing Western calendar. The old dates are also used in subsequent chapters when the scene of action is Russia. The Western calendar was adopted by the Soviet government in February 1918 and thereafter the dates correspond. The old dates were retained because they have left their mark on the events. For example, the revolution that took place in November 1917 is known as the October Revolution.

The judges' bench at the trial of the St. Petersburg Soviet.
A drawing by Zarudnaya-Kavos, Petersburg artist
sympathetic to the defendants.

The defendants, with their autographs.

Gentlemen of the judiciary, representatives of the estates!

The main issue before the court, as was also the case during the preliminary investigation, is the question of the armed uprising. No matter how strange it may seem to the prosecution, this question was not placed on the agenda of any of the sessions of the Soviet of Workers' Deputies throughout the fifty days of the existence of the Soviet. The question of the armed uprising as such was not posed or discussed at a single session. Furthermore, we did not take up as such the questions of the Constituent Assembly,[1] the democratic republic, or even the general strike and its principled meaning as a method of revolutionary struggle. These fundamental questions which have been debated for a number of years first in the revolutionary press and then at meetings and assemblies were not subjected to review by the Soviet of Workers' Deputies. I shall presently explain this and characterize the attitude of the Soviet of Workers' Deputies toward the armed uprising. But before passing to this question, which is the central one from the standpoint of the court, I take the liberty of calling the court's attention to another question which is more general and less acute in character — the question of the employment of violence in general by the Soviet of Workers' Deputies. Did the Soviet recognize its right to employ violence, repressions, in certain instances, through one or another of its organs? My answer to a question posed in this general form is — Yes!

I am no less aware than the prosecuting attorney that in every "normally" functioning government, regardless of its form, the monopoly of violence and repressions belongs to the ruling power. This is the "inviolable" right of state power; and towards this right the state power maintains an attitude of most jealous solicitude, being always on guard lest some private body infringe upon its monopoly of violence. In this way the state organization struggles for survival. One need only picture modern society concretely, envisage this complex and contradictory commonwealth, say in a vast country like Russia, in order to become immediately aware that in a modern social system, torn by antagonisms, repressions are absolutely inevitable. We are not anarchists, we are socialists. The anarchists call us "statists" because we recognize the historical necessity of the state and, therefore, the historical inevitability of state violence. But under the conditions created by the general strike which essentially consists in this, that it paralyzes the state machinery — under these conditions the old, long-outlived state power against which the political strike was directed proved to be completely impotent. It was absolutely incapable of regulating and safeguarding public order even by resorting to those barbaric measures which alone remained at its disposal. Meanwhile, the strike had propelled hundreds of thousands of workers from the factories into the streets where they began to live a social-political life. Who could lead them and introduce discipline in their ranks? What organ of the old state power? The police? The gendarmes? The departments of the *Okhrana*?[2] I ask myself this question. And there is only one possible answer. No one except the Soviet of Workers' Deputies. No one else!

The Soviet in directing this colossal elemental force set itself the immediate task of reducing internal friction to a minimum, preventing excesses, and limiting the inevitable victims of the struggle to the smallest possible number. And if that is the case, then as a result of the political strike which created it, the Soviet became nothing else but the organ of self-government of the revolutionary masses, *the organ of power.* It wielded command over the parts of the whole by the will of all. It was a democratic power which was obeyed voluntarily. But insofar as the Soviet was the organized power of a great majority, it was inevitably confronted with the necessity of employing repressions against those sections of the masses which were introducing anarchy among the unanimous ranks. To counterpose its power to these elements was deemed as its right by the Soviet of Workers' Deputies. It was its right as a new historical power, as the only power in the period of the complete moral, political, and technical bankruptcy of the old apparatus, as the sole guarantee of the inviolability of the individual and of public order in the best sense of these terms. The representatives of the old power which rests entirely on bloody repressions cannot dare to speak with moral indignation about the violent measures of the Soviet. The historical power in whose name the prosecutor speaks in this court is the organized violence of a minority over the majority! The new power, whose precursor was the Soviet, represents the organized will of the majority calling the minority to order. Because of this distinction the revolutionary right of the Soviet to existence stands above all juridical and moral speculations.

The Soviet recognized its right to employ repressions. But under what circumstances, and within what limits? We have heard hundreds of witnesses on this score. Before resorting to repressions, the Soviet employed arguments and tried to convince. This is the real method of the Soviet, and in applying it the Soviet was untiring. By means of revolutionary agitation, with the weapon of words, the Soviet raised to their feet and brought under its authority ever newer and newer layers of the masses. Whenever it met with opposition from unenlightened or corrupted groups of proletarians, the Soviet said to itself that there was always ample time to render them harmless by physical force. It sought, as you have heard from the testimony of witnesses, other means. It appealed to the common sense of the factory administration, calling upon them to cease operations; it exerted its influence upon the unenlightened workers through technicians and engineers who sympathized with the general strike. It sent delegates to workers in order to take them off their jobs, and only in extreme cases did it threaten to apply force to strikebreakers. But did the Soviet apply force? Gentlemen of the court, such instances are not to be found among the materials of the preliminary investigation, and, despite all the efforts, none was successfully established even during the sessions of this court. Even if one were to take seriously those instances of "violence," more comical than tragic, which have been presented to the court (somebody entered a strange apartment and kept his cap on; somebody arrested somebody else with the latter's consent . . .), then it is only necessary to juxtapose this *cap* which somebody forgot to remove with the hundreds of *heads* which are "removed" by mistake day in and day out by the old power — and the violence of the Soviet of Workers' Deputies will appear before our eyes in its true guise. And that is all we want. Our task is to reestablish the events which then transpired in their true guise; it is precisely for the sake of this, that we defendants have taken active part in the trial.

Did the Soviet of Workers' Deputies — and here I come to another question of importance to the court — did the Soviet of Workers' Deputies take a stand in its actions and declarations on legal grounds, and, in particular, on the grounds of the Manifesto of October 17? What was the relation between the October Manifesto and the Soviet resolutions on the Constituent Assembly and the democratic republic? This question did not occupy us at all at the time — and I say this as emphatically as I can — but this question is now undoubtedly of great importance to the court. We have heard here the testimony of the witness Luchinin. I personally found this testimony extremely interesting, and in some of its conclusions very apt and deep-going. He said among other things that while the Soviet of Workers' Deputies was republican in its slogans, principles, and political ideals, it put into effect actually, directly, and concretely those freedoms which had been in principle proclaimed by the czar's Manifesto, and which were being opposed might and main by precisely those who were the authors of this Manifesto of October 17. Yes, gentlemen of the judiciary and of the estates, we of the revolutionary proletarian Soviet did actually realize and did carry out the freedom of speech, the freedom of assembly, and the inviolability of the person — all of which had been promised to the people under the pressure of the October strike. On the other hand, the apparatus of the old power showed signs of life only in tearing to pieces the already legalized conquests of the people. Gentlemen of the court, this is an incontrovertible fact, already a part of history. It is impossible to controvert it.

If I — or my comrades — were asked did we *subjectively* base ourselves on the Manifesto of October 17, then we would categorically reply in the negative. Why? Because we were profoundly convinced — and we were not mistaken — that the Manifesto of October 17 did not create a legal foundation, did not establish the foundation for new laws because a new legal order arises, according to our convictions, not through manifestos but through a real reorganization of the entire state apparatus. Inasmuch as we took our stand on this materialist viewpoint — the only correct one — we deemed ourselves justified in not cherishing any trust in the immanent power of the Manifesto of October 17. And we stated our views openly. But it seems to me that our subjective attitude as party people, as revolutionists, does not as yet determine for the court our objective relation as citizens toward the Manifesto, the formal foundation of the existing state order. Because the court insofar as it is a court *must* look upon the Manifesto as such a foundation or it must cease to exist.

In Italy there exists, as is well known, a bourgeois parliamentarian republican party which functions on the basis of the country's monarchical constitution. In all the cultured countries socialist parties which are in essence republican legally exist and carry on a struggle. The question is: Does the Manifesto of October 17 apply to us Russian socialist republicans? This question must be decided by the court. It must say whether we Social Democrats were right in arguing that the constitutional Manifesto was only a catalogue of promises which would never be fulfilled voluntarily. The court must say whether we were right in our revolutionary criticism of paper promises, right in calling the people to an open struggle for genuine and complete freedom. Or were we wrong? In that case, let the court tell us that the Manifesto of October 17 constitutes a genuine and legal foundation on the basis of which we republicans are people of law and order — people who have acted "legally" even if contrary to our own conceptions and intentions. Let the Manifesto of October 17 speak to us here through the lips of the court and say in the verdict: "You have denied me but I nevertheless exist for you as well as for the whole country."

I have already stated that the Soviet of Workers' Deputies never posed at its sessions the questions of the Constituent Assembly and the democratic republic. Nevertheless its attitude toward these slogans was quite definitive, as you have heard from the statements of the worker witnesses. How could it have been otherwise? After all, the Soviet did not arise in a vacuum. It appeared after the Russian proletariat had already passed through January 9; through the commission of Senator Shidlovsky;[3] and in general through the long, much too long school of Russian absolutism. Long before the Soviet, the demands for the Constituent Assembly, universal suffrage, and the democratic republic became the central slogans of the revolutionary proletariat, alongside of the demand for the eight-hour working day. That is why the Soviet did not find it necessary to raise even once the questions and discuss them in principle — it simply introduced them into its resolutions as matters that have been decided once and for all. The same thing was in essence true with regard to the idea of an uprising.

Before passing to this central question — the armed insurrection — I must warn that insofar as I understand the attitude of the power that accuses us and, in part, of the judicial authorities, the latter differs from our attitude not only in the political or party sense, not only in the sense of evaluating it — it would be futile to combat this — no, we differ on the very concept of the armed uprising. The concept of the prosecution differs fundamentally, most profoundly, most irreconcilably from the concept held by the Soviet, and which I believe was and is shared with the Soviet by the entire Russian proletariat.

What is an insurrection, gentlemen of the court? Not a palace overturn, not a military conspiracy, but the uprising of the working masses? One of the witnesses was asked here by the court presidium whether he considered a political strike an uprising. I do not recall his answer but I think and I say that a political strike, contrary to the doubts of the presiding judge, is in essence an uprising. This is not a paradox! Although it

might seem to be a paradox from the standpoint of the indictment, I repeat, my concept of the uprising—and I shall
presently demonstrate this—has nothing in common except
the name with the police-prosecution conception. I have said
that a political strike is an uprising. As a matter of fact, what
is a political general strike?

With the economic strike it has only one thing in common:
in both instances the workers suspend work. In everything
else they are absolutely dissimilar. The economic strike has
its own fixed and narrow goal—to exert influence upon the
will of a given employer and to remove him from the ranks
of competition with this goal in mind. Production is halted in
a factory in order to gain changes within the confines of this
factory. The political strike differs profoundly in nature. It
does not at all exercise pressure upon individual employers;
it does not as a rule present partial economic demands—its
demands are directed, over the heads of the employers and consumers who are cruelly affected, to the state power. How does
the political strike act upon the state power? By paralyzing its
vitality. A modern state even in so backward a country as
Russia rests on a centralized economic organism composing a
single body whose skeleton is railways, and whose nervous
system is the telegraph. And if, so far as Russian absolutism
is concerned, the telegraph and railways and generally all the
conquests of modern technology do not serve for cultural-
economic aims, then they are all the more indispensable to it
for the purposes of repression. Railways and the telegraph
are the indispensable instruments for shifting troops from one
end of the country to the other; and for unifying and directing
the activities of the administration in the struggle against dis-
turbances. What does the political strike do? It paralyzes the
economic apparatus of the state, disrupts communication between the various branches of the administrative machine,
isolates the government and renders it impotent. On the other
hand, it unites politically the mass of workers in the mills and
factories and counterposes this army of workers to the state
power. In this is the essence of an uprising. To unite the proletarian masses in a single revolutionary protest and to counterpose them to the organized state power, as one hostile force to
another—that is precisely an uprising, as the Soviet of Workers'
Deputies understood it, and as I understand it. We have already witnessed such a revolutionary clash between the two
hostile sides during the October strike which broke out spontaneously without the Soviet of Workers' Deputies, prior to its
formation, and which itself created the Soviet. The October

strike engendered state "anarchy" and one of the products of this anarchy was the Manifesto of October 17. I hope that this will not be denied even by the prosecution, just as it is not denied by the most conservative politicians and publicists, including the semiofficial *Novoye Vrema* whose editors would very much like to expunge from memory the Manifesto of October 17 which was born out of the revolution, along with other manifestos of similar or contrary nature. Only the other day it was written in *Novoye Vrema* that the Manifesto of October 17 came as the result of government *panic* created by the political strike. But if this Manifesto constitutes the foundation of the existing modern order, then it must be admitted that at the foundation of our existing state order lies panic, and this panic in turn is based on the political strike of the proletariat. So you see that the general strike is something more than a mere cessation of work.

I have said that the political strike the moment it ceases being a demonstration is in essence an uprising. It would be more correct to say that it is the fundamental and the most general method of the proletarian uprising. Fundamental but not exclusive. The method of the political strike has its own natural limits. This was manifested the moment that the workers resumed production at noon of October 21 at the summons of the Soviet.

The Manifesto of October 17 met with a vote of nonconfidence; the masses had good grounds to fear that the government would not introduce the promised freedoms. The proletariat saw the inevitability of a decisive struggle and gravitated instinctively toward the Soviet as the focus of their revolutionary strength. On the other hand, absolutism, having recovered from its panic, began to restore its semishattered apparatus and to reassemble its regiments. As a result it turned out that there were two powers in existence after the October clash: the new people's power basing itself on the masses — this power was the Soviet of Workers' Deputies; and a second, the old official power, basing itself on the army. These two powers could not exist side by side: the entrenchment of one meant death to the other.

The autocracy, resting on bayonets, naturally tried to introduce confusion, chaos, and disintegration into the colossal process of the fusing together of the national forces centering round the Soviet of Workers' Deputies. On the other side, the Soviet, resting on the confidence, discipline, activity, and unanimity of the working masses could not fail to understand the terrible threat to the popular freedom, civil rights, and in-

violability of the person represented by the fact that the army
together with all the material instruments of power in general
had remained in the same bloody hands as prior to October
17. Between these two organs of power begins a titanic struggle
for the influence over the army — that is the second stage of the
developing popular uprising.

On the basis of the mass strike which counterposed the proletariat to absolutism as two hostile forces, there arises an
intense eagerness to attract the troops over to the workers'
side, to fraternize with them, to conquer their souls. This eagerness naturally gives birth to the revolutionary summons to
the soldiers on whom absolutism bases itself. The second strike
in November was a mighty and magnificent demonstration
of solidarity between the factory and the barracks. Of course,
had the army gone over to the side of the people, an uprising
would have been unnecessary. But is such a peaceful transition
of the army into the ranks of the revolution conceivable? No,
it is inconceivable! Absolutism will not wait with folded hands
until the army, free from its demoralizing influence, becomes
a friend of the people. So long as it has not lost everything,
absolutism will itself assume the initiative of the offensive. Did
the Petersburg workers understand this? Yes, they understood.
Did the proletariat think, did the Soviet of Workers' Deputies
think that it would come to an open clash between the two
sides? Yes, the Soviet thought so, it had no doubts on this
score; it was aware, firmly aware that sooner or later the fatal
hour would strike. . . .

Naturally, if the organization of social forces could have
proceeded without interruptions by any attacks of the armed
counterrevolution along the road undertaken under the leadership of the Soviet of Workers' Deputies, then the old order
would have been destroyed without the slightest application
of force. For what did we witness? We saw that the workers
rallied to the Soviet; the peasant alliance, embracing ever larger
masses of the peasantry, sent its deputies to the Soviet; the
railway, postal and telegraph unions united with the Soviet;
the liberal professions, the Union of Unions,[4] gravitated toward
the Soviet; even the attitude of the factory administration
toward the Soviet was one of tolerance, almost friendly. It
seemed as if the entire nation was making a kind of heroic
effort, striving to deliver out of its womb an organ of power
that would create the genuine and unquestionable foundations
of a new order prior to the convocation of the Constituent
Assembly. If the old state power had not interjected itself into
this organic process, if it had not striven to introduce real

anarchy into the national life, if the process of the organization of forces had unfolded quite freely — then a new and resurgent Russia would have been born without violence and without bloodshed.

But the whole point is that we did not for a moment believe that the process of emancipation would unfold in this way. We knew only too well what the old power was. We Social Democrats were certain that despite the Manifesto, which seemed like a complete break with the past, the old state apparatus would not withdraw voluntarily, would not transfer the power to the people, would not surrender a single one of its vital positions. We foresaw and warned the people openly that absolutism would still make many convulsive attempts to retain the remnants of power in its own hands, and even to take back once again everything it had so solemnly granted. That is why, from our point of view, an uprising, an armed insurrection was inevitable — it was and remains a historic necessity in the process of the struggle of the people against a military-police order. In October and November this idea dominated at all the meetings and assemblies; it dominated the entire revolutionary press; it filled the whole political atmosphere; and, for better or worse, it crystallized in the consciousness of every member of the Soviet of Workers' Deputies. That is why it naturally entered into the resolutions of our Soviet; and that is why we did not have to discuss it at all.

As a consequence of the October strike we inherited a tense situation: the revolutionary organization of the masses fighting for its existence, basing itself not upon a body of laws which was nonexistent but upon force insofar as the Soviet existed; and the armed counterrevolution waiting for its hour of revenge. This situation was, if I may be permitted to use such an expression, the algebraic formula of the insurrection. New events would introduce only new arithmetic magnitudes. Contrary to the superficial conclusions of the prosecution, the idea of the armed uprising did not leave its traces only in the motion passed by the Soviet on November 27, i. e., one week before our arrest, where it is expressed clearly and definitively. No, from the very beginning of the activity of the Soviet of Workers' Deputies — in the resolution cancelling the funeral demonstration as well as subsequently in the resolution calling for the cessation of the November strike — in a whole series of other decisions the Soviet spoke of an armed conflict with the government, of the final onslaught or the final battle as an inevitable mo-

ment of the struggle. Thus, under diverse forms but identical
in essence, this idea of an armed uprising runs like a red
thread through all the decisions of the Soviet of Workers'
Deputies.

How were these decisions understood by the Soviet? Did
the Soviet believe that an armed uprising was an undertaking
to be created underground and then transferred ready-made
into the streets? Did the Soviet conceive it as an insurrectionary
act to be accomplished in accordance with a definite plan?
Did the Executive Committee elaborate the technique of the
street struggle?

Of course not! And this cannot fail to stump the author of
the indictment who stands with his mouth agape before a few
dozen revolvers which constitute in his eyes the only genuine
prerequisites for an armed uprising. But the viewpoint of the
prosecution is only the viewpoint of our criminal code which
knows of conspiratorial complicity but has no inkling of mass
organizations; which knows of attempts and mutinies but does
not and cannot know of revolution.

The juridical concepts on which the present trial is based
have lagged many decades behind the evolution of the revolutionary movement. The modern Russian labor movement
has nothing in common with the concept of conspiracy as
defined by our criminal statutes which have remained essentially unaltered since the days of Speransky who lived in
the epoch of the Carbonari. That is why the attempt to
squeeze the activity of the Soviet into the narrow framework
of articles 100 and 101 is absolutely hopeless from the standpoint of juridical logic. [5]

Nevertheless our activity was revolutionary. Nevertheless we
actually did prepare for an armed insurrection.

An insurrection of the masses, gentlemen of the court, is not
something man-made but a historical event. It is the result of
social relations and not the product of a plan. It is impossible
to manufacture it; it is possible to foresee it. Through the operation of causes depending on us as little as they do on czarism,
an open conflict had become unavoidable. Each day brought
us closer and closer to it. For us, preparation for it meant
doing everything in our power to reduce the victims of this
irrepressible conflict to a minimum. Did we think that this required first of all that we prepare arms, draft a plan of military actions, divide the city into specific sections, in a word
do everything that is done by military authorities in expectation of "disorders" when they divide Petersburg into sections,
appoint colonels for each section, assign a certain number of

machine guns and all the necessary equipment? No, that is
not how we understood our role. To prepare for the inevitable
uprising—and we never *prepared an uprising,* as the prosecutor thinks and says, we *prepared for an uprising*—for us, this
meant first and foremost to bring clarity into the minds of the
people; to explain to them that an open conflict was inevitable;
that they would be deprived of everything that had been
granted them; that they could preserve their freedoms only by
force; that a mighty organization of the revolutionary masses
was indispensable; that it was necessary to meet the enemy
head on; that they had to be prepared to go to the end in the
struggle; that there was no other road. For us, this constituted
the essence of the uprising.

What did we believe necessary for the insurrection to be
victorious? The sympathy of the troops! It was necessary first
of all to attract the army to our side. To compel the soldiers
to understand the shameful role they were playing and to
summon them to joint action with the people and for the people—that is the kind of task we set ourselves first and foremost. I have already said that the November strike which
came as an unselfish outburst of direct solidarity with the
sailors who were threatened with a death sentence was likewise of enormous political significance. It attracted the attention and sympathy of the army toward the revolutionary proletariat. This is where the prosecutor should have first of all
sought to find the preparation for the armed uprising. But
naturally the issue could not be decided by a single demonstration of protest and sympathy.

Under what conditions, then, did we think at the time and
do we think now is it possible to expect the army to pass to
the side of the revolution? What is needed for this? Machine
guns? Rifles? Of course, if the workers possessed machine guns
and rifles they would hold an enormous power in their hands.
The very unavoidability of uprising would in large measure
be eliminated thereby. A wavering army would surrender its
weapons at the feet of an armed people. But the masses did
not possess weapons, they did not and could not have them in
large quantities. Does this mean that the masses are doomed
to defeat? No! Important as weapons are, the main power
does not lie in weapons. No, not in weapons. *Not the capacity
of the masses to kill but their great readiness to die*—this is
what, gentlemen of the court, in the last analysis guarantees in
our opinion the victory of the people's uprising.

When the soldiers march into the streets to quell the crowds
and come face to face with the crowds and become convinced

that these crowds, this people will not leave the pavements until they gain what they must have, that they are ready to pile corpses upon corpses — when the soldiers see and are convinced that the people have come to struggle seriously, to the very end, then the hearts of the soldiers, as has happened in every revolution, must inevitably waver because the soldiers cannot fail to become dubious about the stability of the regime they are serving and cannot fail to believe in the victory of the people.

It has become customary to associate insurrections with barricades. If we leave aside the fact that the barricade colors far too strongly the prevailing concept of the insurrection, even in that case it should not be forgotten that the barricade which is so obviously and purely a mechanical element in the uprising plays essentially and primarily a *moral* role. For in all the revolutions the barricades did not at all have the meaning of physical barriers that fortifications have in war. The barricade served the cause of the uprising by forming a temporary physical obstacle to the movement of the army thus bringing the latter into close contact with the people. Here, at the barricade, the soldier heard, perhaps for the first time in his life, honest human language, a fraternal summons, the voice of national consciousness. And here as a result of this communion between soldiers and citizens in the atmosphere of revolutionary enthusiasm, discipline fell apart, dissolved, disappeared. This and this alone assured victory to the people's uprising. That is why we are of the opinion that a people's uprising is "ready" not when the people are armed with machine guns and cannon — for in that case it never would be ready — but rather at a time when they are armed with readiness to die in open street struggle.

But naturally the old power seeing the growth of this great feeling, this capacity to die for the sake of the interests of the native land, the capacity to sacrifice one's life for the happiness of future generations, seeing that the masses were becoming infected by this enthusiasm so alien, strange, and hostile to it — this besieged power could not tranquilly look on the moral regeneration of the people which was taking place before its very eyes. By passive waiting the czarist government could only have doomed itself to extinction. This was clear. What was there left for it to do? Use its last resources and every means to fight against the political self-determination of the people. For this purpose the unenlightened army, the Black Hundred gangs,[6] agents of the police, and the venal press were equally useful. To incite some against others, to cover

the streets with blood, to plunder, violate, burn, sow panic,
spread lies, deceit, and slander—this is what remained for the
old and criminal power. It did all this and is continuing to
do it to this very day. While the open clash was inevitable, it
was not we in any case but our mortal enemies who were
anxious to bring the hour closer.

You have already heard here more than once that the workers were arming themselves in October and November against
the Black Hundreds. To those who know nothing it might
seem absolutely incomprehensible that in a revolutionary country where the enormous majority of the population is on the
side of liberationist ideals and where the popular masses have
openly evinced their readiness to struggle to the bitter end—it
might seem incomprehensible that in such a country hundreds
of thousands of workers should have to arm themselves for
the struggle against the Black Hundreds which represent a weak
and insignificant portion of the population. Are these dregs,
these degenerates recruited from all layers of society really so
dangerous? Of course not! How easy that task would be if
the wretched gangs of the Black Hundred were the only ones
barring the road to the people! But we have heard not only
from the testimony of attorney Bramson but also from hundreds of worker witnesses that behind the Black Hundred there
stands if not the entire state power then a goodly portion of it.
Behind the gangs of thugs who have nothing to lose and who
are not deterred by anything—neither by the gray hair of the
aged, nor defenseless women and children—there stand the
agents of the government who organize and arm the Black
Hundreds and do so, one must presume, at the expense of the
state budget.

After all, didn't we know all this before the present trial?
Didn't we read the papers? Didn't we hear the reports of eye-
witnesses? Didn't we receive letters? Didn't we see it with our
own eyes? Are we unacquainted with the shocking revelations
of Count Urusov?[7] The prosecution believes none of this. It
cannot believe it. For in that case it would have to direct the
barb of its accusations against those whom it is now defending;
it would have to admit that a Russian citizen in arming himself with a revolver against the police is taking the necessary
measures of self-defense. But it is in the nature of things im-
material whether the court believes or disbelieves in the pogrom
activities of the authorities. So far as the court is concerned, it
is sufficient that we believe it, that hundreds of thousands of
workers who armed themselves at our summons are convinced
of it. For us it was unquestionable that behind the decorative

facade of the hooligan gangs was the guiding and august
hand of the ruling clique. Gentlemen of the court, we see this
evil hand even here, even now.

The power that accuses us invites you, gentlemen of the court,
to recognize that the Soviet of Workers' Deputies armed the
workers for the direct struggle against the existing "form of
government." If I were categorically asked— Is that true?
I would answer— Yes! Yes, I agree to accept this charge, but
on one condition. I do not know whether this condition will
be acceptable to the prosecution or to the court.

I ask: What does the prosecution understand by the term
"form of government"? Does there really exist among us
a form of government? The government has long ago drifted
away from the nation to its military-police-Black Hundred
apparatus. What we have is not a national power but an au-
tomaton for mass murder. I cannot define in any other way
a governmental machine which is hacking to pieces the living
body of our country. And if I am told that the pogroms, the
murders, the incendiary fires, rapes— if I am told that everything which took place in Tver, Rostov, Kursk, Sedlez— if I
am told that Kishinev, Odessa, Bialystok, constitute the form of
the Russian empire, then I will acknowledge together with the
prosecution that during October and November we armed
immediately and directly against the form of government of
the Russian empire.

2

Zimmerwald Manifesto Against the War

Trotsky and fourteen of the other defendants were sentenced in November 1906 to deportation to Siberia for life. This time Trotsky made his escape en route to the site of his deportation and began his second exile which was to last until revolution flared in Russia again in 1917.

For the next seven years he, Natalia Sedova, and their two sons lived in Vienna. His activity assumed a different character: lecturing about the meaning of the 1905 revolution and current events; editing a paper, Pravda [Truth], which was smuggled into Russia; acting as a military correspondent for a Kiev paper in the Balkans, where local warfare foreshadowed the explosion of World War I.

As Russian citizens they had to leave Austria, Germany's ally, when Germany declared war against Russia in August 1914. Their itinerary during the next three years included Switzerland, France, Spain, and the United States.

The outbreak of the war produced a deep-going crisis for the international socialist movement. The Second International and its affiliated parties had all pledged undying opposition to the war, but when it came, most of the Social Democratic parties on both sides capitulated and not only supported but even hailed the war. For Trotsky and the other revolutionary socialists, the Second International was finished as a progressive force. What was needed now was a regroupment of the vanguard that would lead the struggle against the war and for a new International.

At the end of 1914 Trotsky moved from Zurich to Paris to resume the job of military correspondent for the Kiev paper. He also became coeditor of a daily Russian antiwar paper, Nashe Slovo [Our Word] and a participant in the antiwar wing of the French labor movement, which enabled him to play an important role in the first wartime international conference against the war.

*In September 1915, thirty-eight delegates from eleven coun-
tries assembled for the conference to be held in the Swiss
village of Zimmerwald, high in the Alps. "The delegates, filling
four stagecoaches, set off for the mountains," Trotsky wrote
in* My Life. *"The passers-by looked on curiously at the strange
procession. The delegates themselves joked about the fact that
half a century after the founding of the first International,
it was still possible to seat all the internationalists in four
coaches. But they were not skeptical. The thread of history
often breaks — then a new knot must be tied. And that is what
we were doing in Zimmerwald.*

*"The days of the conference, September 5 to 8, were stormy
ones. The revolutionary wing, led by Lenin, and the pacifist
wing, which comprised the majority of the delegates, agreed
with difficulty on a common manifesto of which I had prepared
the draft. The manifesto was far from saying all that it should
have, but, even so, it was a long step forward. Lenin was on
the extreme left at the conference. In many questions he was
a minority of one, even within the Zimmerwald left wing, to
which I did not formally belong, although I was close to it
on all important questions. In Zimmerwald, Lenin was tight-
ening up the spring of the future international action. In a
Swiss mountain village, he was laying the cornerstone of the
revolutionary International."*

*Although the manifesto drawn up by Trotsky was not a
speech, it has a speech-like quality, and is reprinted here in
the translation by Moissaye J. Olgin from the 1930 edition
of Lenin's* Collected Works, *Volume XVIII, where it appears
as an appendix along with other Zimmerwald documents.*

Proletarians of Europe!

The war has lasted more than a year.[1] Millions of corpses
cover the battlefields. Millions of human beings have been
crippled for the rest of their lives. Europe is like a gigantic
human slaughterhouse. All civilization, created by the labor
of many generations, is doomed to destruction. The most savage barbarism is today celebrating its triumph over all that
hitherto constituted the pride of mankind.

Irrespective of the truth as to the direct responsibility for
the outbreak of the war, one thing is certain: the war that
has produced this chaos is the outcome of imperialism, of

the attempt on the part of the capitalist classes of each nation
to foster their greed for profit by the exploitation of human
labor and of the natural resources of the entire globe.

Economically backward or politically weak nations are thereby subjugated by the great powers who, in this war, are seeking to remake the world map with blood and iron in accord
with their exploiting interests. Thus entire nations and countries like Belgium, Poland, the Balkan states, and Armenia
are threatened with the fate of being torn asunder, annexed
as a whole or in part as booty in the game of compensations.

In the course of the war, its driving forces are revealed in
all their vileness. Shred after shred falls the veil with which
the meaning of this world catastrophe was hidden from the
consciousness of the people. The capitalists of all countries,
who are coining the gold of war profits out of the blood shed
by the people, assert that the war is for defense of the fatherland, for democracy, and the liberation of oppressed nations.
They lie! In actual reality, they are burying the freedom of
their own people together with the independence of the other
nations on the fields of devastation. New fetters, new chains,
new burdens are arising, and it is the proletariat of all countries, of the victorious as well as of the conquered countries,
that will have to bear them. Improvement in welfare was proclaimed at the outbreak of the war — want and privation, unemployment and high prices, undernourishment and epidemics
are the actual results. The burdens of war will consume the
best energies of the peoples for decades, endanger the achievements of social reform, and hinder every step forward.

Cultural devastation, economic decline, political reaction —
these are the blessings of this horrible conflict of nations.

Thus the war reveals the naked figure of modern capitalism
which has become irreconcilable not only with the interests
of the laboring masses, not only with the requirements of historical development, but also with the elementary conditions
of human intercourse.

The ruling powers of capitalist society who held the fate
of the nations in their hands, the monarchic as well as the
republican governments, the secret diplomacy, the mighty business organizations, the bourgeois parties, the capitalist press,
the church — all these bear the full weight of responsibility
for this war which arose out of the social order fostering them
and protected by them, and which is being waged for their
interests.

Workers!

Exploited, disfranchised, scorned, they called you brothers

and comrades at the outbreak of the war when you were to be led to the slaughter, to death. And now that militarism has crippled you, mutilated you, degraded and annihilated you, the rulers demand that you surrender your interests, your aims, your ideals—in a word, servile subordination to civil peace. They rob you of the possibility of expressing your views, your feelings, your pains; they prohibit you from raising your demands and defending them. The press gagged, political rights and liberties trod upon—this is the way the military dictatorship rules today with an iron hand.

This situation which threatens the entire future of Europe and of humanity cannot and must not be confronted by us any longer without action. The Socialist proletariat has waged a struggle against militarism for decades. With growing concern, its representatives at their national and international congresses occupied themselves with the ever more menacing danger of war growing out of imperialism. At Stuttgart, at Copenhagen, at Basle, the International Socialist congresses indicated the course which the proletariat must follow.[2]

Since the beginning of the war Socialist parties and labor organizations of various countries that helped to determine this course have disregarded the obligations following from this. Their representatives have called upon the working class to give up the class struggle, the only possible and effective method of proletarian emancipation. They have granted credits to the ruling classes for waging the war; they have placed themselves at the disposal of the governments for the most diverse services; through their press and their messengers, they have tried to win the neutrals for the government policies of their countries; they have delivered up to their governments Socialist ministers as hostages for the preservation of civil peace, and thereby they have assumed the responsibility before the working class, before its present and its future, for this war, for its aims and its methods. And just as the individual parties, so the highest of the appointed representative bodies of the Socialists of all countries, the International Socialist Bureau has failed them.[3]

These facts are equally responsible for the fact that the international working class, which did not succumb to the national panic of the first war period or which freed itself from it, has still, in the second year of the slaughter of peoples, found no ways and means of taking up an energetic struggle for peace simultaneously in all countries.

In this unbearable situation, we, the representatives of the Socialist parties, trade unions, or of their minorities, we Germans, French, Italians, Russians, Poles, Letts, Rumanians, Bulgarians, Swedes, Norwegians, Dutch, and Swiss, we who stand not on the ground of national solidarity with the exploiting class, but on the ground of the international solidarity of the proletariat and of the class struggle, have assembled to retie the torn threads of international relations and to call upon the working class to recover itself and to fight for peace.

This struggle is the struggle for freedom, for the reconciliation of peoples, for socialism. It is necessary to take up this struggle for peace, for a peace without annexations or war indemnities. Such a peace, however, is only possible if every thought of violating the rights and liberties of nations is condemned. Neither the occupation of entire countries nor of separate parts of countries must lead to their violent annexation. No annexation, whether open or concealed, and no forcible economic attachment made still more unbearable by political disfranchisement. The right of self-determination of nations must be the indestructible principle in the system of national relationships of peoples.

Proletarians!

Since the outbreak of the war you have placed your energy, your courage, your endurance at the service of the ruling classes. Now you must stand up for your own cause, for the sacred aims of socialism, for the emancipation of the oppressed nations as well as of the enslaved classes, by means of the irreconcilable proletarian class struggle.

It is the task and the duty of the Socialists of the belligerent countries to take up this struggle with full force; it is the task and the duty of the Socialists of the neutral states to support their brothers in this struggle against bloody barbarism with every effective means. Never in world history was there a more urgent, a more sublime task, the fulfillment of which should be our common labor. No sacrifice is too great, no burden too heavy in order to achieve this goal: peace among the people.

Workingmen and workingwomen! Mothers and fathers! Widows and orphans! Wounded and crippled! We call to all of you who are suffering from the war and because of the war: Beyond all borders, beyond the reeking battlefields, beyond the devastated cities and villages —

Proletarians of all countries, unite![4]

Signature du Titulaire

Leon Trotsky

Trotsky's French passport during World War I.

3

The February Revolution and Its Results

Toward the end of 1916 the French government, prodded by its czarist ally, banned Nashe Slovo, *ordered Trotsky to leave the country "forever," and its police hustled him across the border into Spain. The Spanish government was no more hospitable than the French. Unable to secure entry into any other European country, Trotsky and his family boarded a ship for the United States which at that time had an open door for political refugees. The ship docked in New York in January 1917, just two months before the news that a revolution had begun in war-weary Russia (occurring in March, it is also called the February revolution because of the Russian calendar's thirteen-day lag behind the Western).*

The important thing now was to get back to Russia. While passports and visas were being arranged, Trotsky appeared at many excited mass meetings organized by the Russian colony and the socialist movement in New York, explaining what was happening in Russia and predicting with remarkable accuracy the political battles that would be fought there in the ensuing months. Isaac Deutscher, in The Prophet Armed, *quotes a Menshevik opponent of Trotsky, Dr. G. A. Ziv, as saying about these meetings: "Trotsky's speech was the main event and the natural climax. Meetings were sometimes delayed for hours because Trotsky was taking part in many gatherings convened simultaneously . . . but the public patiently waited for him, thirsting for the words that would throw a light on the momentous event that had occurred in Russia."*

These speeches were not transcribed, but fortunately their political essence and part of their style were preserved in a series of articles Trotsky wrote for the New York Russian-language daily, Novy Mir [New World], *and which were printed in its issues of March 13, 17, 19, and 20, 1917. The first English translation, made by Moissaye J. Olgin, is taken from the collection of Trotsky's articles published in 1918 under the title* Our Revolution.

On the Eve of a Revolution

The streets of Petrograd[1] again speak the language of 1905. As in the time of the Russo-Japanese war,[2] the masses demand bread, peace, and freedom. As in 1905, streetcars are not running and newspapers do not appear. The workingmen let the steam out of the boilers, they quit their benches, and walk out into the streets. The government mobilizes its Cossacks.[3] And as in 1905, only those two powers are facing each other in the streets — the revolutionary workingmen and the army of the czar.

The movement was provoked by lack of bread. This, of course, is not an accidental cause. In all the belligerent countries the lack of bread is the most immediate, the most acute reason for dissatisfaction and indignation among the masses. All the insanity of the war is revealed to them from this angle: it is impossible to produce necessities of life because one has to produce instruments of death.

However, the attempts of the Anglo-Russian semiofficial news agencies to explain the movement by a temporary shortage in food, or by snowstorms that have delayed transportation are one of the most ludicrous applications of the policy of the ostrich. The workingmen would not stop the factories, the streetcars, the printshops and walk into the streets to meet czarism face to face on account of snowstorms which temporarily hamper the arrival of foodstuffs.

People have a short memory. Many of our own ranks have forgotten that the war found Russia in a state of potent revolutionary ferment. After the heavy stupor of 1908-1911, the proletariat gradually healed its wounds in the following years of industrial prosperity; the slaughter of strikers on the Lena River in April 1912 awakened the revolutionary energy of the proletarian masses. A series of strikes followed. In the year preceding the world war, the wave of economic and political strikes resembled that of 1905. When Poincare,[4] the president of the French republic, came to Petersburg in the summer of 1914 (evidently to talk over with the czar how to free the small and weak nations) the Russian proletariat was in a stage of extraordinary revolutionary tension, and the president of the French republic could see with his own eyes in the capital of his friend, the czar, how the first barricades of the second Russian revolution were being constructed.

The war checked the rising revolutionary tide. We have witnessed a repetition of what happened ten years before, in the Russo-Japanese war. After the stormy strikes of 1903, there

had followed a year of almost unbroken political silence—
1904—the first year of the war. It took the workingmen of
Petersburg twelve months to orient themselves in the war and
to walk out into the streets with their demands and protests.
January 9, 1905, was, so to speak, the official beginning of
our first revolution.

The present war is vaster than was the Russo-Japanese war.
Millions of soldiers have been mobilized by the government
for the "defense of the fatherland." The ranks of the proletariat have thus been disorganized. On the other hand, the
more advanced elements of the proletariat had to face
and weigh in their minds a number of questions of unheard-
of magnitude. What is the cause of the war? Shall the proletariat agree with the conception of "the defense of the fatherland"? What ought to be the tactics of the working class in
wartime?

In the meantime, czarism and its allies, the upper groups
of the nobility and the bourgeoisie, had during the war completely exposed their true nature—the nature of criminal plunderers, blinded by limitless greed and paralyzed by want
of talent. The appetites for conquest of the governing clique
grew in proportion as the people began to realize its complete
inability to cope with the most elementary problems of warfare, of industry and supplies in wartime. Simultaneously, the
misery of the people grew, deepened, became more and more
acute—a natural result of the war multiplied by the criminal
anarchy of Rasputin czarism.[5]

In the depths of the great masses, among people who may
have never been reached by a word of propaganda, a profound bitterness accumulated under the stress of events. Meantime the foremost ranks of the proletariat were finishing
digesting the new events. The socialist proletariat of Russia
came to after the shock of the nationalist fall of the most influential part of the International, and decided that new times
call us not to let up, but to increase our revolutionary struggle.

The present events in Petrograd and Moscow are a result
of this internal preparatory work.

A disorganized, compromised, disjointed government on top.
An utterly demoralized army. Dissatisfaction, uncertainty, and
fear among the propertied classes. At the bottom, among the
masses, a deep bitterness. A proletariat numerically stronger
than ever, hardened in the fire of events. All this warrants
the statement that we are witnessing the beginning of the second Russian revolution. Let us hope that many of us will
be its participants.

Two Faces —
Internal Forces of the Russian Revolution

Let us examine more closely what is going on.

Nicholas[6] has been dethroned and, according to some information, is under arrest. The most conspicuous Black Hundred leaders have been arrested. Some of the most hated have been killed. A new ministry has been formed consisting of Octobrists, liberals, and the radical Kerensky.[7] A general amnesty has been proclaimed.

All these are facts, big facts. These are the facts that strike the outer world most. Changes in the higher government give the bourgeoisie of Europe and America an occasion to say that the revolution has won and is now completed.

The czar and his Black Hundred fought for their power, for this alone. The war, the imperialistic plans of the Russian bourgeoisie, the interests of the Allies were of minor importance to the czar and his clique. They were ready at any moment to conclude peace with the Hohenzollerns and Hapsburgs,[8] to free their most loyal regiment for war against their own people.

The Progressive Bloc of the Duma[9] mistrusted the czar and his ministers. This bloc consisted of various parties of the Russian bourgeoisie. The bloc had two aims: one, to conduct the war to a victorious end; another, to secure internal reforms — more order, control, accounting. A victory is necessary for the Russian bourgeoisie to conquer markets, to increase their territories, to get rich. Reforms are necessary primarily to enable the Russian bourgeoisie to win the war.

The progressive imperialistic bloc wanted *peaceful* reforms. The liberals intended to exert a Duma pressure on the monarchy and to keep it in check with the aid of the governments of Great Britain and France. They did not want a revolution. They knew that a revolution, bringing the working masses to the front, would be a menace to their domination, and primarily a menace to their imperialistic plans. The laboring masses, in the cities and in the villages, and even in the army itself, want peace. The liberals know it. This is why they have been enemies of the revolution all these years. A few months ago Miliukov[10] declared in the Duma: "If a revolution were necessary for victory, I would prefer no victory at all."

Yet the liberals are now in power — through the revolution. The bourgeois newspapermen see nothing but this fact.

Miliukov, already in his capacity as a minister of foreign affairs, has declared that the revolution has been conducted in the name of a victory over the enemy, and that the new government has taken upon itself to continue the war to a victorious end. The New York Stock Exchange interpreted the revolution in this specific sense. There are clever people both on the stock exchange and among the bourgeois news-papermen. Yet they are all amazingly stupid when they come to deal with mass movements. They think that Miliukov manages the revolution, in the same sense as they manage their banks or news offices. They see only the liberal govern-mental reflection of the unfolding events, they notice only the foam on the surface of the historical torrent.

The long pent-up dissatisfaction of the masses has burst forth so late, in the thirty-second month of the war, not be-cause the masses were held by police barriers — those barriers had been badly shattered during the war — but because all liberal institutions and organs, together with their social-patriotic shadows,[11] were exerting an enormous influence over the least enlightened elements of the workingmen, urging them to keep order and discipline in the name of "patrio-tism." Hungry women were already walking out into the streets, and the workingmen were getting ready to uphold them by a general strike, while the liberal bourgeoisie, accord-ing to news reports, still issued proclamations and delivered speeches to check the movement — resembling that famous heroine of Dickens who tried to stem the tide of the ocean with a broom.

The movement, however, took its course, from below, from the workingmen's quarters. After hours and days of uncer-tainty, of shooting, of skirmishes, the army joined in the revolution, from below, from the best of the soldier masses. The old government was powerless, paralyzed, annihilated. The czar fled from the capital "to the front." The Black Hun-dred bureaucrats crept, like cockroaches, each into his corner.

Then, and only then, came the Duma's turn to act. The czar had attempted in the last minute to dissolve it. And the Duma would have obeyed, "following the example of former years," had it been free to adjourn. The capitals, however, were already dominated by the revolutionary people, the same people that had walked out into the streets despite the wishes of the liberal bourgeoisie. The army was with the people. Had not the bourgeoisie attempted to organize its own government, a revolutionary government would have emerged from the revolutionary working masses. The Duma of June 3[12] would never have dared to seize the power from the hands of czarism. But it did not want to miss the chance offered by interregnum: the monarchy had disappeared, while a revolutionary government was not yet formed. Contrary to all their part, contrary to their own policies and against their will, the liberals found themselves in possession of power.

Miliukov now declares Russia will continue the war "to the end." It is not easy for him to speak so: he knows that his words are apt to arouse the indignation of the masses against the new government. Yet he had to speak them—for the sake of the London, Paris, and American stock exchanges. It is quite possible that he cabled his declaration for foreign consumption only, and that he concealed it from his own country.

Miliukov knows very well that *under given conditions he cannot continue the war, crush Germany, dismember Austria, occupy Constantinople and Poland.*

The masses have revolted, demanding bread and peace. The appearance of a few liberals at the head of the government has not fed the hungry, has not healed the wounds of the people. To satisfy the most urgent, the most acute needs of the people, *peace* must be restored. The liberal imperialistic bloc does not dare to speak of peace. They do not do it, first, on account of the Allies. They do not do it, further, because the liberal bourgeoisie is to a great extent responsible before the people for the present war. The Miliukovs and Guchkovs, not less than the Romanov camarilla,[13] have thrown the country into this monstrous imperialistic adventure. To stop the war, to return to the antebellum misery would mean that they have to account to the people for this undertaking. The Miliukovs and Guchkovs are afraid of the liquidation of the war not less than they were afraid of the revolution.

This is their aspect in their new capacity, as the government of Russia. They are compelled to continue the war, and they can have no hope of victory; they are afraid of the people, and the people do not trust them.

This is how Karl Marx characterized a similar situation:

"From the very beginning ready to betray the people and to compromise with the crowned representatives of the old regime, because the bourgeoisie itself belongs to the old world; . . . keeping a place at the steering wheel of the revolution not because the people were back of them, but because the people pushed them forward; . . . having no faith in themselves, no faith in the people; grumbling against those above, trembling before those below; selfish towards both fronts and aware of their selfishness; revolutionary in the face of conservatives, and conservative in the face of revolutionists, with no confidence in their own slogans and with phrases instead of ideas; frightened by the world's storm and exploiting the world's storm — vulgar through lack of originality, and original only in vulgarity; making profitable business out of their own desires, with no initiative, with no vocation for world-wide historic work . . . a cursed senile creature condemned to direct and abuse in his own senile interests the first youthful movements of a powerful people — a creature with no eyes, with no ears, with no teeth, with nothing whatever — this is how the Prussian bourgeoisie stood at the steering wheel of the Prussian state after the March revolution."[14]

These words of the great master give a perfect picture of the Russian liberal bourgeoisie as it stands at the steering wheel of the government after *our* March revolution. "With no faith in themselves, with no faith in the people, with no eyes, with no teeth." . . . This is their political face.

Luckily for Russia and Europe, there is another face to the Russian revolution, a genuine face: the cables have brought the news that the Provisional Government is opposed by a Workmen's Committee which has already raised a voice of protest against the liberal attempt to rob the revolution and to deliver the people to the monarchy.

Should the Russian revolution stop today as the representatives of liberalism advocate, tomorrow the reaction of the czar, the nobility, and the bureaucracy would gather power and drive Miliukov and Guchkov from their insecure ministerial trenches, as did the Prussian reaction years ago with the representatives of Prussian liberalism. But the Russian revolution will not stop. Time will come, and the revolution will make a clean sweep of the bourgeois liberals blocking its way, as it is now making a clean sweep of czarist reaction.

The Growing Conflict

An open conflict between the forces of the revolution, headed by the city proletariat, and the antirevolutionary liberal bourgeoisie temporarily at the head of the government is more and more impending. It cannot be avoided. Of course, the liberal bourgeoisie and the quasi socialists of the vulgar type will find a collection of very touching slogans as to "national unity" against class divisions; yet no one has ever succeeded in removing social contrasts by conjuring with words or in checking the natural progress of revolutionary struggle.

The internal history of unfolding events is known to us only in fragments, through casual remarks in the official telegrams. But even now it is apparent that on two points the revolutionary proletariat is bound to oppose the liberal bourgeoisie with ever-growing determination.

The first conflict has already arisen around the question of the form of government. The Russian bourgeoisie needs a monarchy. In all the countries pursuing an imperialistic policy, we observe an unusual increase of personal power. The policy of world usurpations, secret treaties, and open treachery requires independence from parliamentary control and a guarantee against changes in policies caused by the change of cabinets. Moreover, for the propertied classes the monarchy is the most secure ally in its struggle against the revolutionary onslaught of the proletariat.

In Russia both these causes are more effective than elsewhere. The Russian bourgeoisie finds it impossible to deny the people universal suffrage, well aware that this would arouse opposition against the Provisional Government among the masses, and give prevalence to the left, the more determined wing of the proletariat in the revolution. Even that monarch of the reserve, Michael Alexandrovich,[15] understands that he cannot reach the throne without having promised "universal, equal, direct, and secret suffrage." It is the more essential for the bourgeoisie to create right now a monarchic counterbalance against the deepest social revolutionary demands of the working masses. *Formally,* in words, the bourgeoisie has agreed to leave the question of a form of government to the discretion of the Constituent Assembly. Practically, however, the Octobrist-Cadet Provisional Government will turn all the preparatory work for the Constituent Assembly into a campaign in favor of a monarchy against a republic. The character of the Constituent Assembly will largely depend upon the character of those who convoke it. It is evident, therefore, that right now the revolutionary proletariat will have *to set up its own organs, the Councils of Workingmen's, Soldiers', and Peasants' Deputies, against the executive organs of the Provisional Government.* In this struggle the proletariat ought to unite about itself the rising masses of the people, with one aim in view — *to seize governmental power.* Only a revolutionary labor government will have the desire and ability to give the country a thorough democratic cleansing during the work preparatory to the Constituent Assembly, to reconstruct the army from top to bottom, to turn it into *a revolutionary militia,* and to show the poorer peasants in practice that their only salvation is in support of a revolutionary labor regime. A Constituent Assembly convoked after such preparatory work will truly reflect the revolutionary, creative forces of the country and become a powerful factor in the further development of the revolution.

The second question that is bound to bring the internationally inclined socialist proletariat in opposition to the imperialistic liberal bourgeoisie is *the question of war and peace*.

War or Peace?

The question of chief interest, now, to the governments and the peoples of the world is: What will be the influence of the Russian revolution on the war? Will it bring peace nearer? Or will the revolutionary enthusiasm of the people swing towards a more vigorous prosecution of the war?

This is a great question. On its solution depends not only the outcome of the war, but the fate of the revolution itself.

In 1905, Miliukov, the present militant minister of foreign affairs, called the Russo-Japanese war an adventure and demanded its immediate cessation. This was also the spirit of the liberal and radical press. The strongest industrial organizations favored immediate peace in spite of unequaled disasters. Why was it so? Because they expected internal reforms. The establishment of a constitutional system, a parliamentary control over the budget and the state finances, a better school system and, especially, an increase in the land possessions of the peasants would, they hoped, increase the prosperity of the population and create a *vast internal market* for Russian industry. It is true that even then, twelve years ago, the Russian bourgeoisie was ready to usurp land belonging to others. It hoped, however, that abolition of feudal relations in the village would create a more powerful market than the annexation of Manchuria or Korea.

The democratization of the country and liberation of the peasants, however, turned out to be a slow process. Neither the czar, nor the nobility, nor the bureaucracy were willing to yield any of their prerogatives. Liberal exhortations were not enough to make them give up the machinery of the state and their land possessions. A revolutionary onslaught of the masses was required. This the bourgeoisie did not want. The agrarian revolts of the peasants, the ever-growing struggle of the proletariat, and the spread of insurrections in the army caused the liberal bourgeoisie to fall back into the camp of the czarist bureaucracy and reactionary nobility. Their alliance was sealed by the coup d'etat of June 3, 1907. Out of this coup d'etat emerged the Third and the Fourth Dumas.

The peasants received no land. The administrative system changed only in name, not in substance. The development of an internal market consisting of prosperous farmers, after the American fashion, did not take place. The capitalist classes, reconciled with the regime of June 3, turned their attention to the usurpation of foreign markets. A new era of Russian imperialism ensues, an imperialism accompanied by a disorderly financial and military system and by insatiable appetites. Guchkov, the present war minister, was formerly a member of the Committee on National Defense, helping to make the army and the navy complete. Miliukov, the present minister of foreign affairs, worked out a program of world conquests which he advocated on his trips to Europe. Russian imperialism and its Octobrist and Cadet representatives bear a great part of the responsibility for the present war.

By the grace of the revolution which they had not wanted and which they had fought, Guchkov and Miliukov are now in power. For the continuation of the war, for victory? Of course! They are the same persons who had dragged the country into the war for the sake of the interests of capital. All their opposition to czarism had its source in their unsatisfied imperialistic appetites. So long as the clique of Nicholas II was in power, the interests of the dynasty and of the reactionary nobility were prevailing in Russian foreign affairs. This is why Berlin and Vienna had hoped to conclude a separate peace with Russia. Now, purely imperialistic interests have superseded the czarist interests; pure imperialism is written on the banner of the Provisional Government. "The government of the czar is gone," the Miliukovs and Guchkovs say to the people, "now you must shed your blood for the common interests of the entire nation." Those interests the imperialists understand as the reincorporation of Poland, the conquest of Galicia, Constantinople, Armenia, Persia.

This transition from an imperialism of the dynasty and the nobility to an imperialism of a purely bourgeois character can never reconcile the Russian proletariat to the war. An international struggle against the world slaughter and imperialism are now our task more than ever. The last dispatches which tell of antimilitaristic propaganda in the streets of Petrograd show that our comrades are bravely doing their duty.

The imperialistic boasts of Miliukov to crush Germany, Austria, and Turkey are the most effective and most timely aid for the Hohenzollerns and Hapsburgs. . . . Miliukov will now serve as a scarecrow in their hands. The liberal imperialistic government of Russia has not yet started reform in its own army, yet it is already helping the Hohenzollerns to raise the patriotic spirit and to mend the shattered "national unity" of the German people. Should the German proletariat be given a right to think that all the Russian people and the main force of the Russian revolution, the proletariat, are behind the bourgeois government of Russia, it would be a terrific blow to the men of our trend of mind, the revolutionary socialists of Germany. To turn the Russian proletariat into patriotic cannon fodder in the service of the Russian liberal bourgeoisie would mean *to throw the German working masses into the camp of the chauvinists and for a long time to halt the progress of a revolution in Germany.*

The prime duty of the revolutionary proletariat in Russia is to show that there is *no power* behind the evil imperialistic will of the liberal bourgeoisie. The Russian revolution has to show the entire world its real face.

The further progress of the revolutionary struggle in Russia and the creation of a revolutionary labor government supported by the people will be a mortal blow to the Hohenzollerns because it will give a powerful stimulus to the revolutionary movement of the German proletariat and of the labor masses of all the other countries. If the first Russian revolution of 1905 brought about revolutions in Asia — in Persia, Turkey, China — the second Russian revolution will be the beginning of a powerful social revolutionary struggle in Europe. Only this struggle will bring real peace to the blood-drenched world.

No, the Russian proletariat will not allow itself to be harnessed to the chariot of Miliukov imperialism. The banner of Russian Social Democracy is now, more than ever before, glowing with bright slogans of inflexible internationalism:

Away with imperialistic robbers!

Long Live a Revolutionary Labor Government!

Long Live Peace and the Brotherhood of Nations!

4

All Power to the Soviets

Less than three months after their arrival in New York Trotsky and his family were again aboard ship, headed for Russia. They were delayed when the British interned him for a month at a German prisoner-of-war camp in Nova Scotia, Canada. When he arrived in Petrograd he found a situation that can be summarized as follows:

After the February uprising and the abdication of the czar, there were two centers of authority in the country. One was the Soviets, elected by the workers and soldiers, and later the peasants, which had reappeared in the first days of the revolution (sometimes called "the democracy" or "the organs of the democracy"). The other was the Provisional Government (the "government"), which had been put together by a frightened ruling class but whose only claim to authority derived from the fact that it was supported by the Soviets.

The idea that the Soviets should rule alone was bitterly opposed by the right wing of the Soviets—the Mensheviks and the Social Revolutionaries (the SRs), the main peasant party. In order to raise the sagging prestige of the Provisional Government, the Mensheviks and Social Revolutionaries joined the capitalist politicians in May in creating a coalition cabinet for the Provisional Government, consisting of ten capitalist and six "socialist" ministers. The main posts were filled by the chief bourgeois party, the Constitutional Democrats (Cadets); the socialist seats were taken by the Mensheviks and Social Revolutionaries, whose apologetics for the government earned them the epithet "Compromisers."

The Petrograd Soviet had already accepted its right wing's endorsement of the coalition cabinet on May 5 when Trotsky made his first speech to that body, a day after his arrival in Petrograd.

"The official speakers [at the May 5 session] didn't arouse much interest . . ." reports the Left Menshevik N. N. Sukhanov,

in his eyewitness account, The Russian Revolution 1917. *"Accidentally turning around I saw Trotsky behind me. [N. S.] Chkheidze [the Menshevik president of the Soviet], behaving differently from the way he behaved with his friends, ignored Trotsky's appearance and didn't propose a welcome to the distinguished revolutionary, who had, moreover, just returned from imprisonment. But Trotsky had already been pointed out, and the hall resounded with cries of 'Trotsky! We want Comrade Trotsky!' . . . He was warmly greeted. And, with characteristic brilliance, he made his first speech—on the Russian Revolution and its influence in Europe and overseas. . . ."*

More important, Trotsky, by calling for "all power to the Soviet of Workers' and Soldiers' Deputies," was aligning himself with its left wing, which was led by the Bolsheviks and supported by other opponents of the class-collaborationist coalition cabinet.

The text printed here is the translation used in Frank A. Golder's collection, Documents of Russian History, 1914-1917. *Since Isaac Deutscher refers to the speech as a "long argument," the text that survives may be only a summary or excerpts.*

News of the Russian Revolution found us in New York but even in that great country, where the bourgeoisie dominates as nowhere else, the Russian Revolution has done its work. The American laborer has had some unfavorable things said about him. It is said that he does not support the revolution. But had you seen the American workman in February, you would have been doubly proud of your revolution. You would have understood that it has shaken not only Russia, not only Europe, but America. It would have been clear to you, as to me, that it has opened a new epoch, an epoch of blood and iron, not in a war of nations, but in a war of the oppressed classes against the domineering classes. [*Tumultuous applause.*] At all the meetings, the workers asked me to give you their warmest greetings. [*Applause.*] But I must tell you something about the Germans. I had an opportunity to come in close contact with a group of German proletarians. You ask me where? In a prisoner-of-war camp. The bourgeois English government arrested us as enemies and placed us in a prisoner-of-war camp in Canada. [*Cries: "Shame!"*] About one hundred German officers and eight hundred sailors were there. They

asked me how it happened that we, Russian citizens, became
prisoners of the English. When I told them that we were prisoners not because we were Russians, but because we were
socialists, they said that they were slaves of their government,
of their William.[1] We got very close together with the German proletarians. . . .

This talk did not please the German officers, and they made
a complaint to the English commander that we were undermining the loyalty of the sailors to the kaiser. The English
captain, anxious to preserve the allegiance of the German
sailors to the kaiser, forbade me to lecture to them. The sailors protested to the commander. When we departed, the sailors
accompanied us with music and shouted "Down with William!
Down with the bourgeoisie! Long live the united international
proletariat!" [*Great applause.*] That which passed through the
brains of the German sailors is passing through in all countries. The Russian Revolution is the prologue to the world
revolution.

But I cannot conceal that I do not agree with everything.
I regard it as dangerous to join the ministry. I do not believe that the ministry can perform miracles. We had, before,
a dual government, due to the opposing points of view of
two classes. The coalition government will not remove opposition, but will merely transfer it to the ministry. But the revolution will not perish because of the coalition government.
We should, however, keep three precepts in mind: 1. Trust
not the bourgeoisie. 2. Control our own leaders. 3. Have confidence in our own revolutionary strength.

What do we recommend? I think that the next step should
be the handing over of all power to the Soviet of Workers' and
Soldiers' Deputies. Only with the authority in one hand can
Russia be saved. Long live the Russian Revolution as the
prologue to the world revolution. [*Applause.*]

5

President of the Petrograd Soviet

Coalition cabinets (the one in May was the first of a series) left the real power in the hands of the capitalists, who were determined to continue the hated war and stop the revolution. Such devices extended the Provisional Government's lease on life, but solved nothing.

Trotsky was seeing his theory of permanent revolution confirmed in life: the only way the revolution could develop was by the working class taking power through the establishment of a workers' state, supported by the peasantry. The socialist revolution beginning in backward Russia would impel the workers of the more advanced countries to take the same road.

Lenin's thinking now ran along the same lines. He and Trotsky had always had a common attitude toward the liberals. But he had expected, after the downfall of the monarchy, that the next stage in Russia would be bourgeois democracy under "a democratic dictatorship of the working class and the peasantry." In the concrete circumstances of the war and the revolution, Lenin changed his position. Returning to Russia in early April, he steered the Bolshevik Party onto the course of proletarian revolution in Russia as an integral part of the international revolutionary struggle against the imperialist world war.

Since Trotsky and the Bolsheviks now agreed that all power should be taken by the Soviets, and that only a government based on the workers in alliance with the peasants could end the war, give the land to the peasants, and save the revolution, Trotsky began to collaborate with the Bolsheviks. With his group, the Mezhrayontzi (Interdistrict Organization), he joined the Bolshevik Party in July, just as the government unleashed a vast slander campaign against Lenin's party, charging its leaders with being German agents and with responsibility for an unsuccessful, semispontaneous, mass armed demonstration. Trotsky was included among the victims of this campaign of repression, being arrested and put in the same jail he had occupied in 1905. Lenin went into hiding, the Bolshevik press was suppressed, and thousands of Bolsheviks were arrested or terrorized.

The tide turned, however, at the end of August when a section of the capitalist class, including the Cadets, overreached itself. They organized a counterrevolutionary military coup around General Lavr Kornilov to overthrow the Provisional Government, now headed by Kerensky of the Social Revolutionaries.

Kerensky had previously appointed Kornilov commander-in-chief as a bolster against the left. Now, to save himself, Kerensky had to turn to the Bolsheviks for help. They responded by arming the workers and appealing to Kornilov's troops to desert— so effectively that in a few days Kornilov's march on Petrograd disintegrated.

This ended the isolation of the Bolsheviks. Trotsky was released from prison on September 4; five days later the Bolsheviks won a majority in the Petrograd Soviet for the first time; on September 23 Trotsky was elected president of that body, whose new presiding committee reflected the new relation of forces— thirteen Bolsheviks, six Social Revolutionaries, three Mensheviks.

The first of the following three speeches was made September 25, on accepting his new post as president.

It was translated for this book by George C. Myland from Volume I of Trotsky's work, 1917.

Acceptance Speech

The new presidium is commencing its work at a moment which must be acknowledged to be not only strained to the highest degree, but also tragic.

Permit me to remind you of the moment in 1905 when I had to open the session of the Petrograd Soviet instead of Khrustalev, who had been arrested.[1] At that time the Petrograd Soviet was going through a critical moment, which ended in our defeat. On the third of December 1905, the whole Soviet was arrested by soldiers of the Izmailovsky Regiment.

But the Izmailovsky Regiment of that time and of the present are entirely different. We feel that we are on much firmer ground than we were then. The new list of ministers published in the evening newspapers, which is a challenge to the democracy, bears witness to the fact that the revolution has approached a serious moment. We are convinced that the new presidium will have occasion to work at the time of a new upsurge of the revolution.

We are all members of parties, and we will be carrying on our work, and more than once we will have to cross swords.

But we will conduct the work of the Petrograd Soviet in the spirit of justice and of full freedom for all factions, and the hand of the presidium will never be the hand which suppresses the minority.

The Petrograd Soviet is closing its ranks and each of us, in the factories and in the military detachments, will carry out in life the decisions which have been adopted in the Soviet.

Long live the Petrograd Soviet of Workers' and Soldiers' Deputies! [*Stormy applause.*]

The following speech was also made on September 25 in answer to the arguments of Matvei Skobelev, a Menshevik who had served as minister of labor in the Provisional Government. He had begun his stint in office by promising to cut down profits "100 percent" but in less than two weeks had concentrated on cutting down strikes.

Skobelev was now advising the Soviet to support the coalition which had just been put together made up of six capitalist and ten "socialist" ministers. To provide a semblance of support for this government now seated in the czar's Winter Palace, a pre-Parliament had been convened, stacked with right-wing socialists, cooperators, and Cadets. But to no avail; this was to be the last coalition government.

This speech was also translated by George C. Myland from Volume I of 1917.

Answer to Skobelev

Comrades! The former minister of labor considered it necessary to recall that the revolution is beginning anew for him, for he is again in the Petrograd Soviet. All I see is that *former* ministers are more willing to appear among us than *present* ones.

The latter have shown up extremely rarely, and from this we have drawn the conclusion that the coalition with the bourgeoisie that Skobelev recommends to us so much reconciles itself very badly with the appearance of the existing ministers before us. The main demand of the Cadet bourgeoisie is the independence of the ministers from the organs of the democracy and the Cadet bourgeoisie always won out on this point, for the history of the coalition ministry was the history of the gradual freeing of the ministers from the control of the organs of revolutionary democracy.

Now, after this freedom has been achieved, even a quite dubious "de facto responsibility" of the government to the pre-Parliament seems to be a great conquest to former ministers. . . . That's how much demands have been lowered, now that they have trampled their responsibility to the Soviets underfoot.

Today Skobelev came to us and again, as before, offered us *advice,* but we, also as before, would like to hear a *report.* [*Applause.*]

Why didn't he tell us who compelled him to make his concessions at the expense of the workers during his stay as a minister? Clearly the coalition, for the coalition is an institution where the Skobelevs serve the Konovalovs.[2]

Skobelev advises us: be aware of your responsibility.

But there are two kinds of responsibility. There is the responsibility of a minister to the bourgeois state, and there is responsibility to the proletariat.

In order to mask the responsibility of the ministers to the bourgeoisie, the term "statesmanship" was also introduced. But we know well that in Western Europe, when the minister-socialists moved over into the camp of the bourgeoisie, they also covered themselves with the term "statesmanship." However, Marx taught us that the state always bears a class character. We want *our* statesmanship—one which gives power to the working masses and land to the peasants. Now, however, the government is in the hands of our class enemies with whom we will be bound not by mutual responsibility, but by merciless struggle.

According to Skobelev, we have inherited a Petrograd Soviet which is strong thanks to the policy of coalition. No, our Soviet developed not in subservience to the bourgeoisie but in struggle with it. We regenerated the Soviet in the spirit of enmity and merciless struggle against the impending dictatorship of the liberal bourgeoisie.

And we can say: as czarism educated the Russian Revolution,

so the policies of Citizen Skobelev and others educated the present Petrograd Soviet.

We understand that our responsibility has grown, that each word of ours now has greater weight; but, having become the majority of the Soviet, we still have not become a government party, we remain the organization of the revolutionary proletariat—the irreconcilable class enemy of the state. The Mensheviks,[3] however, want to transform the Soviet into a government organ.

Therefore, they turned away from us and united with . . . the cooperators, the new "social base" of the revolution.

Up until now we never heard of cooperative democracy.

What kind of a new class is this? The circumstance that certain people serve as functionaries in peasant cooperatives, for example, still does not mean that they express the revolutionary political will of the peasants, just as a doctor who treats the workers still does not express their political will. Cooperators must be good organizers, merchants, bookkeepers, but for the defense of their class rights the peasants, like the workers, trust the Soviets.

In fact, however, the cooperators have been called to create a revolutionary power, which their constituency did not at all empower them to do.

We are convinced that we will find greater support among the peasantry than the cooperators. Let us take an example. If a revolutionary government immediately transferred the land to the land committees and the rent payments for the land to the soldiers, then the whole peasant democracy would support such a government. But the Berkenheims and Prokopoviches[4] are against this!

When we bring forth the slogan "All power to the Soviets" we know that it will not instantly heal all ills.

We need a power which has been created on the lines of the trade unions, which give the strikers everything they can, conceal nothing, and when something is impossible, openly acknowledge it.

We need a power which comes from the ranks of the peasants, workers, and soldiers, which rests on them and is responsible to them. Under such a power the railroad workers would not have to resort to a strike. They would know beforehand that this power will give them everything it can.

A truly great danger threatens us at the time of demobilization, when the tormented, hungry army floats through the country. But repressions are not the remedy for the so-called "anarchy." It is necessary that every honest Russian soldier know that an honest, people's power holds all the resources of the country in its hands and is distributing them without deception, without indulgence to marauders. Only a power which they trust, and rightly trust, can save us from fratricidal struggle, from cruel chaos. And they talk, as if about a success, about that shame—yes, shame—that some upstarts in the Winter Palace are bargaining with us over the degree to which they will be irresponsible to us. And this is what you call the result of the revolution?

Skobelev's resolution comes down to this, that, maybe, if we conduct ourselves decorously in the pre-Parliament—who knows?—the ministers will agree to be responsible, and even will abolish capital punishment.

This is a complete misunderstanding of the situation and of the moods of the masses. The government has already mobilized against us, against the people, and tomorrow it will no doubt declare a holy war against the Soviets. And then, when Kerensky, along with Konovalov and Tretiakov, resting on the pre-Parliament, begin their campaigns against the Soviets, where will Skobelev's party be? With the punitive expedition against the Soviets or with the Soviets?

We, the Petrograd Soviet, appealed at our last session to all Soviets to be on the alert against the impending counterrevolutionary attempts.

In this struggle, to which we are being provoked, we will not be with those who are smashing the democratic organs in the localities, and not with those who are defending the people who are smashing them, but with those who are defending to the end the organs of the Russian Revolution and lead it forward.

As president of the Petrograd Soviet, Trotsky was in a better position to influence developments outside of Petrograd. The Bolsheviks now launched a campaign calling for the Second All-Russian Congress of Soviets (which the Compromisers kept putting off) and tied this up with their demand for all power to the Soviets. As part of this campaign, a congress was held of the Soviets of the Northern Region.

In a speech to the regional congress on October 11 Trotsky condemned the attempts of the government to move the revolutionary troops from Petrograd. The government's maneuvers

*with the Petrograd garrison were to play a prominent role
in the showdown two weeks later.*

*The translation for this book was made by A. L. Preston
from Volume II of 1917.*

To the Soviets of the Northern Region

We represent the party which gives the Soviets its character
and if, after the collapse of early hopes, we still have a powerful Soviet it is because it is armed with a new program of
merciless struggle against our class enemies. Fundamentally,
the Petrograd Soviet is engaged in a struggle against the government and those parties which support it.

You know that when the danger at the front became absolutely clear the Provisional Government wanted to move to
Moscow. Together with it, our "defensists," who would have
left Petrograd defenseless, would have earned good marks for
their defensist policy in Moscow.

This plan was dictated by hatred for revolutionary Petrograd.

Our government can flee from Petrograd, but the revolutionary people will never leave Petrograd; they will defend it to
the end.

Petrograd, as they say in the Evangel, is "the city on the
mountain," seen by all. Everyone knows our opinions and
our works.

And now the General Staff puts forward a plan to evacuate
two-thirds of its garrison from Petrograd. That is the problem
posed before us. The Soviet "authorities" have decided to support the General Staff although they have no confidence in those
who want to evacuate troops.

The Baltic fleet says otherwise. It has declared it does not
believe one single word of the Provisional Government, that
government which in reality is betraying the people—and nevertheless the Baltic fleet is dying in defense of the revolutionary
cause.

The military authorities demand that the soldiers be evacuated; we don't know where but we do know from where—from
revolutionary Petrograd. On the eve of Kornilov's conspiracy
they also issued an order to evacuate the troops, and then
also they argued to us it was for strategic reasons.

We are not able to say, as do the defensists, who have not
a grain of the defense of the revolution in them, that if the
authorities demand it we must obey. The Petrograd Soviet

can not accept in any way such a responsibility, and does not.

This problem will be posed in the near future in a practical fashion for each unit in the Petrograd garrison, and we are aware of our responsibility to Russia and its people.

The matter concerns the fate of Petrograd, and we wish to decide it in concert with you, the representatives of the regional Soviets.

We must take on ourselves the defense of the country as a whole. The best defense of the country will be an offer of immediate peace to the peoples of the whole world, over the heads of their imperialist governments.

Are we going to entrust the conduct of the war to those who are unable to wage war or conclude peace?

There is no one except the Soviets of Workers' and Soldiers' Deputies who can bring this matter to an end, because outside of the Soviets there are only Kornilovists, semi-Kornilovists, or political bankrupts who have broken with the revolutionary people.

There is only one way out—the power must pass into the hands of the All-Russian Soviet of Workers' and Soldiers' Deputies.

6

Organizing the Insurrection

The Second All-Russian Congress of Soviets was called for October 25 at which there was a strong possibility that the Bolsheviks would have a majority. Lenin proposed that the Bolsheviks prepare an insurrection; this was approved by the party leadership, despite the disagreement of the prominent Bolsheviks, Kamenev and Zinoviev; meantime, the Petrograd Soviet set up a Military Revolutionary Committee headed by Trotsky.

The Bolsheviks made no secret of their intention to have the Second Congress of the Soviets take power and set up a new government. What the Provisional Government did not know was only whether the Bolsheviks would really have the audacity to suit their actions to their words, and when. The situation was further complicated by the fact that Kamenev and Zinoviev, breaking party discipline, wrote a letter in the non-Bolshevik press opposing any insurrection. The air was therefore full of rumors and guesses. At the same time, weapons were needed, and it was impossible to conceal the fact that the Soviet was gathering them.

How Trotsky handled these problems—denying a press account claiming that the insurrection would come on October 22 and at the same time justifying armed struggle as a defensive measure of the revolution—is shown in the following speech he gave to the Petrograd Soviet on October 18.

Like the subsequent speeches and resolutions in this chapter, it has been translated for this book by John Fairlie and A. L. Preston from Volume II of 1917. (The material in 1917 was taken from newspaper accounts, and some of the following speeches contain summary comments which were made by the reporters.)

In Answer to a Rumor

During the last days the press has been full of communications, rumors, and articles about an impending "action"; sometimes this action is attributed to the Bolsheviks, sometimes to the Petrograd Soviet.

The decisions of the Petrograd Soviet are published and made known to everybody. The Soviet is an elective institution; each of its members is responsible to the workers or soldiers who elected him. This revolutionary parliament of the proletariat and the revolutionary garrison cannot make a decision which is not known to the workers and soldiers.

We hide nothing. I declare in the name of the Soviet that no armed action has been settled upon by us, but if the Soviet in the course of events should be obliged to set the date for an action the workers and soldiers would come out to the last man at its summons.

The bourgeois press has set the day of the action for October 22. All the papers have repeated this "subtle" prophecy. But October 22 has been unanimously arranged by the Executive Committee as a day of agitation, of propaganda, of bringing out the masses under the banner of the Soviet, and as a collection day on behalf of the Soviet.

Further, they say that I signed an order for five thousand rifles from the Sestroretsk factory. Yes, I signed it—by virtue of the decision already taken in the Kornilov days concerning the arming of the workers' militia. And the Petrograd Soviet will continue to organize and arm the workers' guard.

But all this news, all these "facts" are surpassed by the newspaper *Den* [*The Day*].

Comrade Trotsky reads from yesterday's issue of *Den* the "plan" of the Bolshevik action. This plan outlines the route to be followed by the Bolshevik "armies" on the following night and indicates the places to be occupied. Nor was it forgotten to point out that the insurgents were to bring with them "hooligan elements" from Novaya Derevnya. [*Laughter in the hall during the reading.*]

I beg you to listen carefully so that each army will know the route it has to follow! . . . [*Laughter.*]

Comrades—this news needs no comment just as the newspaper which published it needs no description.

The plan of the campaign is clear.

We are in conflict with the government on a question which may become extremely sharp. It is on the question of the evacuation of the troops. The bourgeois press wants to build up round the Petrograd workers an atmosphere of hostility and suspicion, and to provoke the hatred of the soldiers at the front for Petrograd.

Another sharp question is that of the Soviet Congress. The government circles know our views on the fundamental role of the Soviet Congress. It is known to the bourgeoisie that the Petrograd Soviet is going to propose to the Congress of Soviets that they take the power, offer a democratic peace to the belligerent peoples, and give the land to the peasants. So they are trying to disarm Petrograd by evacuating its garrison; and while the congress is arming itself, they arm those who obey them in order to be able to throw all their forces against the representatives of the workers, soldiers, and peasants, and break them up.

As an artillery barrage precedes an army's attack, the present campaign of lies and calumnies precedes an armed attack on the Soviet Congress.

We must be prepared. We are entering a period of bitter struggles. We must always expect an attack from the counterrevolution.

But at its first attempt to break up the Soviet Congress, at the first attempt at an attack, we shall answer with a counterattack which will be ruthless and which we shall carry through to the end.

A government is in bad shape when it cannot rely on its own troops. In The Russian Revolution, *Marcel Liebman tells how the Military Revolutionary Committee learned on October 23 that the Peter and Paul garrison, whose guns commanded the Winter Palace, had refused to recognize the Military Revolutionary Committee. Some thought it would be necessary to disarm and oust the garrison by force. "Trotsky said that the job could be done much better by political persuasion. He accordingly went to the fortress, called for a general meeting, and so fired those present with his own zeal that he swung them round completely. As a result the Bolsheviks gained not only the fortress itself, but also the nearby Kronverksky arsenal containing 100,000 rifles — all without firing a single shot.*

"This feat was typical not only of the October insurrection but of the entire Bolshevik Revolution. It involved no bril-

*liant displays of military strategy, no spectacular show of
force— the seizure of power was a political rather than a military achievement. It was compounded not of a tissue of dark,
Machiavellian plots but of thousands of acts of persuasion
and propaganda repeated with indefatigable patience. By refusing the temptation of a frontal attack, by going unarmed
to the Peter and Paul Fortress to plead with the soldiers in
person, Trotsky did the work of a true revolutionary: he chose
conversion rather than conspiracy, argument rather than guns,
agitation rather than bludgeoning."*

*Two days before the incident described by Liebman, an
extraordinary meeting of the military committees of the Petrograd garrison adopted three resolutions written by Trotsky:*

Three Resolutions

1. On the Military Revolutionary Committee

Welcoming the setting up of a Military Revolutionary Committee attached to the Petrograd Soviet of Workers' and Soldiers' Deputies, the garrison of Petrograd and its environs
promises the Military Revolutionary Committee full support
in all its steps to link closely the front and the rear in the
interests of the revolution.

2. October 22 Day

The garrison of Petrograd and its environs declares:

October 22 is to be a day devoted to a peaceful review of
the forces of the Petrograd soldiers and workers and of col-
lecting funds for the revolutionary press.

The garrison appeals to the Cossacks: BEWARE OF PROV-
OCATION BY OUR COMMON ENEMIES. We are your brothers. Together let us struggle for peace and freedom.

We invite you to our meetings tomorrow. You are welcome,
brother Cossacks!

The Petrograd garrison also declares:

The entire garrison together with the organized proletariat
assumes the maintenance of revolutionary order in Petrograd.
Any provocative act by the Kornilovists and the bourgeoisie
to bring disturbance and disorder into the revolutionary ranks
will meet with A RUTHLESS COUNTERBLOW.

3. The All-Russian Congress of Soviets of Workers' and Soldiers' Deputies

Endorsing all the political decisions of the Petrograd Soviet of Workers' and Soldiers' Deputies, the Petrograd garrison declares:

THE TIME FOR WORDS HAS PASSED. The country is on the edge of ruin. The army demands peace, the peasants demand land, the workers demand work and food. The coalition government is against the people. It is a tool in the hands of the enemies of the people. The time for words has passed. The All-Russian Congress of Soviets must take the power and give the people peace, land, and food. The safety of the revolution and the people demands it.

ALL POWER TO THE SOVIETS!

IMMEDIATE ARMISTICE ON ALL FRONTS!

LAND TO THE PEASANTS!

HONEST SUMMONING OF THE CONSTITUENT ASSEMBLY AT THE APPOINTED DATE!

The Petrograd garrison solemnly promises the All-Russian Congress to give all the forces it can, to the last man, in the struggle for these demands.

Rely upon us, authorized representatives of the soldiers, workers, and peasants. We are all at our posts, ready TO CONQUER OR DIE!

October 22 had been designated Petrograd Soviet Day, with big meetings planned all over the city, primarily to make a demonstration of strength. Suddenly and anonymously an announcement appeared that the Cossacks would hold a religious demonstration on the same day. This was an obvious attempt to provoke a clash and the Petrograd Soviet responded quickly— by appealing to the Cossacks for their support.

The Cossack demonstration was called off. Petrograd Soviet Day was celebrated peacefully and massively.

A manifesto circulated to the Cossacks the day before, written by Trotsky, follows:

Brother Cossacks!

Brother Cossacks!

The Petrograd Soviet of Soldiers' and Workers' Deputies appeals to you.

You, Cossacks, are being roused against us, workers

and soldiers. It is our common foes who are carrying out this work of Cain: the oppressors of the court, the bankers, landlords, senior officials, former czarist servants. They have always been strong and powerful by dividing the people. They have poisoned the minds of the soldiers against the workers and peasants. They have set the Cossacks on the soldiers. By what means do they achieve this? By lies and slander. The Cossacks, soldiers, sailors, workers, and peasants are brothers. They are all toilers, all poor, they all work hard, they are all oppressed and robbed by the war.

Who's the war good for? Who started it? Not the Cossacks and not the soldiers, not the workers and not the peasants. It's the generals, bankers, czars, and landlords who need the war. They increase their power, their strength, their wealth, by war. They turn the people's blood into their masters' gold.

The people want peace. In all countries the soldiers and workers are thirsting for peace. The Petrograd Soviet of Workers' and Soldiers' Deputies says to the bourgeoisie and the generals: "Move over, tyrants! Let power pass into the hands of the people themselves, and then the people will immediately conclude an honorable peace!"

Is that right, Comrade Cossacks? We do not doubt that you will say: Right! But that's the reason we are hated by all the usurers, the rich, the princes, the courtiers, and the generals, including your Cossack generals. They are ready at any hour to annihilate the Petrograd Soviet, to crush the revolution, and put back the shackles on the people as in the czar's time.

That's why they're telling you slanders about us. They are deceiving you. They say the Soviets want to take away your land. Don't believe them, Cossacks! The Soviet wants to take the land away from all the landowners and hand it over to the peasants, the corn-growers and also the poor Cossacks. Whose hand is raised to take the land away from the worker Cossack?

They tell you the Soviet is intending to make some sort of insurrection on October 22, to fight with you, shoot on the streets, kill. Those who told you that are rogues and provocateurs. Tell them so! On October 22 the Soviet has arranged peaceful meetings, assemblies, and concerts, where the workers and soldiers, sailors and peasants will hear and discuss speeches about war and peace, about the people's lot. We invite you too to these peaceful, fraternal meetings. You are welcome, brother Cossacks!

If any of you doubt this, come along to the Smolny, where the Soviet is.[1] There are always many soldiers there, and Cossacks too. They will explain to the doubters what the Soviet wants, what are its aims and methods. That's what the people overthrew the czar for, to freely discuss their needs and take their affairs into their own hands. Cossacks, throw off the veil that the Kaledins, Bardizhes, Karaulovs[2] and other enemies of the working Cossacks are pulling over your eyes.

Someone has arranged a Cossack religious procession for October 22. It is a matter for the free conscience of each Cossack whether or not to participate in the procession. We shall not interfere in this matter and will cause no trouble to anybody.

However, we warn you, Cossacks: be careful lest under the mask of a religious procession your Kaledins try to incite you against the workers and soldiers. Their goal is to bring about a bloodbath and to drown you and your liberty in brothers' blood.

Be assured: October 22 is Petrograd Soviet Day, a day of peaceful meetings, assemblies, and money collections for soldiers' and workers' newspapers. Join us, Cossacks—join the common family of the working people, for the common fight for freedom and happiness.

We stretch out a brotherly hand to you, Cossacks!

The Petrograd Soviet of Workers'
and Soldiers' Deputies

When the Petrograd garrison went over to the Soviet on October 21, representatives of the Military Revolutionary Committee met with the district commander of the garrison and demanded the right to countersign all staff orders to the garrison. The district commander refused, and the next day the Military Revolutionary Committee sent the following message to the garrison, by Trotsky, alerting all personnel to the deepening crisis:

Message to the Garrison

At its meeting on October 21, the revolutionary garrison of Petrograd rallied to the Military Revolutionary Committee of the Petrograd Soviet of Workers' and Soldiers' Deputies as its leading organ.

Despite that fact, headquarters of the Petrograd military district on the night of October 22 has not recognized the Military Revolutionary Committee, refusing to work with the representatives of the soldiers' section of the Soviet.

Thereby, headquarters has broken with the revolutionary garrison and the Petrograd Soviet of Workers' and Soldiers' Deputies.

Having broken with the organized garrison of the capital, headquarters is a direct armed instrument of the counterrevolutionary forces.

The Military Revolutionary Committee disclaims all responsibility for the actions of headquarters of the Petrograd military district.

SOLDIERS OF PETROGRAD!

1. The defense of revolutionary order against counterrevolutionary attempts falls upon you, under the leadership of the Military Revolutionary Committee.

2. No directives to the garrison are valid unless signed by the Military Revolutionary Committee.

3. All directives for today—Petrograd Soviet Day—retain their full force.

4. On all soldiers of the garrison is imposed the duty of vigilance, steadfastness, and strict discipline.

5. The revolution is in danger! Long live the revolutionary garrison!

> The Military Revolutionary Committee
> of the Petrograd Soviet of Workers'
> and Soldiers' Deputies

Frightened by the defection of the ranks of the Petrograd garrison, the Provisional Government issued some strong directives: troops were ordered not to carry out "unauthorized" orders on "pain of arrest for armed rebellion"; all illegal military activities were threatened with courts-martial; Soviet commissars were informed that they were barred from the garrison; the sailors of the Aurora were ordered out to sea; troops were sent to shut down two papers printed at the Bolshevik printing plant, Rabochii Put and Soldat. The only trouble was that the government already lacked the forces to carry out such orders.

The Petrograd Soviet held an extraordinary session on October 24 at which Trotsky reported on what the government was trying to do and how the Military Revolutionary Committee was handling the situation.

Report to the Extraordinary Session

Giving an account of the conflict with headquarters of the military district, Comrade Trotsky reported a whole series of attempts by the Provisional Government to bring to Petrograd troops against the revolution. But the Military Revolutionary Committee paralyzed all such attempts.

We are not afraid to take over the responsibility for the maintenance of revolutionary order in the city. Today the Military Revolutionary Committee has declared to the people of Petrograd that "the Petrograd Soviet of Workers' and Soldiers' Deputies has taken over the maintenance of revolutionary order against counterrevolutionary and pogrom attempts."

Today we met a delegation from the municipal administration. The delegation asked us what we thought about the maintenance of order in the city. The government has no forces, no power — they see that. The delegation then passed on to the rumor that the government seemed to be ready to pass the power over to the city administration.

To the delegation from the city administration we answered that in the interest of maintaining revolutionary order we were prepared to bring our activity into harmony with that of the city duma. A representative of the Executive Committee had already in the Kornilov days been delegated to the city administration. Moreover, a representative of the city administration had entered the Military Revolutionary Committee.

The delegation then asked us about the uprising and the action. On this matter we told them what has repeatedly been said by us here. In this connection there was not a word to be changed. We answered the delegation:

"All power to the Soviets" is our slogan. At the forthcoming sessions of the All-Russian Congress of Soviets this slogan must be realized. Whether this leads to an uprising or action depends not only and not so much on the Soviets but rather on those who retain the state power in their hands against the united will of the people.

The Military Revolutionary Committee arose not as an organ of insurrection but for the defense of the revolution. When the

Kerensky government wanted to disarm Petrograd and evacuate the troops from there, we said that we would not permit it, in the interest of defending the revolution. When yesterday this government closed down two newspapers which had enormous influence among the Petrograd proletariat and garrison, we said we could not tolerate the stifling of free speech and decided to continue to bring out the papers, placing the honor of protecting the printers of the revolutionary papers on the valiant soldiers of the Lithuanian Regiment and the Sixth Supporting Artillery Battalion.

Is that an insurrection?

We have a semigovernment which does not trust the people and which the people do not trust, because it has no life left in it. This semigovernment is waiting for the broom of history to sweep it away to make room for the real power of the revolutionary people.

The government mobilized the junkers[3] and at the same time gave the cruiser *Aurora* the order to take to the open sea. Why, having ordered up the junkers, did the government move the sailors off? The reasons are clear. The sailors we are talking about are those to whom, in the Kornilov days, Skobelev came, cap in hand, to beg them to defend the Winter Palace from the Kornilovists. The sailors of the *Aurora* carried out Skobelev's request at the time. Now the government is trying to evacuate them. But the comrade sailors have sought the advice of the Military Revolutionary Committee. And today the *Aurora* stays where it was last night.

Tomorrow, the Congress of Soviets will open. The task of the garrison and the proletariat is to put at the disposal of the congress the forces they have gathered by which the government's provocations will be smashed. Our task is to keep these forces intact and undivided until the congress. When the congress says it will organize the power, it will conclude the work done in the whole country. That will mean that, having freed itself from the power of the counterrevolutionary government, the people will have convened their own congress and established their own power.

If the sham authority recklessly tries to reanimate its own corpse, the masses of the people, organized and armed, will offer their determined resistance, and this resistance will be the more powerful the more vicious the attacks of the reaction. If the government, in the twenty-four or forty-eight hours still left to it, wishes to use that time in order to thrust a knife into the back of the revolution, we shall answer blow with blow, iron with steel.

Answering a question about relations with the Left Social Revolutionaries,[4] Comrade Trotsky declared:

Of the five members of the Bureau of the Military Revolutionary Committee, two are Left SRs, Comrades Lazimir and Sakharov. They are working very well and there are no differences of principle between us and them.

This evening we have been informed that the Left SR fraction is leaving the pre-Parliament and is sending its representatives to the Military Revolutionary Committee.

So, in the struggle against the common enemy—the counterrevolution—we have found one another.

At an extraordinary session of the Petrograd Soviet on the afternoon of October 25, Trotsky reported the overthrow of the Provisional Government and then introduced Lenin. His announcement that the fate of the Winter Palace would be settled in a few minutes proved premature; it was not taken until twelve hours later. His prediction that the government ministers would soon be arrested was only partly fulfilled; Kerensky escaped. But his remarks about the lack of bloodshed during the uprising were fully confirmed. Marcel Liebman says, "The only casualties in the whole of Petrograd fell during the capture of the Winter Palace on the night of October 25-26; all five came from the ranks of the insurrectionists."

The Overthrow of the Provisional Government

In the name of the Military Revolutionary Committee, I declare the Provisional Government is no more. [*Applause.*] Some ministers have been arrested. [*Hurrahs!*] The others will be arrested in a few days or a few hours. [*Applause.*]

The revolutionary garrison, which is at the disposal of the Military Revolutionary Committee, has dissolved the meeting of the pre-Parliament. [*Stormy applause. Cries of "Long live the Military Revolutionary Committee!"*]

They have told us that an insurrection of the garrison at the present moment would provoke a pogrom and drown the revolution in torrents of blood. Up till now no blood has flowed. We do not know of a single casualty. I do not know of any other example in history of a revolutionary movement involv-

ing such gigantic masses that was carried through without
bloodshed.

The authority of the Provisional Government, presided over
by Kerensky, was a corpse and only awaited the broom of
history to sweep it away.

We must underline the heroism and self-sacrifice of the Petrograd soldiers and workers. We have been awake here all night,
and at the telephone followed how the detachments of revolutionary soldiers' and workers' guards went about their business
quietly. The populace slept peacefully and did not know that
at this very time one authority was replacing another.

The railway stations, post offices, telegraph stations, the
Petrograd Telephone Agency, the State Bank have been occupied. [*Stormy applause.*]

The Winter Palace is not yet taken, but its fate will be settled
in the course of the next few minutes. [*Applause.*]

The Petrograd Soviet of Workers' and Soldiers' Deputies has
the right to be proud of the soldiers and workers on whom
it relied, whom it led into battle and led to a glorious victory.

The characteristic of bourgeois and petty-bourgeois governments is to deceive the masses.

We, today, we, the Soviet of Soldiers', Workers', and Peasants' Deputies, are going to undertake an experiment unique
in history, the establishment of a government that will have
no other aim than the satisfaction of the needs of the soldiers,
workers, and peasants.

The state must become the instrument of the masses in the
struggle for their liberation from all slavery.

The work cannot be done without the influence of the Soviets.
The best representatives of bourgeois science will understand
that the conditions created by the Soviets of Workers', Soldiers', and Peasants' Deputies are the best for their work.

It is necessary to establish control over production. Peasants,
workers, and soldiers must feel that the nation's business is
their business.

That is the fundamental principle of the establishment of the
authority.

The introduction of universal labor service was one of the
immediate tasks of genuine revolutionary power.

Further, Comrade Trotsky announced that on the agenda
were the report of the Military Revolutionary Committee and
the report on the tasks of Soviet power. The reporter on the
second question would be Comrade Lenin. [*Thunderous applause.*]

Comrade Trotsky announced that those who had been arrested for political reasons had been released and some of them were already carrying out the duties of revolutionary commissars.

Comrade Zinoviev, announced Comrade Trotsky, would be the guest of the Petrograd Soviet in the current session.

In the name of the Petrograd Soviet a telegram had been circulated that night throughout the whole of Russia giving the real state of affairs.

Radiotelegrams had been sent to the forces on active service announcing the fall of the old authority and the imminent establishment of a new one. The first steps of the new authority would require the following: immediate armistice on all fronts; land to the peasants; urgent convocation of a genuinely democratic Constituent Assembly.

The whereabouts of the former minister-president Kerensky are unknown, but we hope it will soon become known to all.

To the question of what the attitude of the front was to the events, Comrade Trotsky replied: We have only been able to send our telegrams. No replies have been received to them, but we have heard here many times the representatives from the front rebuking us for not having taken vigorous steps.

Vladimir Ilyich Lenin has just come in and joined us; because of the course of circumstances he has not been able to come among us until now. Comrade Trotsky describes the role of Comrade Lenin in the history of the revolutionary movement in Russia, and proclaims:

Long live Comrade Lenin who has returned to us!

Later in the same October 25 session, Trotsky answered an objection from the floor that the Bolsheviks were predetermining the will of the Second Congress.

One of the immediate tasks of the Military Revolutionary Committee is to send delegations to tell the front about the revolution that has taken place in Petrograd.

The Petrograd Soviet must select from its midst commissars to be sent to the front. The Military Revolutionary Committee and its members cannot at the moment make reports since they are continuously taken up with urgent work. I can tell you that a telegram has just been received that troops from the front are moving in the direction of Petrograd. It is necessary to send revolutionary commissars over the whole country to tell the broad masses of the people what has happened.

[*A voice: "You are predetermining the will of the All-Russian Congress of Soviets."*]

The will of the All-Russian Congress of Soviets is predetermined by the great fact of the insurrection of the workers and soldiers of Petrograd, which has taken place this night. Now we have only to consolidate our victory.

On October 25 the Military Revolutionary Committee sent the following message, written by Trotsky, to all army committees and Soviets of Soldiers' Deputies:

To the Army Committees and Soldiers' Soviets

The Petrograd garrison and proletariat have overthrown the government of Kerensky, which rose against the revolution and the people. The revolution which removed the Provisional Government took place bloodlessly.

The Petrograd Soviet of Workers' and Soldiers' Deputies triumphantly welcomed the revolution which had taken place and recognized the power of the Military Revolutionary Committee until the setting up of a government of Soviets. In informing the army at the front and in the rear of this, the Military Revolutionary Committee calls on the revolutionary soldiers to watch vigilantly the behavior of their commanding officers. Officers who do not directly and openly associate themselves with the revolution which has taken place are to be arrested immediately as foes.

The Petrograd Soviet sees the program of the new power as being the immediate offer of a democratic peace, the immediate handing over of landowners' lands to the peasants, the transfer of all power to the Soviets, and the honorable convocation of a Constituent Assembly. The people's revolutionary army must not permit unreliable units to be sent from the front to Petrograd, doing so by word and persuasion, and where that does not help, hindering them by the merciless use of force.

This order is to be proclaimed immediately before the military units armed with all types of weapons. Concealment by army organizations of this order from the masses of the soldiers will be treated as a grave crime against the revolution and will be punished with all the severity of revolutionary law.

Soldiers! For peace, for bread, for land, for people's power!
The Military Revolutionary Committee

The Second All-Russian Congress of Soviets, which opened at 11:45 on the night of October 25, found the Mensheviks and Social Revolutionaries in a distinct minority: the Social Revolutionary delegates, caucusing that morning, had split into two wings, the larger favoring collaboration with the Bolsheviks (now the strongest party) and formation of a Soviet government. The right-wing Mensheviks and Social Revolutionaries refused any kind of collaboration with the Bolshevik "party of insurrection" and walked out of the congress.

Martov, representing the Left Mensheviks, proposed that the new government should be based on all the Soviet parties, including those whose representatives had just walked out. Trotsky's reply was sharp: "An insurrection of the popular masses needs no justification; what happened was not a conspiracy but an insurrection. . . . Our insurrection has won. And now we are being asked to give up our victory, to come to an agreement. With whom? With those who have left or with those that make these proposals? You are miserable bankrupts; your part is over. Go to the place where you belong from now on — the dustbin of history!"

At this the Left Mensheviks decided that they were walking out too. On behalf of the Bolsheviks, Trotsky introduced the following resolution:

Walkout of the Mensheviks and Social Revolutionaries

The Second All-Russian Congress of Soviets declares:

The walkout of the Menshevik and SR delegates from the congress is a completely impotent attempt to wreck the plenipotentiary representation of the worker and soldier masses at the very moment when the vanguard of these masses, with weapons in hand, is defending the congress and the revolution against counterrevolutionary attack.

The compromising parties by their past policies have caused incalculable losses to the cause of the revolution and have irreparably compromised themselves in the eyes of the workers, peasants, and soldiers.

The Compromisers prepared and approved the fatal offensive of June 18 which brought the army and the country to the edge of destruction.

The Compromisers supported the government of carnage and punishment and treason to the people. For seven months the Compromisers supported the policy of systematic deception of the peasants on the land question.

The Compromisers supported the suppression of revolutionary organizations, the disarming of the workers, the introduction of Kornilovist discipline into the army and the purposeless dragging out of the bloody war.

The Compromisers in fact helped their bourgeois allies deepen the economic ruin in the land, condemning millions of the toiling masses to famine.

Having lost the confidence of the masses as a result of this policy, the Compromisers, artificially and dishonestly, kept for themselves top positions in the Soviet and army organizations which for a long time had not been up for reelection.

In view of the stated circumstances, the Central Executive Committee[5] has made every effort to wreck the Congress of Soviets, relying for that on the compromising army committees and on the direct support of the governmental authority.

When this policy of obstructing and falsifying the revolutionary class's public opinion suffered a lamentable failure; when the Provisional Government, set up by the Compromisers, fell under the blows of the Petrograd workers and soldiers; when the All-Russian Congress of Soviets showed clearly the predominance of the party of revolutionary socialism; and when insurrection became the only way out for the revolutionary masses, deceived and tormented by the bourgeoisie and their lackeys, then the Compromisers drew the final conclusions for themselves, and broke with the Soviets whose power they had tried vainly to undermine.

The walkout of the Compromisers does not weaken the Soviets but strengthens them as it cleanses the workers' and peasants' revolution of counterrevolutionary ingredients.

Having heard the statements of the SRs and the Mensheviks, the Second All-Russian Congress continues its work whose aims are determined by the will of the toiling people and its insurrection of October 24-25.

Down with the Compromisers! Down with the lackeys of the bourgeoisie! Long live the victorious insurrection of the soldiers, workers, and peasants!

The debate continued on October 26 as the Second Congress moved toward the selection of the new government. In

*answer to a Right Social Revolutionary named Pyanykh, who
came from the Peasants' Executive Committee to protest the
arrest of the socialist ministers in the Provisional Government,
Trotsky said:*

On the Arrest of Socialist Ministers

Here two questions are being confused, comrades. One of
them was settled by us yesterday in businesslike fashion. It
was decided that the socialist ministers, Mensheviks and SRs,
should be temporarily placed under house arrest by the Military
Revolutionary Committee. That is what happened to Prokopovich; that's what we are going to do to Maslov and Salazkin.
The Military Revolutionary Committee is taking every measure
to carry out your decisions to the full, in the shortest possible
time; and if it has not been done yet it is because, comrades,
we are passing through an armed insurrection when another
representative of one of these parties, Kerensky — who is well
known to us — is organizing counterrevolutionary forces to
hurl against us. 6 Occupied till now with saving the victorious
workers' and peasants' revolution, the Military Revolutionary
Committee neglected two socialist ministers in order that the
workers' and peasants' revolution would not suffer harm. [*Applause.*]

The second question is that of the impression made on the
public by these arrests. Comrades, we are passing through
new times when the usual ideas must be discarded. Our revolution is the victory of new classes who have come to power
and who must defend themselves against the organization of
counterrevolutionary forces in which the socialist ministers
participated. But they are only subjected to house arrest until
their participation in the organization of the counterrevolutionary conspiracy is established. By themselves, these two
ministers do not represent any danger to us, either morally,
politically, or in the slightest significant way.

We are told that nothing like this has happened in any other
revolution. Those who say so have short memories because
this very thing happened a few months ago when members of
the Executive Committee of Workers' and Soldiers' Deputies
were arrested with the full connivance and agreement of these
same socialist ministers, and there was no protest, no demand
for their liberation. That is not all: no other than the chairman of the Executive Committee of the Peasants' Deputies,
Avksentiev, posted two men from the Okhrana at the doors

of Alexandra Mikhailovna Kollontai's[7] flat though she had
been set free by the magistrates. Now these same representatives come to tear us away from official work, trouble us in the
middle of most serious matters in which they can take no part,
in order to shout into our ears their impotent threats and lay
before us their tearful indignation. [*Loud applause.*]

*On October 26 the Second Congress elected a workers' and
peasants' government headed by Lenin. The Left Social Revolutionaries, anxious to mediate with those who had walked
out, at this time did not take the places offered them on the
Council of People's Commissars, the directing body of the
Central Executive Committee which, newly elected, consisted
of sixty-two Bolsheviks, twenty-nine Left Social Revolutionaries, and ten others.*

*On the same day the new government passed decrees for
peace and for land to the peasants, and prepared to lay the
basis for a socialist society.*

*Before the elections took place, however, the debate continued
over the composition of the new government. B. V. Avilov, a
representative of the United Internationalists, a group headed
by Maxim Gorky, introduced a resolution proposing that the
government include representatives of all the tendencies that
had attended the congress. His position was supported by
V. A. Karelin, a Left Social Revolutionary. The main answer
to the Avilov-Karelin argument, which was decisively rejected
by the congress, was given in this speech by Trotsky.*

The Organization of Power

The considerations we have heard here have been brought
against us more than once. They have tried to frighten us
again and again with the possible isolation of the left wing.
A few days ago when the question of an insurrection was
openly raised, we were told we were isolating ourselves, we
were heading for destruction, and in fact, if one were to judge
from the political press what the class groupings were, then
an insurrection threatened us with inevitable ruin.

Against us were counterrevolutionary bands and defensists
of all varieties. One wing of the Left SRs worked courageously

with us in the Military Revolutionary Committee. The rest of them took up a position of watchful neutrality. Nevertheless, even under these unfavorable conditions, when it seemed we were abandoned by everybody, the insurrection triumphed, almost without bloodshed.

If we had really been isolated, if the real forces had genuinely been against us, how could it have come about that we gained a victory almost without bloodshed? No, it was not we who were isolated, but the government and the democrats — the pseudodemocrats. It was they who were isolated from the masses. By their wavering, their compromising, they cut themselves off from the ranks of the real democracy.

Our great advantage as a party lies in the fact that we have formed a coalition with the masses, creating a coalition of the workers, soldiers, and poorest peasants.

Political groupings disappear, but the basic interests of classes remain. The party which prevails is the one that is able to understand and to satisfy the basic demands of classes. If a coalition was necessary then that coalition is the coalition of our garrison, chiefly composed of peasants, with the working class. We can be proud of such a coalition. This coalition has been tested in the fire of struggle. The Petrograd garrison and proletariat, as one, entered into the great struggle which will be the classic example of revolution in the history of all peoples.

We have been told here about the Left Bloc set up in the pre-Parliament, but this bloc lasted only one day; evidently it had not been formed in the place where it should have been. Perhaps both the bloc and program were good; nevertheless one collision was sufficient for the bloc to crumble into dust.

Comrade Avilov has spoken of the great difficulties with which we are faced. To remove all these difficulties he proposes the formation of a coalition. But in this he makes no attempt to clarify this formula, to define more accurately what kind of coalition he has in mind. A coalition of groups, or classes, or simply a coalition of newspapers? For, after all, before talking of a coalition, for example, with the old Central Executive Committee, you have to understand that a coalition with the Dans and the Liebers[8] would not strengthen the revolution but would serve as a reason for its ruin. At the most critical moment of the struggle we were left without a telephone, with the connivance of the CEC commissars.

They say that the split in the democracy is a misunderstanding. When Kerensky sends shock troops against us, when they deal us blow after blow, can one really talk of a misunderstanding? If this is a misunderstanding, I am afraid that all the arguments of our opponents — Comrades Avilov and Karelin — are also a political misunderstanding.

Comrade Avilov has told us: There is not much bread; we must have a coalition with the defensists. But will this coalition really increase the quantity of bread? The whole question of bread is a question of the program of action. The struggle against economic collapse demands a definite system of action and not merely political groupings.

Comrade Avilov talked about the peasantry But again, what peasantry is one talking about? We must choose between the different elements of the peasantry. Today, and right here, a representative of the peasants of Tver province demanded the arrest of Avksentiev. We must choose between the Tver peasant who demands the arrest of Avksentiev, and Avksentiev who has filled the prisons with members of the peasant committees. We are with the Tver peasants against Avksentiev. We are with them to the end and indissolubly. We firmly reject coalition with the kulak elements of the peasantry in the name of coalition of the working class and the poorest peasants.

If the revolution has taught us anything then it is this — that it is only by way of agreement, by way of a genuine coalition of these elements that victory can be achieved. Those who chase the shadow of coalition are isolating themselves from life. The Left SRs will lose support among the masses to the extent that they venture to oppose themselves to our party; a party which opposes itself to the party of the proletariat, with whom the village poor have united, isolates itself from the revolution.

Openly and in front of the whole people we raised the banner of insurrection. The political formula of this insurrection was: All power to the Soviets — through the Congress of Soviets. We are told: You did not wait for the congress. No, we would have waited for it but Kerensky did not want to wait; the counterrevolutionaries were not sleeping. We as a party considered it our task to create a real chance for the Congress of Soviets to take power into its hands. If the congress had been surrounded by junkers how could it have taken the power into its hands? To achieve this task, what was needed was a party which would wrest the power from the hands of the counterrevolutionaries and say to you: "Here is the power and you are obliged to take it!" [*Stormy, continuous applause.*]

Despite the fact that the defensists of all shades stopped at nothing in their struggle against us, we did not reject them. We proposed to the congress as a whole to take the power into its hands. How utterly you distort the perspective when you talk about our irreconcilability. How, after all that has happened, is it possible to speak of our irreconcilability? When a party surrounded by a cloud of gunpowder smoke comes to them and says, "Let us take the power together!" they run to the city duma and there unite with open counterrevolutionaries! They are traitors to the revolution with whom we will never unite!

For a successful struggle for peace, said Comrade Avilov, we must have a coalition with the Compromisers. At the same time he said that the Allies do not want to conclude peace; but if we rally to those who are betraying us everything will be fine. The Allied imperialists laughed, says Avilov, at the margarine democrat Skobelev. But nevertheless he advised us: If you form a bloc with the margarine democrats, the cause of peace will be assured!

There are two ways in the struggle for peace. One way is to oppose to the Allied and enemy governments the moral and material forces of the revolution. The other way is a bloc with Skobelev, which means a bloc with Tereshchenko, 9 that is, complete submission to Allied imperialism.

It is pointed out to us that in our proclamation on peace we address ourselves at the same time to the governments and the peoples. This is only a formal equality.

We of course are not thinking of influencing the imperialist governments with our proclamations; but as long as they exist we cannot ignore them. But we rest all our hope on the unleashing of the European revolution by our revolution. If the insurrectionary peoples of Europe do not crush imperialism, we will be crushed — that is beyond doubt. Either the Russian Revolution will raise the whirlwind of struggle in the West or the capitalists of all countries will crush our revolution.

[*"There is a third way,"* says someone from his seat.]

The third way is the way of the Central Executive Committee — which on the one hand has sent delegations to the West European workers and on the other has formed an alliance with the Kishkins and Konovalovs. That is the way of lies and hypocrisy which we will never take.

Of course, we do not say that the first day of the insurrection of the European workers will inevitably be the day of the signing of the peace treaty. It is also possible that the bourgeoisie, frightened by the approaching insurrection of all the oppressed, will hasten to conclude peace. The dates are not set. No concrete forms can be foreseen. It is important and necessary to determine the method of struggle, which in principle is identical in both foreign and domestic policies. The alliance of the oppressed, always and everywhere—that is our way.

The Second Congress of Soviets has elaborated a whole program of measures. Any group that wishes to realize this program in fact, which at this critical moment takes its place on this side of the barricade, will meet with only one statement from us: "Welcome, dear comrades, we are brothers-in-arms and we shall go with you to the end."

[*Stormy and prolonged applause.*]

PART TWO

Defending the Revolution

begins in 1917 with the efforts of the newly appointed commissar of foreign affairs to end World War I or, failing that, to take the new Soviet country out of it; finds him reassigned to the post of commissar of war, in which he organizes the Red Army and leads it to victory in three years of bitter civil war and resistance against imperialist intervention; continues as he turns to problems of socialist construction and creates the Left Opposition to fight the growing bureaucratization and conservatism of the Stalin regime; and concludes, prior to his deportation to Turkey in 1929, as he is about to be expelled from the Communist Party.

Trotsky addressing troops during the civil war.

7

Commissar of Foreign Affairs

*In his post as commissar of foreign affairs on the Council
of People's Commissars Trotsky made skillful use of his talents as educator and propagandist, both at home and abroad.
On November 21, a month after the insurrection, he was back
on the popular meeting grounds of the Modern Circus reporting to an anxious gathering of twelve thousand on the new
Soviet government's efforts to bring peace and on the principles animating its peace proposals.*

This speech is reprinted from The Proletarian Revolution
in Russia *by Lenin and Trotsky, edited by Louis C. Fraina,
published in 1918.*

For Peace — Against Secret Diplomacy!

In this building on October 23 I spoke to a popular meeting at which the question of an All-Russian Congress was
being discussed, and all voices were raised in favor of Soviet
power. The question which had been most emphatically before the people in all the eight months of the revolution was
the question of war and peace, and we maintained that only
a power basing its authority directly on the people could put
an end to the slaughter. We maintained that the secret treaties
must be published, and declared that the Russian people, not
having made these treaties, could not be bound to carry out
the conquests agreed upon therein. Our enemies answered that
this was demagogy. You would never dare if you were in
power, they said, to do this, for then the Allies would oppose
us. But we maintained that the salvation of Russia was in
peace. We pointed out that the prolonged character of the war

was destroying the revolution, was exhausting and destroying the country, and that the longer we should fight the more complete the slavish position we should then occupy, so that at last we should merely be left the choice of picking a master.

We desire to live and develop as a free nation; but for the conclusion of peace, we had to overthrow the power of the bourgeoisie and of Kerensky. They told us we would be left without any supporters. But on October 25 the local Soviet of Petrograd took the initiative upon itself as well as the responsibility and, with the aid of the garrison and the workers, accomplished the insurrection and appeared before the Congress of Soviets then in session and said: "The old power in the country is broken, there is no authority anywhere, and we are obliged to take it into our own hands." We have said that the first obligation devolving upon the new power is the offering of peace parleys on all fronts, for the conclusion of a peace without annexations or indemnities on the basis of self-determination of peoples, that is, each people, through popular elections, must speak for itself the decisive word: Do they wish to enter into a confederation with their present sovereign state, enjoying full autonomy under it, or do they wish to separate themselves from it and have full independence? We must put a stop to a condition in which the strong can by force of arms compel the weak to assume what conditions of life the strong may desire: every people, be it great or small, must be the master of its own fate. Now this is the program not of a party, not of a Soviet, but of the whole people, excepting the predatory party which dares call itself the Party of Popular Liberty[1] but which in reality is an enemy of popular liberty, fighting against peace with all its might, and against which we have declared our implacable hostility — with the exception of this party, the whole Russian people has declared that it will not tolerate the use of force. And this is the spirit in which we issue our peace decree.

On the day on which we passed this decree Krasnov's[2] Cossacks rebelled and danger threatened the very existence of the Soviet power. Yet hardly had they been defeated and the Soviet authority strengthened, when our first act was to turn to the Allied and German authorities, simultaneously, with a proposition for peace parleys on all fronts. Our enemies, the Cadets and their lackeys, said that Germany would ignore us — but it has turned out otherwise and we already have the assent of Germany and Austria-Hungary to the holding of peace parleys and preliminary peace on the Soviet formula. And even before that, as soon as we obtained the keys to the case of secret diplomatic correspondence, we published the secret treaties thus fulfilling an obligation that we had assumed toward the people when we were still an insignificant opposition party. We said then and we say now that a people cannot shed their blood and that of their brothers for treaties that they have not themselves concluded, have never read or even seen. To these words of mine the adherents of the coalition replied: Do not speak to us in this tongue, this is not the Modern Circus. And I answered them that I have only one tongue, the tongue of a socialist, and I shall speak in this tongue to the country and to you, to the Allies and to the Germans.

To the adherents of the coalition, having the souls of hares, it seemed that to publish the secret treaties was equivalent to forcing England and France to declare war on us. But they did not understand that their ruling circles throughout the duration of the war have been talking the people into the idea that the treacherous, cruel enemy is Germany and that Russia is a noble land, and it is impossible within twenty-four hours to teach them the opposite. By publishing the secret treaties we have incurred the enmity of the governing classes in those countries, but we have won their people to our support. We shall not make a diplomatic peace; it will be a people's peace, a soldiers' peace, a real peace. And the outcome of our open policy was clear: Judson appeared at the Smolny Institute and declared, in the name of America, that the protest to the Dukhonin staff against the new power was a misunderstanding and that America had no desire to interfere in the internal affairs of Russia; and, consequently, the American question is disposed of. [3]

But there is another conflict that is not yet settled. I must tell you about it. Because of their fight for peace, the English government has arrested and is now detaining in concentration camp George Chicherin who has devoted his wealth and his knowledge to the peoples of Russia, England, Germany, and France, and the courageous agitator of the English workers, the emigre Petrov. [4] I communicated in writing with the English embassy, saying that Russia was now permitting the presence within her borders of many wealthy Englishmen who are engaged in counterrevolutionary conspiracies with the Russian bourgeoisie, and that we were therefore all the more disinclined to permit Russian citizens to be thrown into English prisons; that, consequently, all those against whom there were no criminal charges should be liberated at once. Failure to comply with this request will mean that we shall refuse passports to English subjects desiring to leave Russia. The people's Soviet power is responsible for the well-being of the entire people; wherever its citizens may be, they shall enjoy its protection. If Kerensky spoke to the Allies like a shop attendant to his boss, we are prepared to show that we shall live with them only on terms of equality. We have more than once said that anyone who counts on the support and friendship of the free and independent Russian people must approach them with respect for them and for their human dignity.

As soon as the Soviets found themselves with power in their hands we proposed peace parleys in the name of the Russian people. We had a right to speak in the name of the people for everything that we proposed, as well as the whole program of the People's Commissars, consists of doctrines and propositions voted on and passed in hundreds and thousands of Soviets, factories and workshops, that is, by the entire people. Our delegation will speak an open and courageous language: Do you agree to the holding of an immediate peace conference on all the fronts? And if they say yes, we shall ask them to invite their governments and allies to send their delegates. Our second question will be: Do you mean to conclude peace on a democratic foundation? If we are forced to make peace alone, we shall declare to Germany that it is inadmissible to withdraw their troops from the Russian front to some other front, since we are offering an honorable peace and cannot permit England and France to be crushed by reason of it.

Secret diplomacy shall not be tolerated for a single moment during the negotiations. Our leaflets and our radio service will keep all the nations informed of every proposition we make and of the answers they elicit from Germany. We shall be sitting in a glass house, as it were, and the German soldiers, through thousands of newspapers in German, which we shall distribute to them, will be informed of every step we take and of every German answer.

We say that Lithuania and Courland must themselves decide with whom they will join forces, and that Germany must, not in words only but in deeds, heed the free expression of the will of the people. And if after these frank and honorable declarations the kaiser refuses to make peace, if the banks and exchanges, which profit by the war, destroy our peace the nations will see on whose side is the right and we shall come out the stronger, the kaiser and the financiers the weaker. We shall feel ourselves to be not the vanquished but the victors, for peace has its victories no less renowned than war. For a nation that has assumed power after having cast out its enemies, such a nation is victorious. We know no other interests than those of the people, but these interests are identical with the interests of the people of all nations. We declare war upon war. The czars are afraid of the conclusion of peace, are afraid that the people will ask for an accounting for all the great sacrifices they have made and the blood they have shed. Germany, in agreeing to peace negotiations, is heeding the will of her people; she knows that they want her to answer, and that if she does not answer the Russian Revolution will become the ally of the German people. France and England ought to come to the discussion on the conclusion of peace, but if they do not their own people, who will know of the course of the transactions, will cast them out with rods. The Russian representatives at the peace table will be transformed into plaintiffs; the people will sit in judgment on their rulers. Our experience of the manner in which the rulers have treated their people in the forty months of the war has not been wasted. In your name we shall say to our brothers: Understand that the moment you turn your revolutionary strength against your bourgeoisie not one Russian soldier will shoot! This promise will be given in your name and you will keep it.

The Allies, opposed to Russia's revolution and withdrawal from the war, rejected the proposals for a general armistice and began intriguing with monarchist, liberal, Menshevik, and Social Revolutionary opponents of the young Soviet government. But formal negotiations for peace were started with Germany on December 9 at Brest-Litovsk, a Polish town occupied by German troops.

Three days before the negotiations began, Trotsky sent this message to the people of Europe. It was typical of those that were widely circulated as leaflets and broadcast by radio. This sort of political warfare did not succeed in bringing an end to the war immediately, but it undoubtedly undermined military morale and hastened the end of the war which came a year later, and it certainly played an indispensable role in the Red Army's victory in the civil war.

The appeal is taken from Soviet Documents on Foreign Policy *in a translation by Jane Degras, the editor, published in 1951.*

Appeal to the Toiling, Oppressed, and Exhausted Peoples of Europe

An armistice has been signed at Brest-Litovsk. Military operations on the eastern front have been suspended for twenty-eight days. This in itself is a tremendous victory for humanity. After nearly three and a half years of uninterrupted slaughter, with no end in sight, the workers' and peasants' revolution in Russia has opened the way to peace.

We have published the secret treaties. We shall continue publishing them in the immediate future. We have declared that these treaties will in no way bind the policy of the Soviet government. We have proposed to all nations the way of open agreement on the principle of the recognition for each nation, great or small, advanced or backward, of the right freely to determine its own destiny. We do not attempt to conceal the fact that we do not consider the existing capitalist governments capable of making a democratic peace. The revolutionary struggle of the toiling masses against the existing governments can alone bring Europe nearer to such a peace. Its full realization can only be guaranteed by the victorious proletarian revolution in all capitalist countries.

While entering into negotiations with the existing governments, which on both sides are permeated through and through with imperialist tendencies, the Council of People's Commissars has never for a moment deviated from the path of social revolution. A truly democratic people's peace will still have to be fought for. The first round in this struggle finds in power, everywhere except in Russia, the old monarchist and capitalist governments which were responsible for the present war, and which have not yet accounted to their duped peoples for the waste of blood and riches. We are forced to begin negotiations with the governments which are now in existence, just as, on the other hand, the monarchist and reactionary governments of the Central Powers are forced to carry on negotiations with the representatives of the Soviet government because the Russian people have confronted them with the fact of a workers' and peasants' government in Russia. In negotiating for peace the Soviet government has set itself a double task: first, to bring to an end as quickly as possible the disgraceful and criminal slaughter which is laying Europe waste; and second, to use all the means at our disposal to help the working class in all lands to overthrow the rule of capital and to seize political power in order to reconstruct Europe and the whole world on democratic and socialist lines.

An armistice has been signed on the eastern front. But on the other fronts the slaughter is still going on. Peace negotiations are only just beginning. It should be clear to socialists in all countries, but especially to socialists in Germany, that there is an irreconcilable difference between the peace program of the Russian workers and peasants and that of the German capitalists, landowners, and generals. If there were nothing but the clash of these two policies, peace would obviously be impossible, for the Russian people have not overthrown the monarchy and bourgeoisie in their own land merely to bow before the monarchs and capitalists of other lands. Peace can only be brought nearer, realized, and guaranteed if the voice of the workers makes itself heard, firmly and resolutely, both in Germany and in the lands of its allies. The German, Austro-Hungarian, Bulgarian, and Turkish workers must oppose to the imperialist program of their ruling classes their own revolutionary program of agreement and cooperation between the laboring and exploited classes in all countries.

An armistice has been signed on one front only. Our delegation, after a long struggle, wrung from the German government, as one of the conditions of the armistice, a commitment not to transfer troops to other fronts. Thus, those German troops which are stationed between the Black Sea and the Baltic are to have a month's respite from the gruesome nightmare of war. The Rumanian army also, against the will of the Rumanian government, adhered to the armistice. But on the French, Italian, and all other fronts the war is still going on. The truce remains partial. The capitalist governments fear peace, because they know they will have to render an account to their people. They are trying to postpone the hour of their final bankruptcy. Are the nations willing to go on patiently enduring the criminal activities of stock exchange cliques in France, Great Britain, Italy, and the United States?

The capitalist governments of these countries conceal their abject and greedy calculations under fine talk about eternal justice and the future society of nations. They do not want an armistice. They are fighting against peace, but you, peoples of Europe, you, workers of France, Italy, England, Belgium, Serbia, you, our brothers in suffering and struggle, do not you, together with us, want peace — an honorable, democratic peace among nations?

Those who tell you that peace can only be guaranteed by victory are deceiving you. In the first place they have been unable, in the course of nearly three and a half years, to give you victory, and show no signs of doing so should the war go on for years longer. And in the second place, if victory should appear possible for one side or the other, it would only mean further coercion of the weak by the strong, thus sowing the seeds of future wars.

Belgium, Serbia, Rumania, Poland, the Ukraine, Greece, Persia, and Armenia can only be liberated by the workers in all belligerent and neutral countries in the victorious struggle against all imperialists, and not by the victory of one of the imperialist coalitions.

We summon you to this struggle, workers of all countries! There is no other way. The crimes of the ruling, exploiting classes in this war have been countless. These crimes cry out for revolutionary revenge. Toiling humanity would be for-swearing itself and its future if it continued meekly to bear on its shoulders the yoke of the imperialist bourgeoisie and militarists, their governments and their diplomacy.

We, the Council of People's Commissars, empowered by the Russian workers, peasants, soldiers, sailors, widows, and or-phans, we summon you to a common struggle with us for the immediate cessation of hostilities on all fronts. May the news of the signing of the armistice at Brest-Litovsk ring like a tocsin for the soldiers and workers in all the belligerent countries.

Down with the war! Down with its authors! The govern-ments opposing peace and the governments masking aggres-sive intentions behind talk of peace must be swept away. The workers and soldiers must wrest the business of war and peace from the criminal hands of the bourgeoisie and take it into their own hands. We have the right to demand this from you because this is what we have done in our own country. This is the only path to salvation for you and for us. Close up your ranks, proletarians of all countries, under the banner of peace and the social revolution!

8

A Word to the Russian Workers and Peasants on Our Friends and Enemies, and How to Preserve and Strengthen the Soviet Republic

Trotsky headed the Soviet delegation at Brest-Litovsk where the negotiations were carried on as "in a glass house." He renounced the czarist war aims, asserted the principle of self-determination against German demands, and continued to direct revolutionary propaganda to the German people, including the soldiers at Brest-Litovsk. But Germany had the upper hand militarily and the Soviet government, faced with the threat of a new assault which it was unable to resist, was forced in March 1918 to sign a treaty on punitive terms.

The respite from war was short. Germany moved into the areas formerly comprising the Russian empire in Eastern Europe. The Allies began to arm and finance Russian counterrevolutionary armies, known as the Whites or White Guards. Even before the world war ended in November 1918, Soviet territory was invaded by British, French, Japanese, United States, and other Allied troops.

Against these formidable foes the young Soviet Republic had a devastated economy, a people weary of war, and no army. But it had a revolutionary leadership that was determined to resist. And Soviet resistance was different from anything ever seen before, unmatched until the people of Vietnam stood up against the American imperialist colossus half a century later.

Trotsky received his new appointment as commissar of war in March 1918 — and set about the task of organizing the Red Army. "Show me another man able to organize almost a model army within a single year and win the respect of military authorities," said Lenin. "We have such a man. We have everything. And we shall work wonders."

Trotsky worked wonders with the Red Army not because he had some secret military doctrine but because his approach was above all political. A speech to a workers' audience in Moscow, on April 14, 1918, shows him explaining the issues of the impending war and seeking to inspire revolutionary discipline, struggle, and sacrifice.

Three nights before this talk anarchist centers in Moscow were surrounded and disarmed; force was used in a few cases where resistance occurred. The question-and-answer exchange that followed Trotsky's talk and the commotion that interrupted it offer a sense of the atmosphere that prevailed.

The translation used here was made by the British Socialist Party in 1920, which published it as a pamphlet under the title "A Paradise in This World."

Comrades—Our country is the only one where power is in the hands of the working class and on all sides we hear the advice: "Leave it alone, you are not equal to the task. Look how many difficulties there are in the way of Soviet power." And that is true, many are the difficulties, every step is beset with impediments. But what is the cause? Let us look around, let us examine the situation, let us count our friends and our enemies, let us look ahead. We inherited from our predecessors, the czar, Miliukov, Kerensky—*a state completely ruined internally as well as externally.* There is not the slightest doubt that at the present moment our country is in a terrible condition. But this condition is only the result of the whole of the preceding historical development and, in particular, of the present war. The czar and Miliukov had dragged us into the war. The czar's army was defeated. The revolution broke out. The toilers of all lands expected that the revolution would give peace. But Miliukov and Kerensky allowed themselves to be led on the leash by the Allied imperialists; they protracted the war, they deceived all expectations, and they compromised the revolution. Then the workers rebelled and took the power into their own hands. We on our part did everything that was possible to raise confidence in the Russian Revolution, to make it clear to the European workers that it was not Miliukov or Kerensky who represented the Russian Revolution, but the working class, the toiling proletariat, the peasant who did not exploit other people's labor.

This is what we did. It is true, comrades, the victory is not yet ours. We deceive neither ourselves nor you. European militarism has proved still too strong, the movement of the working masses has not yet dealt it that blow which will bring salvation to the European workers as well as to us, and European militarism has made the best use of the delay which history has granted it. The Russian Revolution has reached its summit, whereas the European one has not yet begun. It is in these conditions that our negotiations with Germany and Austria-Hungary took place, after the confidence in the Russian Revolution had been undermined by the policy of the Miliukovs, the Kerenskys, the Tseretellis, and the Chernovs.[1] We are told: "You have signed the Brest-Litovsk treaty which is a predatory and oppressive treaty." True, very true, there is no treaty so predatory, so oppressive as the Brest-Litovsk treaty. But what really is this treaty? It is an IOU, an old IOU which had already been signed by Nicholas Romanov, Miliukov, and Kerensky, while we have to pay it.

Was it we who started this war? Was it the working class who unchained this bloody slaughter? No, it was the monarchs, the wealthy classes, the liberal bourgeoisie. Was it we who caused those terrible disasters when our unfortunate soldiers found themselves in the Carpathians without rifles and ammunition? No, that was czarism supported by the Russian bourgeoisie.

And was it we who, on July 1, 1917, threw away in that shameful and criminal offensive the capital of the Russian Revolution, its good name, its authority? No, those were the Compromisers, the Right Social Revolutionaries, the Mensheviks, together with the bourgeoisie. Yet it is we who were presented with the bill for all these crimes, and we with clenched teeth were obliged to pay it. We know that it was a usurer's bill, but, comrades, it was not we who contracted the loans, it is not we who are morally responsible for them before the people. Our conscience is perfectly clear. We stand before the working class of all countries as a party which did its duty to the end. We published all the treaties, we sincerely declared that we were willing to conclude an honest democratic peace. This declaration remains, this idea remains in the consciousness and conscience of the toiling masses of Europe, and there it is accomplishing its deep subterranean work.

It is true, comrades, that at the present moment the frontiers of our country are secure neither in the East nor in the West. Over there in the East, Japan has for a long time past been trying to grab from us the most fertile, the richest parts of

Siberia, and the Japanese press is only concerned as to the territorial limit up to which Japan is called upon to "save" Siberia. The papers actually say so: "We shall have to answer before God and Heaven for the fate of Siberia." Some say that heaven enjoined them to grab Siberia up to Irkutsk, others say, up to the Urals. This is the only point of dispute among the propertied classes of Japan. They had been looking out for all sorts of pretexts to make this raid. As a matter of fact this business began long ago. Already under czarism, and later at the time of Tereshchenko and Kerensky, Russia was complaining in confidential documents that Japan was preparing for the seizure of our Far Eastern dominions. And why? Simply because they are an easy prey. This is indeed the whole essence of international imperialism. All those fine phrases about "democracy," "the fate of small nationalities," "justice," "God's commands"— all these are but words, phrases used for the purpose of cheating the common people; in reality the powers are only looking out for unprotected booty in order to pocket it. This I say is the essence of imperialist policy.

And so, comrades, at first, about six weeks ago, the Japanese spread throughout the world the rumor that the Siberian railway was about to be seized by the German and Austro-Hungarian prisoners who, forsooth, had been organized and armed there, and that two hundred thousand of them were only awaiting the arrival of a German general. Even the name of that general was given— everything was perfectly definite and exact. The Japanese ambassador in Rome spoke about it, and the tidings of the coming seizure of the Siberian railway was circulated by the wireless stations of the Japanese headquarters throughout the length and breadth of America. Thereupon, in order to unveil before the public gaze of the entire world the shameful lie which has been spread for the purpose of preparing a buccaneering raid, I made the following offer to the British and American military missions: "Give me one British and one American officer and I shall send them immediately, together with representatives of our commissariat of war, along the Siberian railway in order that they may see for themselves how many there are of German and Austrian prisoners armed for the purpose of seizing the Siberian railroad."

They were unable, comrades, in all decency to refuse this offer, and the officers appointed by them went, having received from me papers ordering the Siberian Soviets to afford them all possible facilities: let them examine everything, see everything they wanted to see, get complete and free access everywhere. I afterwards was shown their reports every day by direct wire. It goes without saying that nowhere could they find even a trace of armed enemy prisoners. They saw that, different from the Russian railway system, the Siberian line was guarded better, and was working better. They only found six hundred armed Hungarian prisoners who were socialist internationalists, and had put themselves at the entire disposal of the Soviet authorities against all its enemies. That was all they found there. It proved up to the hilt that the Japanese imperialists and the Japanese headquarters had consciously and maliciously misled public opinion in order to justify the predatory raid upon Siberia, in order to be able to say: the Germans had threatened the Siberian line, and we, the Japanese, rescued it by our raid. Well, *this* subterfuge failed; so immediately another was concocted on the spot. At Vladivostok somebody had killed two or three Japanese. No inquiry into the affair had as yet taken place. Who were the murderers? Were they Japanese agents, or common bandits, or German or Austrian spies? Nobody knows to this day. Yet though they were killed on April 4, the Japanese disembarked the first two companies at Vladivostok on April 5. Once the fairy tale about the seizure of the Siberian railway by the German prisoners proved of no avail, the simplest thing was to take advantage of the murder of two or three Japanese—killed, in all probability, on instructions from the Japanese headquarters itself in order to create a plausible pretext for attacking us. Such murders from behind a corner are the accepted practice of international capitalist diplomacy. But here the thing came to a sudden stop; two companies were disembarked and then the landing was discontinued. British, French, and American agents came to our commissariats and declared: "This is not banditry or even a beginning of banditry and annexation, it is just a local incident, a local temporary misunderstanding"; as a matter of fact, it does seem as if the Japanese themselves were hesitating. First, their own country is exhausted by militarism, and an expedition against Siberia is a great, complicated, and costly affair, for the Siberian worker and peasant, the strong and sturdy peasant whom I studied closely enough in previous times and who never knew serfdom, would clearly refuse to let the Japanese take him without an effort. A long and stubborn fight would be necessary there; there is, indeed, in Japan itself a party which fears it. On the other hand, the American capitalists who directly compete with Japan on the shores of the Pacific do not want the strengthening of Japan, their chief enemy.

This, then, comrades, is the advantage of our position: the world bandits and highwaymen are at loggerheads with one another, fighting among themselves for the booty. This rivalry between Japan and the United States on the Far Eastern shores constitutes a great boon to us, for it gives us a respite, gives us an opportunity to gather our forces and to await the moment when the European and world working class will rise to help us.

In the West, comrades, we observe just now a new flaring up of the terrible slaughter which has already lasted five and forty months. It seemed before as if the forces of hell had already been set in motion, that nothing more could be invented, that the war had landed in a blind alley. If the countries, who had fought before with their forces still unimpaired, could not overpower one another, it seemed that there was nothing more to wait for, that no victory could be hoped for anywhere. But that is just the curse, that the wizard of capitalism, having called out this war devil, is powerless to exorcise him again. It is impossible, say, for the German bourgeoisie to come back to their workers and tell them: Well, we have conducted this terrible war for four years; you have borne many sacrifices, and what has this war brought you? Nothing, absolutely nothing! Nor can the British bourgeoisie go back to its workers having a like result to show for all their unheard-of sacrifices.

That is why they are dragging on this slaughter automatically, senselessly, aimlessly, further and further. Just as an avalanche rolls down a mountain, so do they roll down under the weight of their own crimes.

This we observe now once more on the soil of unhappy white-bled France. There, comrades, on the French soil, the front is of a different nature than it was in our country. There every yard is studied beforehand, registered, placed on the map, every square distinctly marked. There colossal means of destruction, colossal monstrous engines for mass murders are collected on both sides on a scale hitherto inconceivable to the most powerful imagination.

Comrades, I lived in France for two years during the war, and I well remember those flowings and ebbings of attacks, and then the slow periods of waiting. An army stands against an army clasped tightly with one another, a trench against a trench, everything calculated, made ready. French public opinion becomes restive. Foch,[2] the bourgeoisie, and the people in general begin grumbling: "How much longer will this terrible constrictor, the front, be sucking the lifeblood of the people? Where is the way out? What are we waiting for? Either stop the war or else vanquish the enemy by an offensive and get peace. Either one or the other." The bourgeois press would then begin its encouragements: "The next offensive, tomorrow, the day after tomorrow, next spring, will deal the Germans a mortal blow."

At the same time no less corrupt and mercenary pens would be writing in the German press for the benefit of the German workers and peasants, for the German mothers, workingwomen, sisters, wives: "Do not despair, one other offensive on the French front and we shall crush France and will give you peace." Thereupon, in fact, an offensive would begin.

Countless victims, hundreds, thousands, millions would perish in the course of a few days or weeks. And the result? As a result, the front would be shifted one way or another a mile or two, perhaps even more, but the two armies would continue as before to press against one another in a death clasp; and so it has happened already five or six times. It was so on the Marne during the first rush upon Paris, the same later, on the Yser, then on the Somme, at Cambrai. The same thing is now taking place in the present colossal battles, such as were never before witnessed throughout the whole of history. Hundreds of thousands, millions are falling there at the present moment, the flower of European humanity is being destroyed senselessly, aimlessly. This shows that there is no salvation on the road on which the ruling classes and their lackeys, the pseudosocialists, walk.

America joined the war more than a year ago, and promised to finish it in the course of the next few months. What did America get by her intervention? She had at first been patiently waiting over there, beyond the ocean, while Germany was fighting England; and then she intervened. Why? What does America want? America wants Germany to exhaust England, and England to exhaust Germany. Then American capital will come forward as an heir who will rob the whole world. And so when America noticed that England was being bent to the ground, and that Germany was getting the upper hand, she said: "So, it is necessary to support England—just as the rope supports the one hanged—in order that they may exhaust each other completely, in order that European capital may be deprived of all possibility to stand up again on its feet." And at the present moment we read that in Washington, according to the new conscription law, one and a half million men are to be called to arms.

America at first thought the business would be a trifling one, would just amount to a little help; but as soon as she placed her feet on the path, the avalanche caught her in its sweep, and now there is no stopping for her either, and she must go to the bitter end. And yet — at the beginning of the war, at the beginning of the American intervention — that happened in January or February of last year — I myself saw a street demonstration in New York, a downright revolt of the American workingmen, caused by a terrible rise of prices. The American bourgeoisie has earned billions from the blood of the European worker; but what did the American housewife, the workingwoman, get? Her share is scarcity, and the tremendous cost of living. It is the same in all countries, whether the bourgeoisie of one or the other country wins or suffers defeat. For the workers, the toiling masses, the result is the same: exhaustion of food stocks, impoverishment, enhanced slavery and oppression, accidents, wounds, cripples — all this pours upon the popular masses. The bourgeoisie itself can no longer choose its way — that is precisely why Germany did not strangle us completely. She stopped at the Eastern front. Why? Because she had yet to settle her accounts with England and America. England has taken Egypt, Palestine, Bagdad, has brought under her sway Portugal, has strangled Ireland, but — England "fights for freedom, for peace, for the happiness of small and weak nationalities." And Germany? Germany has robbed half of Europe, has suppressed scores of small countries, has taken Riga, Reval, and Pskov. Yet read their speeches: they declare that they have concluded peace on the basis of self-determination of peoples! First they bleed the people white, turn it into a corpse, and then they say: Now it has determined itself that Germany should lay her hand upon it.

Such is the position of the Russian Revolution, of the Russian Soviet Republic. Dangers threaten her on all sides: in the East there is the Japanese peril, in the West the German peril, and of course, there is for us also, although not so close, the British and American perils. All these strong, powerful bandits would not at all mind tearing Russia to pieces, and if at the present moment, today, we have some guarantee against it, it consists in the fact that these countries could not come to an understanding with one another, that Japan is compelled to carry on a veiled, underground struggle against such a mighty power as the United States, while Germany is compelled to conduct an open bloody struggle against both England and the United States.

And so, comrades, at a time when the world bandits have come to grips in the last convulsive round, honest people get a chance of having a rest, of recuperating, of refreshing themselves, of arming, in expectation of the hour when the working class will inflict upon these world bandits the mortal blow.

From the very first days of the revolution we said that the Russian Revolution would be able to win and to free the Russian people only on the condition that it marked the beginning of a revolution in all countries, but that if in Germany the reign of capital remained, if in New York the supremacy of the stock exchange continued, if in England British imperialism held its sway as heretofore, then we should be done for, since they were stronger, richer than we, as yet better educated, and their military machines stronger than ours. They would strangle us, because—number one—they were the stronger, and because—number two—they hated us. We had revolted, we had overthrown in our country the rule of the bourgeoisie. That is the source of the hatred towards us on the part of the propertied classes of all countries. Our bourgeoisie cannot be compared to the bourgeoisie of Germany or England. Yonder it is a strong class, it has a past of its own, when it made cultural conquests, developed science, and thought that no one but itself could hold sway, no one but itself could rule the state.

Every genuine bourgeois thinks that nature itself has destined him to dominate, to command, ride on the backs of the toiling masses, while the worker lives day in, day out under a yoke, and his horizon is narrow. With his mother's milk he has imbibed slavish prejudices, and thinks that to govern the state, to hold power is quite beyond him, that he was not meant for it, that he is made of poorer stuff.

But, lo and behold, the workers and poorer peasants in Russia have made the first step—a good firm step, though only the first one—in order to put an end to the propertied classes of their own as well as of all other countries. They have shown that the working masses are made of the same stuff of which people in general are made, and that they want to hold in their own hands the whole power and govern the whole land. Naturally when the bourgeoisie saw that in taking this power we were in dead earnest, that we meant business, namely, to destroy the domination of capital and to put in its place the domination of labor, its hatred towards us began to swell prodigiously. At first the propertied classes, the exploiters, thought that this was only a temporary misunderstanding, that it was only a stray wave of the revolution which had given us a mighty swing, and only, as it were, by accident had lifted us up, that the workers had got hold of the power only for a time, and that all that would end in a week, or two, or three. But later on it dawned upon them that the workers were standing firm at their new posts and while saying that times were hard, that still greater trials were in prospect, still greater ruin, still more intense hunger would have to be suffered, yet once they had assumed power, they would never let it escape from their hands. Never!

The bourgeoisie in all countries then began to notice that a terrible infection was spreading from the east, from Russia. Indeed, after the Russian worker, the most ignorant, most overdriven and harassed of all, has taken the power into his own hands, those of other countries must necessarily say to themselves sooner or later: if the Russian workers, who are so much the poorer, weaker, less organized than ourselves, could take the power into their own hands, then if we, the advanced workers of the whole world, seize the Russian cudgel and shake off our own bourgeoisie, and organize the whole of industry, verily, we shall then be invincible and shall create a universal republic of labor.

Yes, comrades, we are feared; we stand before the conscience of the propertied classes as a specter. The British imperialists fight the Germans, but every now and then they anxiously look round at us with the intent of getting at the throat of the Russian Revolution. In a similar way German imperialism, chained as it is to its enemy, cannot help sending us from time to time a furtive glance, trying to find a favorable opportunity to stab us in the heart. The imperialists of all other countries are of similar mind. No national difference exists on this point, since the common interests of the bandits and beasts of prey unite them all against us, and let me remind you, comrades, that we always told you that if the revolution did not spread to other countries, we shall in the long run be crushed by European capitalism. No escape will be available, and our task at the present moment is to procrastinate, to hold out till the revolution begins in all European countries—to hold out, to consolidate our strength, and to stand firmer on our feet, since at present we are feeble, shattered and morally feeble.

We ourselves know our sins, and we do not need the criticism from outside, from the bourgeoisie and the Compromisers who have undermined the Russian state and economic life;

their criticism is not worth two pence. But we do need our own criticism in order that we may realize our own sins. And in this connection the following must be said above everything else: the Russian working class, the Russian toiling people, must realize that once it took over the power in the state, it assumed the responsibility for the fate of the whole country, of the whole economic life of the whole state.

Of course, even now the bourgeoisie and its lackeys are still trying to put spokes in our wheels. Therefore, each time they stand in our way, we shall as heretofore fling them aside. At Orenburg they are again sending their Dutovs[3] against us; Kornilov, too, tries to attack Rostov. There we shall deal with the gangs of bourgeois White Guards without mercy. This is a matter of course for all of us. In this respect there will be no change in our tactics. If the bourgeoisie still hopes to come back into power we shall once for all knock out of it that hope. If it rises, we shall fling it down again, and if, as a result, it breaks its neck — so much the worse for it. It is its own lookout. It has had its warnings.

We offer it the common fare, the universal labor duty — a labor regime without oppressed or oppressors, and if it does not like it, if it continues to be obdurate and to revolt, the Soviet power must use against it measures of repression.

But, comrades, just because we, all of us as one man, do not want to allow the restoration of the power of the bourgeoisie, of the squires, of the bureaucracy, and because we are prepared to stand up for the power of the working class and the poorest peasants to the last drop of our blood, we must say to ourselves that from today we shoulder the greatest task and must therefore establish in our country a settled order, a new labor regime. We have inherited from the past, from czardom, from the war, from the Miliukov-Kerensky period a complete dislocation of our railways, a dislocation of our factories, and of all the branches of economic and social life, and we must put all this in working order, for we are responsible for it all.

The Soviets, the trade unions, the peasant organizations — these are at the present moment the masters in the country. Formerly, comrades, we were living under a whip, the whip of bureaucracy; but that whip is no more. There are only organizations of workers and the poorest peasants, and these organizations must teach us all to know and to remember that every one of us is not an isolated unit, but before all a part of the working class, of a common great association the name of which is "Toiling Russia" and which can only be saved by common labor. When the railwaymen surreptitiously carry a load; when depots or, in general, state property is plundered by individuals, we must denounce it as the greatest crime against our people—against the revolution. We must keep a sleepless watch and tell such betrayers "You rob the propertyless classes—not the bourgeoisie, but yourself, your own people!" At the present moment every one of us, whatever post he occupies in a factory or on the railways—everywhere he ought to feel himself like a soldier who has been placed there by the workers' army, by his own people, and every one of us must discharge his duty to the end.

This new labor discipline, comrades, we must create at all costs. Anarchy will destroy us; labor order will save us. In the factories we must create elected tribunals to punish the shirkers. Every worker, once he has become the master of his country, must distinctly remember his labor duty and his labor honor. Every one of us must fulfill one and the same obligation: "I work a certain number of hours a day with all the energy, with all the application I am capable of for now my labor is for the common good. I work in order to equip the peasant with the necessary implements of labor. I create for him winnowing machines, ploughs, scythes, nails, horseshoes, everything that is necessary for agriculture, and the peasant must give me bread."

Here, comrades, we are approaching the question of corn—the most acute question with us at the present moment. There is a lack of corn. The towns are starving, yet the present bourgeoisie, the usurers somewhere in the Tula, Orel, Kursk, or other provinces have concentrated in their hands enormous quantities of corn, tens of millions of poods, and resolutely refuse to surrender it, keep it in their grasp and resist all attempts at requisition.

They let the corn rot, while in the towns and cornless provinces the workers and peasants starve. At the present moment the village bourgeoisie is becoming the chief enemy of the working class. It wants to defeat the Soviet resolutions by means of starvation, in order to usurp the land. They, the village usurers, the bloodsuckers, understand that the socialist revolution spells death for them. There are many, these village usurers, in various parts of the country, and our task at present is to show the poorest peasants everywhere that their interests are deadly opposed to the interests of the rich peasants, and that if the village usurers win, they will grab all the land,

and new squires will appear — this time not members of the nobility, but of the class of village usurers. It is necessary that in the villages the poorest peasants should unite with the town workers against the village and town bourgeoisie, against the village usurers and bloodsuckers. These usurers hold up the corn, hoard up the money, and try to grab all the land; and if they succeed, the poorest peasants and the entire revolution are done for. We warn the village usurers that we shall be ruthless towards them. It is here a question of the feeding of the towns, of not allowing our children in the towns, our old mothers, our old men, our workingmen and women in the towns, and our breadless provinces to go without their daily bread. Once it is a question of life or death for the toilers, we shall allow no jokes. We shall not be stopped by the interests of the village bourgeoisie, but, together with the town and village poor, we shall lay a heavy hand upon the property of the village bourgeoisie and shall forcibly requisition without compensation its corn stores in order to feed the poor in the towns and villages.

But in order to carry out a firm policy with respect to our enemies, we must introduce a firm order into our own midst. The thing is, comrades, that a lot of frivolity, inexperience, and dishonesty has appeared in the midst of the uneducated sections of the working class. We must not shut our eyes to it. Some workers argue: "Why should I try my hardest now? Everything is broken up, and whether I do or don't work hard, things won't change on account of that." Such an attitude is criminal. We must strengthen within us the sense of responsibility, so that every one of us should say: "If I do not fulfill my duty, the whole machine will work still worse." All must create a sense of labor discipline, of labor duty, and joint responsibility. I am instructed, comrades, by the Central Executive Committee to undertake the task of creating a properly equipped army for the defense of socialist Russia. But the Red Army will be powerless, thrice powerless, if our railways are bad, if our mills and factories are ruined, and if food is not brought in from the villages to the towns.

It is necessary to get to work to strengthen Soviet Russia on all sides, conscientiously and honestly. A firm order must be established everywhere. Our Red Army must be permeated by the new aim of being the armed advance guard of the laboring people. The mission of the Red Army is to defend the state authority of the workers and peasants. This is the highest possible mission. And for such a mission discipline is necessary, a firm, an iron discipline. Formerly there existed a discipline for the defense of the czar, the landowners, the capitalists, but now every Red soldier must say to himself that the new discipline is one in the service of the working class; and we together with you, comrades, shall introduce a new Soviet socialist oath, not in the name of God or czar, but in the name of the laboring people, that in case of violation of, or raid, or attack upon the rights of the laboring people, upon the power of the proletariat and the poor peasants, he will be prepared to fight to the last drop of his blood. And you, all of you, the whole working class, will be witnesses of this oath, witnesses and participators of this solemn vow.

The first of May is approaching, comrades, and on that day we shall again gather together with the Red Army in great meetings, and shall take stock of what has been done, and ascertain what there is still to be done. And there is still a lot to be done.

Comrades, in preparation for the first of May, the Soviet government has decreed, where possible, the removal from the streets of the old czarist monuments, the old stone and metal idols which remind us of our slavery of the past. We shall then endeavor, comrades, to erect in the near future on our squares new monuments, monuments to labor, monuments to workers and peasants, monuments which will remind every one of you: look, you were a slave, you were nothing and now you must become everything, you must rise high, you must learn, you must become the master of all life.

Comrades, the misfortune of women is not only that they are ill-fed, ill-clothed—this is of course the greatest misfortune, but also that they are not allowed to rise mentally, to study, to develop. There are many spiritual values, lofty and beautiful. There are the sciences and the arts—and all this is inaccessible to the toilers, because workers and peasants are compelled to live like convicts, chained to their wheelbarrow. Their thought, their consciousness, their feelings, must be freed.

We must see to it that our children, our younger brothers have the opportunity of getting acquainted with all the conquests of the mind, with the arts and sciences, and be able to live as befits a human being who calls himself "lord of creation," and not, as hitherto, like a wretched slave, crushed and oppressed. It is of all this that we shall be reminded by May Day when we must meet together with the Red Army and declare: We have taken the power into our hands and we shall not give it up, and this power is for us not an end in itself, but a means—a means for another grand object, which is to reconstruct the whole of life, to make all wealth, all the possibilities of happiness, accessible to the whole people; to establish at last, for the first time, such an order upon this earth as would do away, on the one hand, with the man bent and oppressed and, on the other, with him who rides on the back of his fellow men; to establish firmly a common cooperative economic system, a common labor party, so that all shall work for the common good, that the whole people shall live as one honest loving family.

All this we can and shall realize completely only when the European working class supports us.

Comrades, we should be wretched, blind men of little faith, if we even for one single day were to lose our conviction that the working class of other countries will come to our aid, and following our example, will rise and bring our task to a successful conclusion. You need only call to mind what the toiling masses are living through at the present moment— the soldier masses of Germany on the Western front, where a raging, hellish offensive is going on, where millions of our brothers are perishing on both sides of the front. Does not the same blood which runs in our veins run in the veins of the German workers? Do not the German widows weep in exactly the same way when their husbands perish, or the orphan children when their fathers are killed? The same poverty, the same starvation stalk there; the same unhappy cripples come back from the trenches into the towns and villages and wander like wretched worn-out shadows. Everywhere the war produces the same consequences. Dire want and poverty reign supreme in all lands. And the final result will be, in the long run, everywhere the same: the rising of the laboring masses.

The task of the German working class is more difficult than ours, because the German state machine is stronger than ours, is made of stronger material than was the state of our czar of blessed memory. There the noblemen, the capitalists are robbers, just as ours, just as cruel; only there they are not drunkards, not idlers, not embezzlers of public funds, but efficient robbers, intelligent robbers, earnest robbers. There they have constructed a strong state boiler, which is pressed on all sides by the laboring masses, a boiler made of sound material, and the German working class will have to develop a good deal of steam before it explodes. The steam is already accumulating, as it was accumulating here, but since the boiler is stronger, more steam is needed. The day, however, will come, comrades, when that boiler will blow up, and then the working class will get hold of an iron broom and will start sweeping the dust out of all corners of the present German empire, and will do it with German thoroughness and steadiness, so that our hearts will rejoice watching them doing it.

But in the meantime we say: "We are passing through hard, strenuous times, but we are prepared to suffer hunger, cold, rain, and many other calamities and misfortunes, because we are only part of the world working class and are fighting for its complete emancipation. And we shall hold out, comrades, and shall carry our fight to a successful end, we shall repair the railways, the locomotives, we shall put production on a firm basis, straighten out the food supply, do all that is necessary — if only we keep in our bodies a cheerful mind and a strong stout heart. So long as our soul is a living one, our Russian land is safe, and the Soviet Republic stands firm."

Let us then, comrades, remember and remind the less conscious of us that we stand as a city on the mount, and that the workers of all countries look at us and ask themselves with bated breath, whether we shall tumble off or not, whether we fail or stand our ground. And we on our part call out to them: "We vow to you that we shall stand our ground, that we shall not fail, that we shall remain in power to the end." But you, workers of other countries, you, brothers, do not exhaust our patience too much, hurry up, stop the slaughter, overthrow the bourgeoisie, take the power into your hands, and then we shall turn the whole globe into one world republic of labor. All the earthly riches, all the lands, and all the seas — all this shall be one common property of the whole of humanity, whatever the name of its parts: English, Russian, French, German, etc. We shall create one brotherly state: the land which nature gave us. This land we shall plough and cultivate on cooperative principles, turn into one blossoming garden, where our children, grandchildren, and great-grandchildren will live as in a paradise. Time was when people believed in legends which told of a paradise. These were vague and confused dreams, the yearning of the soul of oppressed man after a better life. There was the yearning after a purer, more righteous life, and man said: "There must be such a paradise, at least in the 'other' world, an unknown and mysterious country." But we say, we shall create such a paradise with our toiling hands *here,* in *this* world, upon *earth,* for all, for our children and grandchildren and for all eternity!

[The chairman: It is evident that there is no opposition. Comrade Trotsky will answer questions.]

Comrades, there are a great number of questions here, but I shall answer only those which are of general interest.

"Is it true that you wanted to introduce a ten-hour labor day?"

No, comrades, that is not true. Although this is spread, broadcast by the Mensheviks and the Right SRs, it is nevertheless a lie. It has arisen in the following way. At one of the meetings I said, "Of course, if we should all of us work now eight hours a day conscientiously, as one ought to, and if we should put into the harness also the bourgeoisie and those who destroyed us yesterday on the strict principle of labor service, we could raise the wealth of our country to a very high degree in a very short time." It is necessary, said I, to raise between ourselves a feeling of responsibility for the fate of the whole country, and to work with all our might, without rest or haste, just as in a family, for instance, where there is no bickering over the work to be done. If it is a good, honest family, its members will not say: "I have done today more than you." If any member should have more strength, he will work harder. At the same time everyone works in such a manner that if needs be they work sometimes even sixteen hours a day, since they work not for a master, nor for a capitalist, but for themselves. That is how the statement arose, that I wanted to substitute a ten- or even a sixteen-hour day for an eight-hour day. It is sheer nonsense. We say: there is no necessity for it. It will be sufficient if we could establish, through the trade unions and the Soviets, such a firm discipline that everybody should work eight hours — by no means more, and as soon as possible, even seven hours — and that the work should be done conscientiously, that is, that every particle of labor time should be really filled with work, that everyone should know and remember that he works for a common association, for a common fund — that is all we are striving for, comrades.

I am asked further: *"You call yourselves socialist Communists, and yet you shoot and imprison your comrades, the anarchist Communists?"*

This is a question, comrades, which, indeed, requires elucidation — a serious question, no doubt. We, Marxist Communists, are deeply at variance with the anarchist doctrine. This doctrine is erroneous, but that would not in any way justify arrests, imprisonment, not to speak of shootings.

I will first explain in a few words wherein the mistake of the anarchist doctrine lies. The anarchist declares that the working class needs no state power; what it does need is to organize production. State power, he says, is a bourgeois service. State power is a bourgeois machine, and the working class must not take it into its hands. This is a thoroughly mistaken view. When you organize your economic life in a village, generally in small areas, no state power, indeed, is required. But when you organize your economic system for the whole of Russia, for a big country—and however much they robbed us, we are still a big country—there is need for a state apparatus, an apparatus which was hitherto in the hands of a hostile class that exploited and robbed the toilers. We say: in order to organize production in a new manner, it is necessary to wrest the state apparatus, the government machine from the hands of the enemy and grasp it in our own hands. Otherwise nothing will come of it. Where does exploitation, oppression, come from? It comes from private property in the means of production. And who stands up for it, who supports it? The state, so long as it is in the hands of the bourgeoisie. Who can abolish private property? The state, as soon as it falls into the hands of the working class.

The bourgeoisie says: don't touch the state—it is a sacred hereditary right of the "educated" classes. And the anarchists say: don't touch it—it is a hellish invention, a devilish machine, keep away from it. The bourgeoisie says: don't touch—it is holy; the anarchists say: don't touch—it is sinful. Both say: don't touch. But we say: we shall not only touch it, but take it over into our hands and run it in our own interests, for the abolition of private property, for the emancipation of the working class.

But, comrades, however mistaken the doctrine of the anarchists, it is perfectly inadmissible to persecute them for it. Many anarchists are perfectly honest champions of the working class; only they don't know how the lock can be opened, how to open the door into the kingdom of freedom, and they crowd at the door, elbowing one another, but unable to guess how to turn the key. But this is their misfortune, not their fault—it is not a crime, and they must not be punished for it.

But, comrades, during the period of the revolution, under the flag of anarchism—as everybody knows, and the honest idealist anarchist better than anybody else—a host of all sorts of hooligans, jailbirds, thieves, and night bandits have crowded in. Only yesterday the man served his term of hard labor for rape, or of prison for stealing, or was deported for banditry, and today he declares: "I am an anarchist—a member of the club," the "Black Crow," the "Tempest," the "Storm," the "Lava," etc., etc., a lot of names, a great lot.

Comrades, I have talked about it to the idealist anarchists, and they themselves say: "A lot of these jailbirds, hooligans, and criminals have smuggled themselves into our movement. . . ."

You all know what occurs in Moscow. Whole streets are forced to pay tribute. Buildings are seized over the heads of the Soviets, of the labor organizations, and it happens also that when the Soviets occupy a building, these hooligans under the mask of anarchists break into the building, fix up machine guns, seize armored cars and even artillery. Lots of plunder, heaps of gold have been discovered in their nests. They are simply raiders and burglars who compromise the anarchists. Anarchism is an idea although a mistaken one, but hooliganism is hooliganism; and we told the anarchists: You must draw a strict line between yourselves and the burglars, for there is no greater danger to the revolution than when it begins to decay at any point, the whole tissue of the revolution will then go to pieces. The Soviet regime must be of firm texture. We took power not in order to plunder like some highwaymen and burglars, but in order to introduce a common labor discipline and an honest labor life.

I hold that the Soviet authorities acted quite correctly when they said to the pseudoanarchists: "Don't imagine that your reign has come, don't imagine that the Russian people or the Soviet state is now a carrion upon which the crows alight to peck it to pieces. If you want to live together with us on the principles of common labor, then submit with us to the common Soviet discipline of the laboring class, but if you put yourselves in our way, then don't blame us if the labor government, the Soviet power, handles you without mittens."

If the pseudoanarchists or, to be plain, the hooligans will attempt in the future to act in the same way, the second chastisement will be thrice, ten times as severe as the first. It is stated that among these hooligans there are a few who are honest anarchists; if that is true—and this looks as if it were true with respect to a few men—then it is a great pity, and it is necessary to render them their freedom as quickly as possible. It is necessary to express to them our sincere regret, but at the same time to tell them—Comrades, anarchists, in order that no such mistakes should occur in the future you must put between you and those hooligans a sort of watershed, a hard line in order that you should not be mixed up one with another, that one should know once for all: that is a burglar, and this is an honest idealist. . . .

[*At this point a commotion, a noise, and a general confusion interrupt the speaker.*]

[The chairman: Nothing extraordinary has happened. Some fifteen anarchists demonstratively left the hall.]

Order, comrades.

Well, comrades, we have just now seen, in a small way, an example of how a small group of men can break up solidarity and order. We were calmly discussing our common problems here. The platform was open to all. The anarchists had the right to demand their turn and speak, if they wanted. I spoke of the true anarchists without animosity or bitterness, as everybody can testify; more than that, I said that among the anarchists there are many mistaken friends of the working class, that they must not be arrested or shot. Against whom did I speak with rancor? Against the hooligans, who put on the mask of anarchism in order to destroy the order and life and labor of the working class. I don't know to what camp these persons belong who thought it possible to create at a crowded meeting a provocative scene of this sort, which frightened many of you and brought in confusion and chaos at our popular meeting.

I am also asked, comrades, *"Why is the elective principle being abolished in military service?"* I shall say a few words about it presently. It was necessary in our old army, which we inherited from czardom, to dismiss the old chiefs, generals and colonels, for in the majority of cases they had been the tools in the hands of a class hostile to us, in the hands of czardom and of the bourgeoisie. Hence when the soldier-workers and soldier-peasants need to elect commanders for themselves, they elected not military chiefs, but simply such representatives who could guard them against attacks of counterrevolutionary classes. But at the present time, comrades, who is building up the army? The bourgeoisie? No, the workers' and peasants' Soviets, i.e., the same classes which compose the army. Here no internal struggle is possible. Let us take as an instance the trade unions. The metal workers elect their committee, and the committee finds a secretary, a clerk, and a number of other persons who are necessary. Does it ever happen that the workers should say: "Why are our clerks and treasurers appointed, and not elected?" No, no intelligent workers will say so. Otherwise the committee would say: "You yourselves have chosen the committee. If you don't like us, dismiss us, but once you have entrusted us with the direction of the union, then give us the possibility of choosing the clerk or the cashier, since we are better able to judge in the matter than you, and if our way of conducting the business is bad, then throw us out and elect another committee." The Soviet government is the same as the committee of a trade union. It is elected by the workers and peasants, and you can at the All-Russian Congress of the Soviets, at any moment you like, dismiss that government and appoint another. But once you have appointed it, you must give it the right to choose the technical specialists, the clerks, the secretaries in the broad sense of the word and, in military affairs, in particular. For is it possible for the Soviet government to appoint military specialists against the interests of the laboring and peasant masses? Besides there is no other way at the present, no other way open, but the way of appointment. The army is now only in the process of formation. How could soldiers who have just entered the army choose the chiefs! Have they any vote to go by? They have none. And therefore elections are impossible.

Who appoints the commanders? The Soviet government appoints them. Registers are kept of former officers and prominent individuals from among the ranks and noncommissioned officers who have shown capacity. Candidates receive their appointments out of this register. If they do represent some danger, there are the commissars to look after them. What is a commissar? The commissars are appointed from among Bolsheviks or the Left SRs, that is from the parties of the working class and of the peasantry. These commissars do not intervene in military affairs. These are managed by military specialists, but commissars keep a sharp eye on them that they may not abuse their position against the interests of the workers or the peasants. And the commissars are invested with large powers of control and prevention of counterrevolutionary acts. If the military leader issues an order directed against the interests of the workers and peasants, the commissar will say, Stop! and will lay his hand on the order and the military leader. If the commissar will act unjustly, he will answer for it in strict accordance with law.

In the first period, comrades, up to October and during October we fought for the power of the laboring masses. Who stood in our way? It was, among others, the generals, the admirals, the sabotaging bureaucrats. What did we do? We fought them. Why? Because the working class was marching to power, and nobody ought to have dared prevent it from taking it. Now the power is in the hands of the working class. And so we say: "Kindly step forward, gentlemen saboteurs, and place yourselves in the service of the working class." We want to make them work, for they also represent a certain capital. They have learned something which we have not. The civil engineer, the medical man, the general, the admiral — they have all studied things which we have not studied. Without the admiral we could not manage a ship; we could not cure a sick person without the physician; and without the engineer we could not build a factory. And we say to all these persons: "We need your knowledge and we shall summon you to the service of the working class." And they will know that if they work honestly to the best of their abilities they will have the fullest scope for their work, and nobody will interfere with them. Quite the contrary: the working class is a sufficiently mature class and will give them every assistance in their work. But if they attempt to use their posts in the interests of the bourgeoisie and against us, we shall remind them of the October and other days.

The social order which we are now establishing is a labor social order, a regime of the working class and of the poorest peasants. We need every specialist and every intellectual if he is not a slave of the czar or of the bourgeoisie, and, if he is really a capable worker, he can come to us and we shall receive him openly and honestly. We shall work with him hand in hand, because he will serve the laboring master of his country. But as for those who sabotage, intrigue, idle, and lead a parasitical life — comrades, give us but the chance of putting our organization in good order, and we shall immediately pass and carry into effect a law for them: he who does not work, who resists, who sabotages — neither shall he eat. We shall take away the bread cards from all saboteurs, from all who undermine the labor discipline of the Soviet Republic.

I am also asked: *"Why are we not introducing free trade in corn?"* If at the present moment, comrades, we introduced free trade in corn, we should in a fortnight stand before the dreadful specter of starvation. What would happen? There are provinces where there is plenty of corn, but where the peasant bourgeoisie does not sell it at the present time at fixed prices. If prices were freed from control, all the speculators, all the dealers would rush into those corn-producing provinces, and the corn prices would rise in the course of a few days or a few hours, and reach 50, 100, or 150 rubles a pood.

Then these speculators would start snatching the corn from one another, flinging it on the railways, and snatching the trucks from one another. At present there is among our railway workers, especially of the higher grade, a lot of corruption; they sell wagons for money and take bribes. If free trade in corn were to be proclaimed, the speculators would pay still higher prices for the wagons, and we should get a still greater disorganization on the railways. And the corn which would arrive into the towns would be quite out of your reach, workers.

Of course, fixed prices for corn will not bring us salvation if firm discipline on the railways is not established. It is necessary to establish a stricter regime for the higher-grade workers and those who encourage bribery, embezzlement, and rapacity among them. And it is also necessary that the whole railway staff should redouble its energy.

Then we must show the village usurers that we are not in a mood for jesting; that it is their duty to surrender their stocks of corn at fixed prices. If they do not surrender them, these must be taken away from them by force—by the armed force of the poor peasants and workers. It is the life and death of the people which is in question and not the speculators and usurers.

The situation is distressing in the highest degree—and not only with us. Holland, for instance, is a neutral country. It did not take part in the war. Yet the other day telegrams arrived stating that in Amsterdam the ration has been reduced for the whole population, and a hunger riot took place in the streets. Why? Because instead of ploughing, sowing, and cutting, scores of millions of men throughout the world have been destroying one another all these last four years. All countries have been impoverished and exhausted, and so it is with us. Therefore, a certain time—a year or two—must pass before we renew our corn stocks, and in the meantime only labor, discipline, order and severe pressure upon the village usurers, the speculators, and the freebooters will help us. If we establish all this, then we shall hold out.

And now let me reply to the last question, comrades: *"Who is going to pay the indemnity to Germany in accordance with the Brest treaty?"*

How shall I say it, comrades? If the Brest-Litovsk treaty holds,[4] then of course, the Russian people will pay. If in other countries the same governments remain which are in existence now, then our revolutionary Russia will be well coffined and buried, and the Brest treaty will be followed by a new one, a Petrograd or Irkutsk treaty which will be thrice or ten times worse than the Brest treaty. The Russian Revolution and European imperialism cannot live side by side for a long time. For the present we exist because the German bourgeoisie carries on a bloody litigation with the English and French bourgeoisie. Japan is in rivalry with America and, therefore, in the meantime its hands are tied. That is why we keep above water. As soon as the plunderers conclude peace, they will all turn against us. And then Germany, together with England, will split the body of Russia in two. There can be no shadow of doubt about it. And the Brest-Litovsk treaty will have to go. A much more grievous, severe, more merciless treaty will be forced upon us. That is the case if European and American capitalists remain where they are, that is, if the working class will not budge from its present place. Then we are done for. And then, of course, the laboring Russian people will pay for everything, will pay with its blood, its labor, will pay during scores of years, from generation to generation. But, comrades, we have no right whatever to assume that after this war everything will remain in Europe as it was.

The working class in every country was deceived by their pseudosocialists, their own Right SRs, Mensheviks, the Scheidemanns, the Davids, and equivalents of our own Tseretellis, Kerenskys, Chernovs, Martovs.[5] They have declared to the workers: "You are not ripe yet for taking the power into your own hands, you must support the democratic bourgeoisie." And the democratic bourgeoisie supports the big bourgeoisie, which supports the noblemen who in their turn support the kaiser. This is how the European Mensheviks and Right SRs found themselves chained to the chair of the kaiser, or to that of Poincare during the war. And so, four years have passed. It is impossible to admit for one moment that after such a terrible experience of bloodletting, calamities, deceit, and exhaustion of the country, the working class, on leaving the trenches, all again humbly return to the factories and all slavishly, as in the days gone by, turn the wheel of capitalist exploitation. No. On coming out of the trenches it will present a bill to its masters. It will say: "You have exacted from us a tribute of blood, and what have you given us instead? The old oppressors, the landowners, the oppression of capitalism, the bureaucracy!"

I repeat: If in the West capitalism remains, a peace will be forced upon us which will be ten times worse than the Brest-Litovsk peace. We shall not be able to stand on our legs. It is said that he who hopes for a European revolution is a utopian, a visionary, a dreamer. And I say: "He who does not hope for a revolution in all countries prepares a coffin for the Russian people." He virtually says: "The party which possesses the most effective killing machine will oppress and torture with impunity all the other peoples." We are weaker economically and technically—that is a fact. Therefore are we doomed? No, comrades, I don't believe it, I don't believe the whole of our European culture is doomed to perdition, that capital will destroy it with impunity, will sell it by auction, bleed it white, crush it. I don't believe it. I believe, comrades, and I know by experience and in the light of Marxist theory, that capitalism is living through its last days. Just as a lamp, before its extinction, flares up brightly for the last time and then all at once goes out, so, comrades, has this mighty lamp of capitalism flared up in this terrible bloody slaughter to illuminate the world of violence, oppression, and slavery in which we have hitherto lived, and to cause the toiling masses to shudder in horror and to awake. We revolted, so will the European working class revolt. And then not only the Brest-Litovsk treaty will fly to the very bottom of hell, but a lot of other things, too: all the crowned and uncrowned despots, the imperialist bandits and usurers, and a reign of liberty and fraternity among all peoples will ensue.

9

Civil War

The civil war lasted three years. In addition to the counter-revolutionary armies of the Whites and the imperialists, the government had to contend with political harassment and insurrectional violence by the other anti-Bolshevik forces.

An attempted assassination of Lenin by Social Revolutionary Dora Kaplan on August 30, 1918, occurred at a moment of grave military threat. The Soviets had lost Kazan, a city on the Volga River, which opened the way for the enemy to Moscow. Trotsky was at the front but left for Moscow where he spoke at the All-Russian Central Executive Committee of the Soviets, three days after Lenin had been shot.

John G. Wright's translation is taken from Fourth International, *January 1943.*

Lenin Wounded

Comrades, your brotherly greetings I explain by the fact that in these difficult days and hours we all feel deeply as brothers a need of closer union with each other and with our Soviet organizations, and the need of closing our ranks more tightly under our Communist banner. In these days and hours so filled with anxiety, when our standard-bearer, and with perfect right it can be said the international standard-bearer of the proletariat, lies on his sickbed fighting with the terrible shadow of death, we are drawn closer to one another than in the hours of victory. . . .

The news of the attack on Comrade Lenin reached me and many other comrades in Svyazhsk on the Kazan front. We suffered blows there, blows from the right, blows from the left, blows between the eyes. But this new blow was a blow in the back from ambush deep in the rear. This treacherous blow has opened a new front, which for the present moment is the most distressing, the most alarming for us: the front where Vladimir Ilyich's life struggles with death. Whatever defeats may await us on this or that front—and I am like you firmly convinced of our imminent victory—no single partial defeat could be so onerous, so tragic, for the working class of Russia and the whole world, as would be a fatal issue of the fight at the front that runs through the breast of our leader.

One need only reflect in order to understand the concentrated hate that this figure has called forth and will continue to call forth from all the enemies of the working class. For nature produced a masterpiece when it created in a single individual an embodiment of the revolutionary thought and the unbending energy of the working class. This figure is Vladimir Ilyich Lenin. The gallery of proletarian leaders, revolutionary fighters, is very rich and varied, and like many other comrades who have been in revolutionary work for three decades, I have had the opportunity to meet in different lands many varieties of the proletarian type of leader—the revolutionary representatives of the working class. But only in the person of Comrade Lenin have we a figure created for our epoch of blood and iron.

Behind us lies the epoch of so-called peaceful development of bourgeois society, during which contradictions accumulated gradually, while Europe lived through the period of so-called armed peace, and blood flowed almost in the colonies alone where predatory capital tortured the more backward peoples. Europe enjoyed her so-called peace of capitalist militarism. In this epoch were formed and fashioned the outstanding leaders of the European working-class movement. Among them we saw such a brilliant figure as that of August Bebel.[1] But he reflected the epoch of the gradual and slow development of the working class. Along with courage and iron energy, the most extreme caution in all moves, the painstaking probing of the ground, the strategy of watchful waiting and preparation were peculiar to him. He reflected the process of the gradual molecular accumulation of the forces of the working class—his thought advanced step by step, just as the German working class in the epoch of world reaction rose only gradually from the depths, freeing itself from darkness and prejudices. His spiritual figure grew, developed, became stronger and rose in stature—but all this took place on the selfsame ground of watchful waiting and preparation. Such was August Bebel in his ideas and methods—the best figure of an epoch which lies behind us and which already belongs to eternity.

Our epoch is woven of different material. This is the epoch when the old accumulated contradictions have led to a monstrous explosion, and have torn asunder the integument of bourgeois society. In this epoch all the foundations of world capitalism are being shattered to the ground by the holocaust of the European peoples. It is the epoch which has revealed all the class contradictions and has confronted the popular masses with the horrible reality of the destruction of millions in the name of the naked greed for profits. And it is for this epoch that the history of Western Europe has forgotten, neglected, or failed to bring about the creation of *the* leader— and this was not due to chance: for all the leaders who on the eve of the war enjoyed the greatest confidence of the European working class reflected its past but not its present. . . .

And when the new epoch came, this epoch of terrible convulsions and bloody battles, it went beyond the strength of the earlier leaders. It pleased history—and not by accident!— to create a figure at a single casting in Russia, a figure that reflects in itself our entire harsh and great epoch. I repeat that this is no accident. In 1847, backward Germany produced from its milieu the figure of Karl Marx,[2] the greatest of all fighters and thinkers, who anticipated and pointed out the paths to new history. Germany was then a backward country, but history willed it that Germany's intelligentsia of that time should go through a revolutionary development and that the greatest representative of this intelligentsia, enriched by their entire scientific knowledge, should break with bourgeois society, place himself on the side of the revolutionary proletariat, and work out the program of the workers' movement and the theory of development of the working class.

What Marx prophesied in that epoch, our epoch is called upon to carry out. But for this, our epoch needs new leaders who must be the bearers of the great spirit of our epoch in which the working class has risen to the heights of its historic task, and sees clearly the great frontier that it must pass if mankind is to live and not rot like carrion on the main highway of history. For this epoch Russian history has created a new leader. All that was best in the old revolutionary intelligentsia of Russia, their spirit of self-denial, their audacity and hatred of oppression, all this has been concentrated in this figure, who, in his youth, however, broke irrevocably with the world of the intelligentsia on account of their connection with the bourgeoisie, and embodied in himself the meaning and substance of the development of the working class. Relying on the young revolutionary proletariat of Russia, utilizing the rich experience of the world working-class movement, transforming its ideology into a lever for action, this figure has today risen in its full stature on the political horizon. It is the figure of Lenin, the greatest man of our revolutionary epoch.

I know, and you know too, comrades, that the fate of the working class does not depend on single personalities; but that does not mean that personality is a matter of indifference in the history of our movement and in the development of the working class. A personality cannot model the working class in his own image and after his likeness, nor point out to the proletariat arbitrarily this or that path of development, but he can help the fulfillment of the workers' tasks and lead them more quickly to their goal. The critics of Karl Marx have pointed out that he forecast the revolution much sooner than was actually the case. The critics were answered with perfect right that inasmuch as Marx stood on a lofty peak, the distances seemed shorter to him.

Many including myself have criticized Vladimir Ilyich too, more than once, for seemingly failing to take into account many secondary causes and concomitant circumstances. I must say that this might have been a defect for a political leader in an epoch of "normal" gradual development; but this is the greatest merit of Comrade Lenin as leader of the new epoch, during which all that is concomitant, superficial, and secondary falls away and recedes to the background, leaving only the basic, irreconcilable antagonism of the classes in the fearful form of civil war. To fix his revolutionary sight upon the future, to grasp and point out the most important, the fundamental, the most urgently needed — that was the gift peculiar to Lenin in the highest degree. Those to whom it was granted, as it was to me in this period, to observe Vladimir Ilyich at work and the workings of his mind at close range could not fail to greet with open and immediate enthusiasm — I repeat, with enthusiasm — the gift of the penetrating, piercing mind that rejected all the external, the accidental, the superficial, in order to mark out the main roads and methods of action. The working class is learning to value only those leaders who, after uncovering the path of development, follow it without hesitation, even when the prejudices of the proletariat itself become temporarily an obstacle along this path. In addition to this gift of a powerful mind Vladimir Ilyich also was endowed with an inflexible will. And the combination of these qualities produces the real revolutionary leader, who is the fusion of a courageous, unwavering mind and a steeled and inflexible will.

What good fortune it is that all that we say, hear, and read in our resolutions on Lenin is not in the form of an obituary. And yet we came so near that. . . . We are convinced that on this near front, here in the Kremlin, life will conquer and Vladimir Ilyich will soon return to our ranks.

I have said, comrades, that he embodies the courageous mind and revolutionary will of the working class. One ought to say that there is an inner symbol, almost a conscious design of history in this, that our leader in these difficult hours when the Russian working class fights on the outer front with all its strength against the Czechoslovaks, the White Guards, the mercenaries of England and France—that our leader is fighting those wounds which were inflicted on him by the agents of these very White Guards, Czechoslovaks, the mercenaries of England and France. In this is an inner connection and a deep historical symbol! And just as we are all convinced that in our struggle on the Czechoslovak, Anglo-French, and White Guard front we are growing stronger every day and every hour— I can state that as an eyewitness who has just returned from the military arena, yes, we grow stronger every day, we shall be stronger tomorrow than we are today, and stronger the day after than we shall be tomorrow; I have no doubt that the day is not distant when we can say to you that Kazan, Simbirsk, Samara, Ufa, and the other temporarily occupied cities have returned to our Soviet family— in exactly the same way we are hopeful that the process of recovery of Comrade Lenin will be swift.

But even now his image, the inspiring image of our wounded leader who has left the front for a time, stands clearly before us. We know that not for a moment has he left our ranks, for, even when laid low by treacherous bullets, he rouses us all, summons us, and drives us onward. I have not seen a single comrade, nor a single honest worker, who let his hands drop under the influence of the news of the traitorous attack on Lenin, but I have seen scores who clenched their fists, whose hands sought their guns; I have heard hundreds and thousands of lips that vowed merciless revenge on the class enemies of the proletariat. You need hardly be told how the class-conscious fighters at the front reacted when they learned that Lenin was lying with two bullets in his body. No one can say of Lenin that his character lacks metal; but now there is metal not only in his spirit, but in his body, and thereby he is even dearer to the working class of Russia.

I do not know if our words and heartbeats can now reach Lenin's sickbed, but I have no doubt that he senses them. I have no doubt that he knows even in his fever how our hearts too beat in double, threefold measure. We all realize now more clearly than ever that we are members of a single Communist Soviet family. Never did the life of each of us seem such a secondary or tertiary thing as it does at the moment when the life of the greatest man of our time is in mortal danger. Any fool can shoot a bullet through Lenin's head, but to create this head anew — that is a difficult task even for nature itself.

But no, he will soon be up again, to think and to create, to fight side by side with us. In return we promise our beloved leader that as long as any mental power remains in our own heads, and blood runs through our hearts, we shall remain true to the banner of the Communist revolution. We shall fight against the enemies of the working class to the last drop of blood, to our last breath.

Trotsky returned to the front and Kazan was recaptured about a week later. This first decisive military test for the Soviets and the Red Army helped to introduce discipline and develop the will and the confidence to win. But victory was still a long way off. Before the war was over, fighting took place on many battlefronts with a circumference of more than five thousand miles. Trotsky traveled to the fronts across Russia in the train which he made his command headquarters and home for two and a half years.

Now he was in Petrograd speaking at a meeting of the Soviet, appealing for volunteers for the southern front and motivating this with a detailed explanation of the military and political factors that made concentration there necessary. Military service in the Red Army was obligatory by this time, but the volunteers made the best fighters and provided the basic cadre around which the Red Army was constructed.

The date of the speech is uncertain, but from its contents it can be placed in October or November of 1918.

It is reprinted from The Living Age *of April 5, 1919.*

Recruiting the Red Army

Comrades — Two months and a half ago I made a speech here to the Petrograd Soviet and the Congress of Soviets of the Northern Territory. It was just after we had surrendered Siberia to the Czechoslovaks and the White Guards, and a few days before we surrendered Kazan, one of the saddest moments in the history of our young Soviet Republic, that I came to you from Moscow, where it was decided at a meeting of the Soviet of the People's Commissars and at party meetings, at a time of danger — grave danger to the Soviet Republic — to return here where this republic was born, to return to Red Petrograd and say to the Petrograd workmen, to the Petrograd Soviet, "The threatening hour of trial has come, and we await support from you." I remember, and you all remember, that the Petrograd Soviet then unanimously, with true, inmost enthusiasm which bore witness to its determination, responded to the appeal and sent hundreds, many hundreds, of the best sons of Petrograd's working class to the front. I was on the eastern front with them during that month when we were trying to take Kazan, and I watched your representative workingmen, the comrades from Petrograd.

If we took Kazan, if we took Simbirsk, if we cleared the Volga, it was, in an enormous degree, thanks to those workers whom we sent from here. They created our army there under the enemy's fire. We only sent the raw material there, young men, unconsolidated forces. The living soul had to be poured into them. They had to be welded together, they had to be given self-confidence; a united, centralized command had to be created. The personnel for the command had to be attracted; and, where political control was needed over them, authoritative workers were wanted who would be a guaranty to our soldiers that those in command would not deceive them or bring them into trouble. All this was done by representatives of the Petrograd working class. You took Kazan, you took Simbirsk, you cleared the Volga, you, the Petrograd Soviet of Workmen's and Red Army Deputies! I told you then that in our War Council there was no doubt that we could create a strong, forcible, compact army and a strong navy, perhaps not numerous for the time while we are limited in what we can do at sea, but a navy which can be developed when international conditions make that possible, and international conditions are changing every day in our favor. We have created a river flotilla on the Volga where, as I remarked at our meeting here yesterday, our sailors have fought and are fighting with incomparable heroism. Some vessels of the Baltic fleet, of course only the smaller fighting units, have been transferred there with first-class, hardened, revolutionary crews. There the White Guards are retreating down the Volga and on the Kama, and have surrendered the mouth of the Byelaya. In these battles perished, as I have mentioned, one of the best representatives of the Baltic fleet, Nikolay Georgiyevich Markin, the founder of our Volga flotilla, second in command to Comrade Raskolnikov.[3]

We created a Red air fleet. This is the most delicate form of armament; among the airmen were many elements demoralized by the old Grand Ducal regime, and the profession itself was very aristocratic. The airmen do not live as a corporate body but as individuals, and many of them look down on the army. We were told: "You will not have an air fleet, they will fly over to the enemy." There were cases in which they flew over with their machines; there were cases here on the northern front where airmen deserters were caught, and, of course, shot, but I must say that these were isolated cases; they might create a false impression among you as to the actual feeling in our Red air fleet. We had many heroes in our Red Army, among the infantry and cavalry, and among the sailors, but if you obliged me to award the palm of eminence to anyone, I should say that the airmen held the first place in the battles around Kazan. They knew no. danger, and they were engaged there under the most incredible conditions. They undertook reconnaissances of the utmost importance in storm and by night; they established a liaison service and terrorized the enemy by ruthless bombardment.

There fell into our hands the diary of an intelligent White Guard woman, who lived through all this month of strife in Kazan, and there on every page the work of the Red bandits of the air—that means our airmen—is spoken of with horror and hatred. And now they have been spread out on all the fronts: on the southern front against the Cossacks our Red airmen will shortly display their strength. I wanted to tell you that our Red Army is spreading itself in all directions, upward as well. We shall establish a durable, centralized, strong apparatus, morally sound at heart, because the Red Army is bound together by that unity of feeling which the revolutionary representatives of the Petrograd and Moscow proletariat have brought into it. Literally, regiments who came from the villages and were but little educated or enlightened have in the course of two or three weeks been morally regenerated under the influence of leading workmen. I remember one group. The picture just now came up before my eyes. It was one of the saddest and most tragic nights before Kazan, when raw young forces retired in a panic. That was in August, in the first half, when we suffered reverses. A detachment of Communists arrived: there were over fifty of them, fifty-six, I think. Among them were such as had never had a rifle in their hands before that day. There were men of forty or more, but the majority were boys of eighteen, nineteen, or twenty. I remember how one such smooth-faced, eighteen-year-old Petrograd Communist appeared at headquarters at night, rifle in hand, and told us how a regiment had deserted its position and they had taken its place, and he said: "We are Communards." From this detachment of fifty men twelve returned, but, comrades, they created an army, these Petrograd and Moscow workmen, who went to abandoned positions in detachments of fifty or sixty men and returned twelve in number. They perished nameless, as the majority of heroes of the working class generally do. Our problem and duty is to endeavor to reestablish their names in the memory of the working class. Many perished there, and they are no longer known by name, but they made for us that Red Army which defends Soviet Russia and defends the conquests of the working class, that citadel, that fortress of the international revolution which our Soviet Russia now represents. From that time, comrades, our position became, as you know, incomparably better on the eastern front, where the danger was the greatest, for the Czechoslovaks and White Guards, moving forward from Simbirsk to Kazan, threatened us with a movement on Nijny in one direction, and, in another, with one toward Vologda, Yaroslavl, and Archangel, to join up with the Anglo-French expedition. That is why our chief efforts were directed to the eastern front, and these efforts gave good results. The Volga has now been cleared from its source to its mouth. And if the Krasnov bands did attempt to cut in again between Tsaritsyn and Astrakhan, near Tsaritsyn, Svetly Yar, and Sarepta, well, as you all know, this effort was crushed by our Steppe army, which overthrew Krasnov's numerous forces, overthrew the maneuvering battalion of officers, took the staff prisoner, seized all the artillery, and, according to the latest information, was pursuing the troops that were fleeing in panic in

Lenin and Trotsky.

Trotsky, with staff, inspecting troops in Moscow in 1921.

all directions. The Volga has been freed at Samara and Syzran, and our affairs on the Urals are going incomparably better than before, for on the Volga we have freed important forces that are moving far on to the east. On the Urals we have approached Orenburg and Ufa after taking Bugulma. The fall of Ufa and Orenburg is certain in the near future, and Ekaterinburg's fate is a foregone conclusion.

It is true that while advancing to the east we lengthen our communications, and this always causes more difficulty. But we must take into consideration the fact that while advancing to the east we are seizing important military bases, for the enemy is retiring everywhere in a panic and is leaving at our disposal enormous military stores, and, what is more important, valuable works which serve for the production of munitions. The result is that not only we, but our military bases, are advancing, and our military position is improving, not becoming more difficult.

Archangel and the Murmansk front represented a great danger for us until we became convinced that that expedition could not join hands with the Czechoslovaks and the White Guards on the Volga and on the Urals. This danger may now be regarded as past. It is true that in their communiques the White Guards say that they have evacuated Kazan, Simbirsk, Volsk, Khvalynsk, Syzran, and Samara for strategic reasons. We, of course, cannot make any objection to all this dirt having cleared out of the territory of the Soviet Republic for strategic reasons connected with their operations. But I remember how, when they tried to surround our army in Svyazhsk, they brought from Samara and Simbirsk some officers' maneuvering battalions from newly mobilized regiments. Savinkov, Fortunatov, and Lebedev[4] marched at the head of these troops to crush our forces that were struggling near Kazan. They were driven off, suffered a defeat, and issued a communique for the White Guard population: "We fulfilled our task, we retired in complete order in the full sense of the expression." This was not a strategical maneuver, but something else—like the panic-stricken retreat of whipped hounds. So that there is no ground to fear that these two fronts will be joined up. And once this is so, then the Archangel front, to which we, of course, must give our full attention, ceases to be threatening, at any rate for the near future during the winter months. The White Sea will soon freeze, and communication between the expedition and the English metropolis will be interrupted.

They will have to retire to the Murmansk coast that does not freeze. But it will not be difficult for us in this land of starvation, cut off from England by ice, to crush the English expedition with small forces. There remains the southern front, and to it I direct all the attention of the Petrograd Workmen's and Red Army Deputies' Soviet. It is quite natural that, here, you concentrated all your attention on the northern and northeastern fronts, sent your best forces thither and were occupied in sustaining, morally and physically, the forces dispatched to those parts.

And now, comrades, we are living in times when the lines of international politics are changing their course with immense, with catastrophic swiftness. England thought Savinkov's White Guards were stronger than they proved to be. In the French legation and in the French embassy I was told that the former French ambassador, Noulens, just before the Yaroslavl revolt summoned Savinkov and told him that on such and such a date he must raise a revolt in Yaroslavl. Savinkov answered that this was a hopeless affair. Noulens, in reply, showed him that they must join hands with the Czechoslovaks, whose armies were already disintegrating, and, therefore, Savinkov's help was essential. Noulens formulated it in this way: "We do not give millions to your organizations in order that you should refuse to do what we want, and when we want it." And then Savinkov organized the Yaroslavl revolt.

At that time we were weak, but, nevertheless, the Yaroslavl revolt was crushed and all the Entente[5] missions were swept out of Vologda. A strict revolutionary regime was set up there; the counterrevolutionary plots were cut off, and the northern operations of the Franco-English imperialists were uprooted.

They are now turning all their attention to the south, not only because they have suffered defeat in the north and northeast, but, first of all, because for the time being the interrelation of forces has changed. Germany, having brought into subjection the Balkan peninsula, Rumania, the Ukraine, and Transcaucasia, was trying to effect a dictatorship in the Northern Caucasus.

Now the situation has radically changed, and the Anglo-French and American plunderers have discounted this to begin with. The orientation is now changing in all the Balkan countries. Previously, they were the vassals, the mercenaries, of Germany; now they are making ready to become, within twenty-four hours, or twenty-four minutes if required, the subject or half-willing vassals and mercenaries of Anglo-French imperialism. This has already happened in Bulgaria, it is happening in Turkey, it may happen tomorrow in Rumania, and it has been for a long time in preparation in the Ukraine. To the landowning and bourgeois classes there, it makes no difference whether Skoropadskyism[6] is on a German or an Anglo-French basis. The Ukraine knows that she cannot expect thanks from Skoropadsky, that he will sell Ukrainian land and Ukrainian grain to Germany just as he would to the Anglo-French imperialists.

Then, the Caucasus too, at present, is a place where the endeavors of English imperialism and the weakening endeavors of German imperialism are at cross purposes. Baku was seized by the Turks, but there is reason to think that it will pass tomorrow into the hands of the English. After Baku it will be Astrakhan's turn, and then that of Ciscaucasia. The Krasnovites, who at present are shooting German ammunition from German rifles, will tomorrow aim all their artillery according to the dictates of English imperialism. Krasnov will carry out these measures without hesitation and in this will unite with Denikin, who continues to carry on Alexeyev's business.[7]

Just now, comrades, the chief danger threatens us, not from the north, and not from the east: this is a more distant danger; the months of this winter will roll by and the spring that follows must come before the danger from the Archangel side becomes a real one, or the Japanese can move their divisions toward old Ural, if their warlike imperialistic pretensions go so far.

The danger in the south is much more immediate; if the Straits are opened by England's and France's fleets, if an Anglo-French expedition appears on the shores of the Black Sea, this will mean a radical change of Krasnov's front, a change of the whole of southern Russia, on the signal of danger from the Anglo-French mercenary bands, supported by Russian White Guard bands; this means a blow at Soviet Russia from the south.

Germany is too weak just now to be a menace to us. England and France account themselves sufficiently strong still; they are at present passing through such a period as that which Germany passed through during the Brest-Litovsk negotiations, and the conclusion of the treaty.

Germany needed six months to fall a victim to her own crimes. England and France, who reached their culmination six months after Germany, require perhaps six or eight weeks, because history works at a feverish rate, and because the patience of the popular masses is being the more exhausted and indications of a catastrophe are visible in imperialistic politics.

It may be hoped that in a few months, and it may be in a few weeks, the Anglo-French will be weaker than at present, but in the next few weeks they are an immediate and menacing enemy to us. This enemy threatens in a much greater degree from the south than from the north, therefore, all our attention must be directed toward the south. Our first and chief problem is not to allow Krasnov to cross the front, not to give him an opportunity to join hands with the Anglo-French and receive military support from them.

How is this to be achieved? It is very simple: Krasnov's and all these bands must be wiped off the face of the earth in the next two or three weeks. The Ukraine, as you know, during her negotiations with us, refused to define the frontier with us and stated that it was the territory of the Don Republic there and this did not concern Soviet Russia. Now, when we clear the Don Republic of the Krasnov bands, we shall have no frontier with the Ukraine; she herself did not want to have this frontier; and we will seek it in conjunction with the Ukrainian workmen and peasants. The evacuation of the Don territory will be a deathblow to all the Ukrainian bourgeoisie and to both of the counterrevolutions: to the already waning German scheme, because this will be the ruin of Krasnov, to whom Skoropadsky appealed for military help in establishing Ukrainian Cossackdom; it will also mean ruin to the Anglo-French scheme, because it reckoned on Krasnov for the best reasons. In this way it will be a deathblow to the whole Ukrainian counterrevolution. There can be no doubt that, when the Red Army regiments enter Rostov and Novocherkask, Soviet barricades will be erected in the streets of Kiev and Odessa. A revolution in the Ukraine, which, of course, we do not regard with indifference — and we shall occupy the post that becomes Soviet Russia — means a mighty concussion for Rumania and the whole Balkan peninsula. Austria, which is now too closely bound up with the Ukraine if only from the fact that Austrian, as well as German, troops are quartered there, is being more and more drawn into the rapids of the Ukrainian revolution. The knot of European imperialism, or even of world imperialism, is tied in the south of Russia, and especially on the Don front. The knot of the European revolution is tied there, together with it, at present, and this knot we must cut in the shortest possible time. We have transferred to that part a sufficient quantity of military forces, we are stronger than our enemy, and we hope to show this very soon indeed; but we need those same Soviet workers whom we had and have on the northern and eastern fronts, where, by their work, they secured the victories we have gained. So far there are in the south but few of you, Petrograd comrades! There is not yet in the political or military organization of the administration of the front that revolutionary temper, that hardness and determination which can only be given to the Red Front by the Petrograd and Moscow proletariat, that, with or without rifles, says, "I am a representative of the Petrograd Soviet, I am a Communard, and I know my post, which I will not desert, nor will I allow others to desert the posts assigned by the republic."

I have been again sent to you, to report that the center of attention of the Soviet Republic is now the south, which is farther away than the north, but cannot be farther from your political consciousness and your revolutionary preparations, because it is there that the fate of Soviet Russia and the world revolution is now to be decided. I reported here yesterday to the leading comrades of Red Petrograd, and they, of course, quite rightly drew my attention to the fact that Petrograd has given many men to all fronts; and everywhere I am always being accosted in the train by some Petrograd or Moscow workman who is now president of the Executive Committee or of the Extraordinary Commission, or is district commissioner — a youth of nineteen or twenty. I know that you have given many men, and those not the worst, to all the fronts in the provinces, but still I feel myself too much a man of Petrograd and a member of your Soviet not to know your strength and what you can do. I know that Petrograd is a Red hydra; cut off a hundred heads and in their place thousands of new ones will grow. I come again to you and say: Comrades, before the spring thaw which makes the fields impassable to military movements, before the spring thaw which makes the advance difficult, we must achieve decisive operations. We must enter Rostov and Novocherkask, clear the Don and plant a firm foundation for the predominance of Soviet power in all the Northern Caucasus. From the military point of view, comrades, we have done all that we could. We now need firm revolutionary support. Give us your Petrograd proletariat, gladiators, ready to go into fire and water and carry whole masses with them; insure our young forces against signs of cowardice and hesitation, give us, in a word, true representatives of the Petrograd Soviet, give us all you can of such workers, and you will see that over Rostov and Novocherkask will float the Red standard of the Soviet Republic.

Trotsky kept in close touch with the ranks of the Red Army, in person when possible or by written orders and appeals, explaining what was being done, praising, criticizing, and educating. An appeal published July 30, 1919, is one example of these messages.

It is reprinted here in the translation that first appeared in Soviet Russia, *February 14, 1920.*

Strike the Enemy, Spare the Prisoner!

At the time of our retreat, the counterrevolutionary bands of Denikin were committing indescribable crimes against the workers and peasants in the territories temporarily seized by them.

The Red Army, together with the whole population, is full of hatred.

While the armies on the southern front are taking the offensive, there is ground for fear that their just indignation may in some cases bring about the killing of White Guard officers taken as prisoners.

I deem it my duty to address myself to all the fighters on the southern front, with the following admonition:

Comrades of the Red Army, Commanders, Commissars: Let your just indignation direct itself only against the enemy with arms in his hand. Save the prisoners, even those that are clearly rogues.

Among the prisoners and deserters there will be found a considerable number of such as had joined the Denikin army through lack of understanding, or under compulsion.

We are annihilating only enemies. The one who will confess his guilt, or will go over to our side, or will fall into our hands as a prisoner — he will be spared.

The commanders and the commissars are instructed to secure the strictest observance of the present order.

All cases of violation of it are to be reported in accordance with military regulations, for the immediate relegation of the revolutionary war tribunal to the place of the commitment of the crime.

> President of the Revolutionary War Council
> of the Republic, People's Commissar for
> Military and Naval Affairs,
> *L. Trotsky*

10

Tasks of the Twelfth Congress of the Russian Communist Party

The fighting in the last stage of the civil war, with Poland, terminated at the end of 1920 and was followed by the treaty of Riga in 1921. Trotsky remained at the head of the armed forces. But as a member of the Political Bureau and Central Committee of the Communist Party (renamed in 1918), he now turned his attention to the problems of developing the workers' state in a socialist direction. The obstacles were no less imposing than they had been in 1917.

The country was in an acutely critical condition, much of its resources destroyed. Many of the best leaders of the revolution had been killed in the civil war. Worst of all, the European revolution, to which the Bolsheviks had looked for indispensable support, had suffered a series of defeats (as in Germany, Hungary); at the very least, aid from this direction had been postponed for a number of years.

In these conditions of extreme material scarcity, cultural backwardness, and continuing isolation, the way was prepared for the emergence and the growth of a privileged bureaucratic caste which took control of the party and state apparatus and began to transform the Russian Communist Party and the Communist International from revolutionary organizations into structures serving the narrow interests of this bureaucracy.

Lenin, critical of the bureaucrats and self-seekers in the state administration, realized in 1922 that the Communist Party itself was falling under the control of these elements and that Stalin, in his post of general secretary, was the representative and promoter of this bureaucracy inside the party.

Resolving to fight the policies of the Stalin machine at the party's forthcoming Twelfth Congress, slated for April 1923, he enlisted the support of Trotsky who shared his opinion and alarm. But he was able only to write some critical notes and articles and to conclude his bloc with Trotsky before he was totally incapacitated in March by the last in a series of strokes which ended in his death on January 21, 1924.

As a result of Lenin's illness an open struggle did not take place at the Twelfth Congress. Stalin made numerous concessions to avoid it, and Trotsky was not prepared to undertake the fight without Lenin.

However, in the precongress discussion, Trotsky raised the issues Lenin had intended to fight on, referring to and drawing on Lenin's notes and articles. This speech, made in Kharkov at a conference of the Communist Party of the Ukraine on April 5, 1923, is a lucid examination of the major problems facing the workers' state once the civil war had ended.

The translation by Brian Pearce from a pamphlet published in Moscow in 1923 was first printed in International Socialist Review, *Fall 1965.*

Comrades! The party congress is held once a year.[1] That means, formally speaking, that the task of the congress is first and foremost to evaluate the experience of the past year and to lay down the fundamental line for work in the year that lies ahead. But our party is not a party of political empiricism, that is, it is not a party that lives from case to case and from day to day. We are the party of Marxism, of scientific socialism; our methods, ideas, and evaluations of events embrace not just a year but a whole great period of history, and therefore we evaluate the experience of the past year and the tasks of the year before us from the standpoint of our view of the entire epoch through which we are passing — not in order to lose ourselves and dissolve our ideas in commonplaces and generalities, but, on the contrary, in order to deduce from a general evaluation certain quite specific and clearcut directives for our conduct in the period immediately in front of us.

If, comrades, we look at the question in the perspective which I have just shown, then we shall be obliged to ask in the first place whether in the year which has elapsed since the Eleventh Congress of the Russian Communist Party there have been any *basic* changes, any changes *affecting principles,* in the international or the domestic situation, any changes which would call for a radical revision of our tasks.

Would such changes be possible in general? Certainly. The Tenth Party Congress, two years ago, marked a very important landmark, and your corresponding Ukrainian congresses carried out the same work—a review of the road traversed, a reevaluation of tasks and methods. From the policy of War Communism we went over, in connection with the international and domestic situation, to what was called the New Economic Policy,[2] which has now developed into an entire historical epoch with a particular grouping of forces and with particular methods of work.

We are living in this epoch today, and we have to ask ourselves: Since the Tenth Congress, and since the Eleventh Congress, which merely rendered more precise and more profound the tasks set forth by the Tenth Congress, have there been any radical changes in the international and domestic situation? This, comrades, is the central question, since we want to evaluate correctly the work of our party as a whole, both on the scale of the Ukraine and on that of the work of the Central Committee of the Russian Communist Party, by whose instructions I am giving this address.

What does "the international situation" mean? For us the international situation is first and foremost the aggregate of those conditions which hasten or delay the international revolution. Has this international situation changed or not? Certainly it has changed. But has it changed *in principle, qualitatively,* since the Tenth Congress? No, it has not changed.

This is the essence of the matter. What was the origin of the great historical turn which we carried through at the Tenth Congress, placing the party under the sign which it still lives under to this day? This turn sprang—and we must not forget this fact for a single minute, otherwise we shall sink into provincialism and national limitedness—from the slowness in the rate of development of the world revolution. In 1917, 1918, and 1919, and to some extent still in 1920, when we were advancing on Warsaw, we estimated differently, not the general course of development of the world revolution, but its tempo, its speed, not as we estimate this today.

It has become clear, however, in terms of facts, that the world revolution, understanding thereby both the struggle of the proletariat for power in the West and the struggle of the colonial and semicolonial peoples of the East for national liberation—these two wings, two sides of one and the same struggle, directed against imperialism—it has become clear, I say, that the world revolution is obliged in its preparatory stage to overcome very much greater obstacles than we were all inclined to suppose at the end of the imperialist war and immediately thereafter.

Yes, this is the essence of the matter. It became clear to us during 1920 and 1921, with absolute clarity, that the Union of Soviet Republics would have to go on existing, perhaps for a rather long time, in the midst of capitalist encirclement. We shall still not receive tomorrow any direct and immediate aid from a proletariat organized in a state, a state of a much higher type and with greater economic might than ours. That is what we told ourselves in 1920. We did not know whether it would be a matter of one, two, three, or ten years, but we knew that we were at the beginning of an epoch of serious and prolonged preparation.

The basic conclusion from this was that, while awaiting a change in the relation of forces in the West, we must look very much more attentively and sharply at the relation of forces in our own country, in the Soviet Union. The chief relation of forces at home here is the relation between the working class and peasantry. The working class is the only class which is capable not only of leading our country in the future to socialism but also of directly saving it from ruin, disintegration, and devastation. But in numbers this class is a small minority, side by side with an overwhelming majority of peasants.

The fundamental task, as it was defined by Comrade Lenin at the Tenth Congress, is to establish correct economic and political relations between the working class and the peasantry, for to make a mistake in this field means to risk a mortal fall. And this is all the more dangerous because up to the present nobody is as yet ready to support us, nobody in the West will hold us up if we stagger and are about to fall; the proletariat is not yet in power over there. Now, let us ask ourselves whether, from this point of view, there have been any radical, basic changes in the world situation—and I have already said that the world situation means for us the aggregate of conditions which hasten or delay the progress of the proletarian revolution.

Let us recall the fundamental facts: the triumph of fascism, the coming to power of the Conservative imperialists in Great

Britain, the victory of the extreme imperialist wing of the national bloc in France, and the occupation of the Ruhr by the French, which has led in the last few days to the shooting of workers in Essen by French soldiers.[3] These are four outstanding facts from this year! They signify that on the political plane the movement of forces during this year has gone in favor of a strengthening of the dictatorship of imperialism, in the shape of its most extreme wing, with the using of the most extreme and ruthless methods of militarism. That is how we can sum up the political process which has developed in Europe during the past year.

Pessimistic and gloomy conclusions would appear to follow from this, at first sight. It would seem that the bourgeoisie has grown stronger during this year than it was at the time of the Eleventh Congress. As regards form and appearance this is true, but in essence it is not true. The day after the imperialist war the bourgeoisie felt incomparably weaker than now, while the proletariat felt revolutionary and pressed forward spontaneously. That's how it was all over Europe— more so in some countries, less in others. The collision between the classes found expression in various forms. The proletariat convinced itself, however, through hard experience, that it did not possess sufficient power to overthrow the bourgeoisie, because it lacked leadership, organization, cohesion, experience. The bourgeoisie convinced itself that it was still standing firm, that the proletariat would not easily overthrow it — and so there took place a shift in the consciousness of these two classes.

From 1919 onward the bourgeoisie began to be strengthened more and more in its class self-confidence. The European proletariat which in 1918-1919 was spontaneously pressing forward against the bourgeois state began in the mass to doubt whether it possessed what was needed to take power, to change the social order. And these two waves — the wave of consolidation of the political self-confidence of the bourgeoisie and the wave of the spontaneously revolutionary mood of the proletariat now ebbing — have been flowing before our eyes during the last three years. These are two processes of prime importance. Whoever does not take them into account is not taking into account the international situation.

But Marx taught us that a class does not always think itself to be what it really is — a class can already be powerful in its position in production, in the role it plays, and yet not understand that this is so. A class can have forfeited half or three-quarters of its economic power and yet keep itself in position through its experience, through inertia, through the habitual procedures of the state. And that is the situation we have in Europe today. The bourgeoisie considers itself, after the experience of 1918-1919, very much stronger than it is in fact, for its economy has not been restored to health, the breakdown of capitalism continues, and the bourgeoisie has no methods at its disposal other than predatory ones, methods of grabbing and smashing, as in the Ruhr, and a class which cannot advance production is a class which is doomed. The bourgeoisie imagines itself, as a result of the experience of 1918 and 1919, much stronger than it is in reality.

The proletariat of Europe, on the contrary, feels after that experience, so far as the overwhelming majority is concerned, much weaker than it really is. Europe is passing through its Stolypin period,[4] a period of imaginary strength, before coming to its Kerensky period. This is now the key to the entire political situation — the lack of correspondence between the political awareness of the classes and their objective position and objective strength.

Comrades, whoever has not mastered this, whoever has not thought it out to the end, will lose his bearings through day-to-day newspaper reports, will be unable to find either the main key to the world situation or the day-to-day keys, and he may fall into pessimism. The process which is taking place in Europe may push official policies still further to the right, towards imperialist monopoly rule by the extremist groups of the bourgeoisie, but this very shift rightwards of the official bourgeois apparatus will create a still bigger gulf not only between the bourgeoisie and the proletariat but also between the bourgeois state and the basic elementary needs of the economy and the standard of living of the whole people and thereby will prepare a fatal, inevitable revolutionary catastrophe.

The catastrophe is being prepared both in the West and in the East — more slowly than we expected in 1918. I said "and in the East" because, while the struggle of the Indians, the struggle of China and the other colonial and semicolonial peoples belongs to another historical epoch, a much more backward one, than the struggle of the proletariat for power, yet these two epochs are today united in practice in a single epoch. The Indian is fighting against the same imperialism which the advanced proletariat of Britain is fighting against. And therefore in the scales of history, in the scales of our Communist International,[5] the struggle of the oppressed colonial peoples and that of the advanced European proletariat constitute two parts of one and the same struggle, merely waged with different types of weapons.

For us, therefore, the colonial and national struggle is not an echo from some ancient epoch which we have half forgotten, but a condition for the victory of the proletarian revolution throughout the world. I was recently looking through the report of the Eleventh Party Congress and, among others, I noticed Comrade Skrypnik's[6] speech in which he declared with undoubted correctness that the question of our national policy inside the country, within the RSFSR, within the entire Union which exists today (there was at that time no Union but only a formless federation),[7] is a question of our world policy in relation to the East, and the East, that is, the struggle of the oppressed nations for equality and freedom, is a colossal factor in the world revolution. This is especially true now, and to this matter I shall return.

Time, comrades, plays an enormous role in politics. Time is an important factor in politics, and it has turned out that the time needed by the backward peoples of Asia and the advanced proletariat of Europe to prepare their revolution is more than we thought. This was what gave rise to the review of our immediate tasks and methods which was carried out at the Tenth Party Congress and the Third Congress of the International, on the world scale. A very big new landmark was set down at the Third Congress of the International: "Win the masses before talking practically about winning power." We have called the phase of politics since the Third Congress the *new stage*. In our internal life, at the Tenth Congress we named our new course the New Economic Policy, NEP for short. But "NEP" can stand not badly both for the new stage[8] and for the New Economic Policy, and this, comrades, is a kind of symbol in verbal form, because the New Economic Policy inside the Soviet countries resulted almost entirely from the new stage on the international scale.

Since the European workers were going to take an undetermined number of years getting ready, since we should not receive German or French technical and organizational aid tomorrow or the day after tomorrow, we said to ourselves, two years and more ago, we shall have to give better and more vigilant attention to what is happening under our own feet, to the relation of forces inside our own country, to the state of the peasants' economy, to its solvency and historical staying-power and, in accordance with this, construct and reconstruct our policy. This gave rise to the new course.

Trotsky speaking at the Fourth Congress of
the Communist International, 1922.

At his desk in Moscow.

And in such a long perspective as this, has the last year given us grounds or data for reconsidering the new course? No. That shifting of forces which began after the defeat of the Italian workers in September, 1919, which continued in 1920 after our retreat from Warsaw, after the March events in Germany, after the defeat of the German proletariat as a result of a premature revolutionary offensive[9] — the shift of forces after these events which put an end to the first spontaneously revolutionary wave is still continuing, has not yet reached its turning point.

These are the basic facts and along with them the basic criteria for evaluating the present moment. We have often, following the example of Vladimir Ilyich, called the new period which began after the end of War Communism the "breathing space." This expression has now gone out of circulation, and not accidentally. Today we use more frequently another expression of Comrade Lenin's, the "bond," in relation to the peasantry. Why do we talk so infrequently now about the breathing space? Because in 1919-20 this new period was not yet defined for any of us in its full magnitude. Yes, there is an interval, we said, and a serious interval, but perhaps it will be exhausted in one or two years, depending on how events go in Germany, on the frontiers of Germany, in France, and so on; in other words, we at that time defined this transitional epoch as shorter than it has proved to be, through our self-confidence in approaching it.

It has turned out, however, that this is not simply a "breathing space" but a big historical pause which has been transformed into a whole epoch. Three years have passed since we adopted our new orientation on the worldwide and domestic scales and we still don't know when this new period will be exhausted, how much time will pass, whether it will be a matter of years or only months. . . . It is impossible to guess, but if you were to ask me whether it will be years or months, then I should answer you (adding again in brackets that it is impossible to guess): If months, they will probably be many, if years, they will probably be not so many [*laughter*]; don't ask for more precision than that in forecasts. But it is unquestionable that this is already not just a breathing space but a whole historical epoch.

And this, comrades, is the explanation of our party's demand, a demand which arises from the experience of last year, that we reexamine, check and ventilate the fundamental questions of our work from this very standpoint that the new stage is dragging out into a whole historical epoch. On the given road, that is, on our Russian cart-track, in the given vehicle, that is, our badly lubricated Russian cart, and in your Ukrainian cart which I don't suppose is much better lubricated than the Russian one [*laughter*], we shall still have to make a considerable historical journey, over, perhaps, a prolonged period of time.

And the party says to itself—let's check up and see what sort of an axle the cart has, what state its wheels are in, and the linchpins, will they hold or won't they; ought anything to be replaced? That is the basic problem before the Twelfth Congress. We are not saying that we have left one epoch behind us and are entering into a new one, which we go on to define. No, we are saying that the epoch which we entered officially as from the Tenth Congress has been prolonged in the West and therefore also in our country. Let us examine our weapons, our ways and means and methods. Will they stand the strain of a prolonged epoch? Let us check our Soviet cart in all its main parts.

That means, above all, the relations between the working class and the peasantry, and the relation between the working class and the peasantry in its broad sense also embraces the problem of industry, for industry in our country rests on a peasant foundation; the relation between the working class and those nationalities which were formerly oppressed, because this is essentially only a subproblem of the basic problem of the relation between the working class and the peasantry; the problem of the mutual relations of the party and the working class; the problem of the mutual relations of the party and the state machine, that is the least well lubricated wheel in our cart. These, comrades, are the main problems. Here you have in essence the whole mechanics of our dictatorship—party and class, working class and peasantry, party and state machine. Industry and the national question are fully linked with the problem of the relation between the proletariat and the peasantry. Testing and sounding these fundamental problems is the task of the Twelfth Congress and also of your conference.

If the NEP epoch is further prolonged, then the conclusion which first and foremost follows from that is that the dangers inherent in this epoch are multiplied, and along with this, that our tasks demand a more accurate and calculated approach on our part. In advance, before we come to deal with particular problems, we can, therefore, say that what we have to do is not to reconsider what our tasks are, for they remain the same, since the aggregate of new conditions remains the same, but to adopt additional *preventative measures* against dangers and to *regulate and systematize* our methods of coping with the fundamental tasks of our epoch. That, as it seems to us, is the general formula for the Twelfth Congress.

Let us check this against particular problems, for then only will it acquire concrete meaning.

The proletariat and the peasantry — this is a problem of our state machine, of its sources of income, of its costs and expenditures, and it was not without reason that Vladimir Ilyich, when he fell ill and before his illness became graver, concentrated all his thinking on two closely connected questions — the first was that of the proletariat and the peasantry as a whole, and the second was the national question. It is to Comrade Lenin's initiative that we owe it that both these questions have been posed so sharply and vividly.

In his articles devoted to the Workers' and Peasants' Inspection, the Central Control Commission and so on — you all remember them, I am sure, and have all had occasion to reread them more than once already — he draws a conclusion which can be formulated like this: Go forward, but don't go too far ahead, remember that we are still in the conditions of the new stage on the world scale and the domestic NEP, that our industry, and along with it our state machine, rest and cannot but rest upon our backward peasant economy and that our state machine and our industry can absorb and demand from the peasantry, in order to make progress, only a limited amount of resources.

What amount? This, of course, cannot be defined theoretically. Here exact calculation is needed and, also of course, to deduce from the problem of how much in a given year the peasantry can contribute to the needs of the state machine, defense and industry, to deduce from this a slogan of ideological struggle, as do certain comrades who talk and write about how we are taking too little from the peasants, that we are "lovers of the peasantry" (I have in mind here, in particular, some articles of Comrade Larin's) is unquestionably a mistake.

The problem of how much the peasants can contribute is a very important one, but it is a practical problem, not one of principle. It is necessary that the peasant should give not less than he is able to give, but also not more. We need to establish the rule: *Take from the peasant so much as will still leave him richer next year than he is this year.* This is a formula which the peasant understands, and this is the basis of our present state policy. It is quite different from the previous formula, which prevailed in the days of War Communism, when we said to the peasant: Hand over all your surplus.

Without a surplus the peasants' holding can't carry on, it won't live but will collapse. Now we say: The peasant needs a surplus in order to develop his holding. Unless agriculture advances there cannot be any industry at all. So then we must measure our cloth seven times before we cut it. But this is not a question of class struggle in our country. Or rather it would be truer to say that the entire wisdom of our party ought to be directed to ensuring that this question is not made a question of class struggle but a question for conciliation, for compromise. Yes, we are conciliators on this question, we are thoroughgoing conciliators on this question of workers' states coming to an agreement with the peasants.

You, peasant, give us the maximum that you can, and after a year or two or three you will be indemnified for this advance, and in any event we will guarantee you against counterrevolution, against White-guardism. In this matter the state is wholly and completely prepared to reach agreement with you, for this is our common interest, to take from you so much as to ensure that next year you — and also the whole state — may be richer than this year. Of course, we may make mistakes in our calculations, and this is inevitable in particular districts and localities, but our basic line is unquestionably correct. This is how the question of the amount of taxation is decided.

But then comes the question of *how* to take from the peasantry. This is also not a simple matter. If they harass the peasant month in and month out, if he finds himself constantly up against our taxation fantasies, both central and local, this upsets his equilibrium. The peasant is very much a man who has to plan his affairs. He lives by the sun, by the stars, by the seasons, and work on his holding requires a plan. We disrupt this plan with our unplanned fiscal harassment. And that is why we say this today.

First, define correctly the total amount of the taxes to be paid by the peasantry. I have tried to give a formula for this. The actual figures are, of course, a matter for our state organs, under the leadership and supervision of our party. Secondly, there must be technique in taxation, all these innumerable varieties of tax must be reduced to uniformity. The taxes must be given the form which is simplest for and most easily understood by the peasant and at the same time most efficient. A balance between taxation in kind and in money must be established in accordance with the special features of the particular district and region, in accordance with the strength or weakness of the peasant.

The question of taxation policy is a very important aspect of the fundamental question of the mutual relations between proletariat and peasantry. Closely connected with this is the question of exports, since we not only have agreed, but consider it necessary, to leave at the disposal of the peasantry ever larger surpluses, however modest they may be. The peasants cannot realize these surpluses on the home front alone, for this means an even more frightful disparity between prices of industrial products and prices of agricultural produce. This disparity results from the state of our industry and from the isolation of our agriculture from the world market. Therefore, open an outlet for the peasants onto the world grain market, enable the peasants to realize their surpluses, which will get bigger year by year, make it possible for them to realize these surpluses in order to raise agriculture to higher levels.

And in this sphere, between the world market and the peasantry, we establish as the link not the speculative export merchant but the working class and its Soviet state, which now comes forward in yet another new, additional role, derived from its old role, as intermediary between the world market and the sellers of agricultural surpluses, the Russian, Ukrainian, and other peasants of our Union. These two questions are closely interconnected. Simplifying, putting in order, and giving a planned character to our taxation policy is closely connected with the exportation of our grain abroad.

And the Tenth Congress of Soviets, if you remember, called for planned organization of all our foreign trade. The monopoly of it in the hands of the workers' state, this immovable condition of the proletarian dictatorship, demands that a planned character be given to our foreign trade, that is, not just proceeding from case to case, selling what you can and buying what you can get, the way we traded, more or less on smuggling lines, in 1919 and 1920. No, bring foreign trade into line with the development of peasant economy, with the inevitable further growth in the potentialities of grain export and with the state of our industry, which we must protect. For we are decidedly supporters of socialist protectionism, otherwise our industry will be plundered by foreign capital.

Hitherto our taxation policy has led us from one case to the next; take what you can, time doesn't wait. There were no regular and orderly methods. Since the situation is being prolonged, that is, since the Soviet state is to remain for a considerable period in direct and severe dependence on the condition of agriculture, we must bring taxation policy within the framework of a serious long-term plan. Don't keep harassing, don't disturb and irritate the peasant, for this is both harmful to him and without benefit to you, but establish a system of planned taxation which looks far ahead and vigilantly. Measure seven times, and be guided by the formula: Take so much that the peasant may be richer next year than this. Give a planned character extending over a number of years to our tax system and our foreign trade—that, comrades, is the very important conclusion which I also want to fix in your memories along with the first basic conclusions.

Let us now proceed, from the same point of view, to consider industry. The main grievances of our industrial executives during the last year, both here in the Ukraine and with us in Moscow, are connected with the question of what are called *circulating media*. Since the time when we went over to the NEP it has not, of course, been my fate alone to talk with dozens of industrial executives to the effect that it would be necessary simply to close down the given enterprise, to which the reply came: "Just give us a little quantity of circulating media and we'll show you that our enterprise will take a turn for the better, will start on the upgrade, and so forth." This is a very widespread reply right down to the present day. Give us circulating media only and we will give you, in exchange for these miserable circulating media, these bits of paper, such splendid things as metal, leather, coal, everything you need. . . .

This attitude to matters is an involuntary carry-over of methods of thinking from the period of War Communism into the conditions of NEP. For what does the shortage of circulating media mean? It means *lack of the necessary market capacity,* understanding by the market both the peasant sector and the state sector of it, for in the last analysis it all comes down to the same thing: since state industry as a whole does not at present create a profit, the state budget basically relies on the peasantry. Outside the state as consumer (for the army, for the railways, and so on) there exists, again, in the main the peasant market. Thus, on the amount of peasants' surplus—regardless of whether it is spent directly by the peasants on buying industrial products or is handed over by them to the state—depends the amount of the media which can be put at the disposal of our industry.

This is a fundamental truth which you can't get away from or jump over. Of course, as we develop, when industry becomes profitable, when it creates surplus value and hands over this surplus value to the state, industry will create its own market, will itself increase its absorption capacity for the realization of its own products. But that is for the future. Today the role of the peasantry as the market remains very important and it will so remain for years and years — getting smaller and smaller of course, as time goes by.

And so long as industry in our country (I say this bluntly and frankly) is running at a loss, so long as, taking light industry and heavy industry together, it lives at the expense of the budget, of the tax system — so long as to say "give me more and more circulating media" means to go in for fantasy — you are trying to lift yourself off the ground by the hair of your own head. Circulating media can be obtained by levelling and deepening the connections between industry and peasant economy, by reducing the cost of production of industrial products, by combining the peasant economy — through an honest and reliable broker, that is, through the workers' Soviet state — with the economy of Western Europe. In this way, and only gradually, we can secure circulating media for industry. Comrades, even if these circulating media were to fall from heaven, would our industry absorb them?

If America were, God preserve us, to give us a billion dollars in gold, our chief care would have to be directed to maintaining a proper correspondence between town and country, so that neither industry as a whole nor any of its branches should be overfed, for industrial indigestion, in the form of a crisis or a series of crises, would also be dangerous; we should have to give the circulating media to the emaciated organism in such doses as to ensure that the blood flowed equally in all the veins. Metal, for example: with our economy, with the state of our transport, it is not so easy to "digest" it. This means, and this is the problem, that we have to observe definite rates of advance, and not rush too far ahead. All the more so now, when nobody is going to present us with any gifts, as far as I can see. . . .

I said, comrades, that our industry works at a loss. I don't doubt that these words will be snatched up by our enemies, both the imperialists and the Menshevik scum of the whole world, and that in every language it will be said that, speaking at a conference in Kharkov, Trotsky admitted that Soviet industry works at a loss and that this means that the dictatorship of the proletariat is threatened with inescapable ruin; for, since industry works at a loss, that is, doesn't grow but rather melts away, this means that the ice floe on which the proletariat stands is melting away under its feet, and so on.

Nevertheless, comrades, I do not take back my words, because it is our habit in general to say what is. Vladimir Ilyich educated the party in that sense, and we cannot repudiate that education; we must tell ourselves the truth about ourselves, we cannot deviate from that. We may make mistakes and we may correct them and go forward, but if we should get into the habit of telling lies to ourselves, touching up the truth for the benefit of party and Soviet congresses, then we should go down without hope of recovery. Our industry as a whole is still working at a loss. I say, as a whole, that is, taking light and heavy industry together.

Some branches of light industry boast that they are making profits. I don't know whether you have checked whether this is so; I haven't, and it would be difficult to check on it today. I wouldn't assume responsibility for such an estimate; but from such partial checks as I have made I have come to the conclusion that, if not always then in a number of cases, the profits of light industry are fictitious and are often obtained at the expense of other branches of the economy. Naturally, when textile manufacturers are in desperate need of circulating media, but the maker won't accept textile goods at prices higher than the cost of production, then prices have to be reduced and how is this done? This is the job of a certain art of black and white magic that is called "calculation" [*laughter*].

It is calculation if you reckon some old cotton at the price at which you bought it some time ago and not at the price it bears today, or what is even more serious, not according to the expenditure you should have to make in order to get a fresh supply of cotton. Obviously the textile industry can really make progress only if we can replace the cotton which we put on the market with fresh cotton. If the old cotton is transformed into fabric, and a profit appears in the balance sheet, but in fact the plantations in Turkestan are declining and the basic resources of raw cotton are being reduced, this means that the profitability is fictitious, it is being reckoned on the basis of old resources which are melting away.

In many other cases light industry is supported by heavy industry, it is nourished by coal, metal, and other forms of raw material, and here, in reality, one should take into account all the expenses involved, starting from the beginning, and then only will it be seen whether there is really a profit here or only a squandering of the basic resources of the state. This is a very complex business, especially with our too mobile ruble, but we need nevertheless to learn how to do it, at all

costs. We used to say: "Socialism is stocktaking." Now we
ought to say: "Socialism is calculation," but not the kind which
resembles white and black magic, no, real calculation, which
is based on economic realities.

A balance sheet is stocktaking, but adapted to the forms of
the New Economic Policy. This translation of stocktaking into
the language of NEP is not very pleasant language, but after
all we still speak this language badly, and we need to learn
to speak properly in the language of the market. The question
of calculation for our industry and the question of balance
sheets is in the last analysis the question whether industry
can reckon up what it costs the peasant and what it gives
him directly or through the workers' state. This is a fundamental question. The balance sheet is not a mere technical
matter — this balance business, say some people, is for ac-
countants, but we are concerned with "high politics." No,
pardon me, calculations and balance sheets constitute the
real check on the stability of the workers' state and the mutual
relations between the proletariat and the peasantry.

Apart from these methods we have and can have no others
which are really reliable. And this is what complicates the tasks
which were set forth by the Tenth Congress. If in the field of
fiscal policy we say, "from the harassment of the peasant we
will go over to a planned system of taxation which looks to
the future"; if in relation to the problem of peasant surpluses
we say, "from our previous talk about the local market we
will go over to a link with the world market through
the workers' state"; then in the field of industry, instead
of cadging from the state from instance to instance, saying
"give me some money, give me some more," we will pass over
to accurate calculation, accurate balance sheets, saying "no
money will be available to you without accurate calculation
and accurate balance sheets — for this is a question of life and
death for our country" [*applause*].

I said that our industry, in general and as a whole, works
at a loss, and I added that all our foes will of course seize
upon this admission. But here it is necessary to give
some general explanation which is not purely economic but
of the historical order. The revolution as a whole has involved
enormous expenses. Our economy in general has been brought
below the level of 1917. You all know that we are now much
poorer than our country was in the last period of the existence
of the old regime. But this is a law of history: Every revolution
results in the new ruling class beginning its rule on an economic
foundation much lower than that on which the previous ruling

class ended its rule. Revolution is devastation, civil war.

It may be said that revolution involves "too great" an expenditure. But that is how these classes reckon against whom the revolution is directed, and also the intermediate classes. The proletariat reckons that this expenditure is in the last analysis repaid a hundredfold; that is why it carries through the revolution. But the revolution is not a single finished turn or overturn. There are turns within the revolution itself. The passage from War Communism to NEP was an important but partial turn within a great revolutionary turn. And every turn has to be paid for. This is how things have been arranged by mother — or stepmother — History: Where you make a turn, there is an obstacle to be overcome. Pay for your training!

For the revolution as a whole the proletariat is paying with a temporary lowering in its general level of production; for the transition from War Communism to NEP, for instruction in the new methods, the working class is paying in this form, that its economic organs are squandering part of that achievement which had survived from the epoch of War Communism, in order to get the industrial machine going. The fact that the workers' state has suffered a definite loss in changing from one set of methods in the economy to another is not in itself tragic for us; on the contrary, it is in the nature of things. But if this is payment for transition from one system of economy to another, it must be a once-for-all payment, not a constant drain. If deficits were to become the norm this would threaten dissipation of the basic resources of the state. We have paid with losses for the transition from War Communism to NEP, but from now on, let there be work which brings profit!

Profitability of industry can be attained only by means of a whole series of measures about which we shall talk in detail when we discuss the relevant point on the agenda. But the general line of these measures is clear; from amateurism and muddle we must go over to systematic, planned work.

Comrades, I have read in your journal *Kommunist* the debates which took place at the Donets provincial conference on Comrade Kviring's report — a much condensed report, of course. There they told how the party organization was obliged to be on the alert at all critical moments — to raise a shout, sound the alarm, and so on — because industry was constantly menaced with financial shocks. This is typical not only of the Donets basin, that is, the heart of our industry, it is typical of our economy as a whole, and from these concussions and shocks, from this unsteadiness and formlessness of economic relations, of course, there is not and cannot be any saving leap into the realm of some sort of absolute planning, but there must be a gradual emergence onto the broad road of planning.

We should, of course, be children after the experience of these years if we were to suppose that we could create an ideal economic plan all by ourselves, the way the spider spins its web, and substitute it for what is done now — that would be a return to the worst illusions of *glavkocracy*[10] when, instead of a comprehensive plan, there was comprehensive economic constipation. It is quite clear that a living and vital plan can be created only on the basis of the experience of that amateurism, those vacillations, those twitchings this way and that, those mistakes and even that accursed black and white magic *under the pretense* of calculation which we have now — only on this basis, not a priori but a posteriori, as the philosophers say, that is, on the basis of experience, testing, correction of errors can we construct a plan and render it more accurate. This task must be set before us clearly and distinctly, in its full dimensions.

The policy of "from one case to the next," the practice of improvisation, economic guerrilla tactics, amateurism, must more and more, under the staunch and stubborn leadership of our party, yield place to planning methods and the principle of planning. Otherwise we shall, in the future as in the past, too often find ourselves straining at gnats while swallowing camels. The expression of planning methods in the field of industry and trade is calculation — calculation which produces correct accounts for the past period, calculation which provides estimates and plans for the period immediately ahead. Not only each separate factory, each separate trust, not only industry as a whole, but our entire state, our entire Union, should go over more and more and more to a real balancing of real resources. This is not just a stunt. It is necessary that this balance correspond to reality, that is, to the resources which we actually have. Better less, more sparingly, but with stability.

The last article Vladimir Ilyich wrote was called "Better Less, but Better."[11] This was on the question of the Workers' and Peasants' Inspection. In relation to the budget and to separate estimates we say: *better less but more solidly.* Cut to the last degree, but so that it may be in firm unity, so that everybody knows what they are standing on! If you've made a mistake let it be corrected in a planned way. The main thing is for each economic organ to know what it has under its feet, so that there may not be this formlessness and precariousness which, together with our poverty, is one of the most damaging

factors in our economic life. A statewide balance, a balance
for each trust, and a balance for each separate enterprise!

As far as I know your debates on the question of the organization of Donbas industry and as far as I can judge the
general trade and industrial expenditure of the Union, we
ought as soon as possible to complete our task, that is, to
emancipate the trusts from those features of *glavkocracy* which
still exist. The different trusts live and will go on living in different ways, supply their enterprises differently with raw material, realize their products differently on the market, but each
enterprise must be connected with its trust by an elastic spring,
not a rigid one. Each enterprise ought to carry out its own
calculation and draw up its own balance—not just a bureaucratic set of accounts but a balance which shows how the given
enterprise lives in the given conditions, how it breathes, to what
extent it absorbs various sorts of nourishing substances, to
what extent it produces goods and to what extent garbage.

Only if there is self-checking by each enterprise in particular
is a really correct and rational organization of the economy
of the trust and of industry as a whole possible. In industry,
as also in finance, it is necessary finally to finish with the
policy of driving *with the lights out.* If the state budget cannot
meet certain expenditure, if you, the enterprise, have had 100
million rubles assigned to you, but I, the state, cannot give
you these 100 million rubles in time and withhold the 100
millions for a month, and then give you 100 millions which
are worth only 25 millions, that is, I break down my own
ruble, changing it into a 25-kopeck piece, but not openly, by
stealth, this is also driving with the lights out: Because it is
very unpleasant to go down from 100 million to 25, you put
the lights out, so as not to see the descent. . . .

No, we say, it is not good to go downhill with the lights
out. And in the estimating work of a particular enterprise or
trust it is the same—better less but more solidly! Contract
working industry but put on a solid basis. We need generally
and firmly to finish with old methods, with the guerrilla approach, with improvisation in fundamental questions of the
economy, we need to learn to approach the economy in a
planned way, looking far ahead. And for this we need the
brightly burning *lights of calculation and accounting*!

In regard to questions of defense of the country it is basically a matter, too, of repeating the same thing. We have no
point on the agenda about defense, but since I am speaking
about the congress in connection with the entire current work

of the Central Committee of the Russian Communist Party I
ought to say a few words about defense, all the more so because this question will probably be touched on at the congress,
even if only partially, in connection with the problem of industry. For three and a half years we built an army by going
from one case to the next, slapdash, one thing today and
another tomorrow; we built crookedly and clumsily, but we
conquered our foes.

Then for a year and a half to two years we reduced the size
of the army, which had been constructed very awkwardly and
unwieldily; we reduced it in the same way as we had built it,
going from one case to the next, here lopping off a bit of the
tail and here a bit of one ear, because our country could not
maintain for a single day longer than necessary an army of
five million men. The army was built by improvisation and
the work of reducing it was also carried out by improvisation.
This was perhaps not only a misfortune but also a fault on
our part. That I am ready to admit at once. Now we have
adopted the approach that the army must be built and developed in a strictly planned way. This is possible and also necessary.

Hitherto we did not know what we should be doing with the
army in a couple of months' time—should we be cutting it
down or should we be whistling all round Russia to all the provincial and district party committees: Give us Communards,
give us horsemen, give us carts, and so forth. But now we
must build the army systematically, solidly, according to sched-
ule, at least over the next five years. We have to draw up a
seriously thought-out program of construction, adapted to present-day conditions. Of course this program cannot be ideally
coordinated, but its fundamental features must correspond to
the general state of the country, its agriculture, the development
of its industry. The army estimates will be drawn up in accordance with this program.

Broadly speaking, the state will give the army so much in
the first half-year, so much percent more in the next half-year,
and so on, in a definite though modest progression. Naturally,
everything may be upset if there is a harvest failure or if we
are attacked in the near future—but even in this event we shall
be better prepared if we work according to a plan. Closely
connected with this is the question of military technique, in
particular, military aviation. We say that, in relation to the
army as well, the principle must be: Better less but solidly,
better less but better, for in relation to the army can we least
of all permit to continue the harassment to which we have sub-

jected it, now cutting off bits, now stitching bits on. Military improvisation is incomparably more costly to the state than planned development of the armed forces.

Let us now proceed to a question of first-class importance, that of the relation between the party and the state machine. In that latest article of Comrade Lenin's which I have mentioned more than once, Comrade Lenin writes about the state machine—and I must say straight out that nobody else would have ventured to utter such words—such words as one doesn't repeat so easily [*laughter*]. Vladimir Ilyich writes about our state machine that it is neither more nor less than very similar to the czarist state machine, anointed, as they say, colored in the Soviet style, but if you examine it, it is the same old bureaucratic machine.

Isn't that nice to hear? It's a real Easter egg for international Menshevism [*laughter*]. It's very much "better" than industry working at a loss. But how are we to understand it? Here, of course, we have one of Lenin's especially emphatic formulations; in order the more firmly to get this into the party's head, to hammer it in as deeply as possible, he doesn't refrain from using drastic words which would earn anybody else a hole in the head. But this is not the sole explanation. We must go more thoroughly into the question. What is our state machine? Did it fall among us from out of the heavens? No, of course it didn't.

Who built it? It grew up on the basis of the Soviets of workers', peasants', Red Army men's and Cossacks' deputies. Who led these Soviets? The Communist Party. What the party is we know well. What the Soviets are we know well also, of course. We said and we say: The Soviets are the best form of government in the interests of the working masses. Our party is the best of parties. It is the teacher of the other parties in the Communist International. That is generally recognized. And here we see, coming into being out of the Soviets, that is, the best representation of the working masses, under the leadership of the party which is the best party in the Communist International, a state machine of which it has been said that it is . . . little different from the old czarist machine.

From this, perhaps, some simple-minded fellow, from the so-called Workers' Truth group,[12] let's say, will draw the conclusion: Should we not take a hammer—just the hammer, without the sickle [*laughter*]—and carry out some mechanical exercises on this machine? Such a conclusion would, however, be groundless, since we should then have to pick up the fragments and begin again. Why? Because this machine, which really is wretchedly bad, nevertheless did not drop onto our shoulders but was created by us under the pressure of historical necessity out of the material which we had to hand. Who is responsible? We all are, and we shall answer for it.

Where has this "quality" of the state machine come from? From this circumstance, that we did not and do not know how to do very much, but we have been forced to do a lot, and often have enlisted people who know, or only half know, but don't want to do it even a quarter properly, and sometimes don't want to do it at all and do it minus a hundred percent. In the operations which we carry out you often cannot distinguish between calculation and magic, but in the state machine there are not a few people who consciously pass off magic as calculation. So here we have been constructing a state machine which begins with a young, selflessly devoted but quite inexperienced Communist, goes on through an indifferent office clerk, and ends with a gray-haired expert who sometimes, under irreproachable forms, engages in sabotage.

Well, now, can we abolish this all at once? Can we do without this machine? Of course we can't. What must we do? Our task is to take this bad machine as it exists and set about transforming it systematically. Not anyhow or slapdash, but in a planned way, calculated to cover a long period. Up to now the state machine has been constructed on the principle of going from one case to the next. First we assembled material, then we reduced it. When an institution had become extremely overgrown, we cut it down. If we have learnt anything in the last five years, Comrade Lenin notes in his article, then it is to estimate time, that is, to appreciate how comparatively little can be done in five years in the sense of replacing the old by the new. And how systematically we must therefore approach our great tasks.

Comrades, this is a very important idea. To take power is one thing, but to reeducate people, to train them in new methods of work, to teach even such a thing (a small thing, but presupposing a displacement of the entire psychology!), such a small thing, I say, as that a Soviet official ought to behave attentively and respectfully to an old, illiterate peasant woman who has come into a big, high-ceilinged hall and gazes around her and doesn't know before which inkstand to beat her forehead on the ground — and there sits our red-tapist, directing her with the tip of his finger to number so-and-so, and she hesitates, turning this way and that, in front of number so-and-so, utterly helpless, and leaves the office without achieving anything.

And if she could formulate her ideas she would formulate them, I think, in Lenin's words, what things were like seven or eight years ago they are also like today; in the same way then she went into the office and in the same way she failed to get what she went for, because they said things to her she couldn't understand in a language she couldn't understand, not trying to help her but trying to get rid of her. This, of course, doesn't go on everywhere and all the time. But if it is only one-third true to life then there is a frightful abyss between the state machine and the working masses. I recently wrote an article about this "tip of a big problem," an article which was transmitted to your newspapers by telephone for reprinting, but, as, alas, Soviet technique is still poor, I only half recognized this article as it appeared here [*laughter*] but the point of this article was what I have just expressed.[13]

Comrades, what is the meaning of Comrade Lenin's plan, which has now already been adopted by an overwhelming majority in the party? This plan means an approach to a *planned* reconstruction of the state machine. The party created the state machine, yes, the party created it, and then it looked at what it had created. . . . Remember what the Bible says: God created, looked at his creation and said that it was good [*laughter*], but the party has created, looked and . . . has shaken its head [*laughter, prolonged applause*]. And now, after this silent shaking of the head along comes a man who has ventured to call what has been constructed by its name, and to do this at the top of his voice.

But this is not the voice of despair—oh, no! The conclusion to be drawn from the situation is this, that whereas we have in five years created this clumsy, creaking machine which to a considerable degree is not "ours," we must now devote a minimum of five years to altering and reconstructing it, so as to make it more like a machine about which there will be no occasion to express oneself so strongly. . . . That is why I pay attention to that phrase which Comrade Lenin puts in parenthesis. Yes, we have now for the first time learned to estimate the "capacity" of the time in which our efforts are confined. A lot of time is needed. And so it is not now just a question of making corrections—we shall, of course, make corrections from case to case in the future as well—but our fundamental task is that of *systematic, planned reconstruction of the state machine.*

Through what agency? Through that which erected it, through the party. And for this party too we need a fresh, improved organ for sounding this machine, a probe which is not only moral but also political and practical—not on the plane of formal state inspection, which has already shown its complete bankruptcy, but on the plane of party penetration into the heart of the matter, to carry out a selection process in the most important fields of work. Again, what this organ will be like at first, how this Central Control Commission will work in conjunction with the Workers' and Peasants' Inspection, is a matter for further experience, and serious-minded workers cannot entertain any illusions about the possibility of rapid changes.

But it would be quite base on our part to say that nothing can come of this planned approach to the problem, to report that "your ears won't grow any higher than your forehead," and so on. It is, of course, a very difficult task, but for just that reason it must be dealt with in a planned way, systematically, not on a case-to-case basis. Precisely for this reason there is needed an authoritative central party-and-Soviet organ which will be able to sound the state machine in a new way both from the angle of its general efficiency and from that of how it responds to a simple illiterate old woman; and all this, perhaps, will be given us by a combined organ of the Central Control Commission and the Workers' and Peasants' Inspection, working on the principle of selecting the best workers and systematically educating them in a combination of formal state-service practices with the methods of the Workers' and Peasants' Inspection—of what is best in it, that is, a small nucleus. This experiment must be made, and we are making it.

Comrades, the question of the state machinery is very closely connected with the role of our party, as are all the fundamental questions which I have mentioned. If there is one question which basically not only does not require revision but does not so much as admit the thought of revision, it is the question of the dictatorship of the party, and its leadership in all spheres of our work. Yesterday we had here a very vivid demonstration by nonparty people in favor of this dictatorship and its leadership. And at the same time we once again signed our names to a very big promissory note, to use the language of NEP.

Yesterday's demonstration by nonparty people signifies that tremendous changes have taken place in the mood of the Ukrainian workers, and this is the most important and valuable achievement of the last two years, but it is also a sign that the working class, while coming towards us more strongly, will more attentively than before follow the progress of our work, that this class will demand from us increased profitability in our state enterprise, ability to bring order into the market, a true bond, that is, in the economic sense between town and country, and so on and so forth, ability to even out rates of wages in the different branches of industry, and so on. And here, comrades, I repeat, we have signed a big promissory note, especially as regards wages, that is, the question which most vitally and acutely concerns the mass of the workers.

It is especially important that the light should shine brightly in this sphere, so that the workers may see the limits of those demands which can be satisfied with the economy in its present state. We must never lose sight of the question of the mutual relations between the proletariat and the peasantry when the party speaks to the nonparty workers because if Menshevik demagogy, which is reviving here and there in the Ukraine in its most Makhnovite[14] form, can win any success in this sphere it will be setting the workers against the peasants on the wages question, so as the better to shove a wedge thereafter between the nonparty workers and the party vanguard.

One of the reasons for the gravitation of nonparty workers toward the party is a certain improvement which has taken place in their material positions — they can breathe more easily, their wages have risen. In heavy industry and in transport wages still lag behind. Where has the increase come from? Not so much from the market as from the budget. In this way we here again and again find ourselves up against the fundamental relationship of classes in Soviet society and, in order to avoid misunderstanding in the future, it is especially important to explain this relationship to the nonparty workers, so that on this fundamental question they think as the party thinks and not fall prey to demagogy. The nonparty workers are drawn to the party, not to the Soviet state, as such. This is a very important circumstance.

The *Smenovekhite*[15] petty bourgeoisie is taking up the Soviet platform because it thinks that communism is a utopia which merely "gets in the way" of the real work of the state. The mass of the workers, on the contrary, are attracted to the Communist Party, and put up with the Soviet state machine in its present form in the hope that the Communist Party will in due course set it to rights. This is the nub of the question. In such conditions as these, can the party allow the thought to enter its head that it might give up its fundamental role as leader of all work, and above all of all the work of the state?

Our party is the ruling party, which, with the confidence of the proletariat and, by and large, of the mass of the peasantry, holds in its hands the helm of state activity. This is a fundamental fact. To allow any changes whatever in this field, to allow the idea of a partial, whether open or camouflaged, curtailment of the leading role of our party would mean to bring into question all the achievements of the revolution and its future. Whoever makes an attempt on the party's leading role will, I hope, be unanimously dumped by all of us on the other side of the barricade. We don't know what awaits us in the future. Only by taking into account the experience of these five years as a whole, not only this very gratifying demonstration we had yesterday, the fraternization of the nonparty workers with the party, but also the experience of the tragic Kronstadt demonstration in February 1921 when the guns of Kronstadt blazed away at us[16] — only a bringing together of all these facts in correct historical perspective can show and make comprehensible what our party is, what role it plays, how and why it has endured what has happened in the past, gone forward to what we have today, and is leading us on to bigger and better things.

This is a fundamental question and the party is unanimous on it. And that is why I mention only in passing and in parentheses that when there appeared the platform which has become known in the party as the "anonymous" platform, a platform which diplomatically and evasively raised the question of liquidating party leadership, it did not find in any of the previous groupings in the party a single comrade who would admit to bearing even a share of responsibility for this platform. You know from the "Discussion Sheet," which has made definite statements on this, that this platform is connected with the ideas of the former "Democratic Centralism" group, [17] but all the comrades who formerly belonged to that group have declared that they have nothing in common with this platform and consider it profoundly pernicious.

If the party has reacted like this to it one can say with confidence that there will be no differences at the Twelfth Congress on this issue. And if the question of the leadership of the party is on our agenda in connection with other questions and especially with Comrade Lenin's proposal, it is there in the sense of how to improve the leadership of the party, how to give it a more systematic and planned character. For not a single serious party member will claim that in the sphere of party leadership we have attained perfect and unchangeable forms, and that as our work inevitably becomes more complicated and subdivided the party will not be threatened with the danger of becoming dissolved in this work and losing the ability to see the forest for the trees. . . .

Up to the present we have built from one case to the next and tested and led in the same way, in all spheres of work; in general this accorded with the character of the past half-decade, and we coped successfully with the main task. But now we must go over more and more in every sphere to systematic and planned work with big schemes and well-thought-out projects. Consequently, the leadership exercised by our party must become more complex and must be carried on by more systematic methods. The creation of the Central Control Commission, of an organ for checking on the state machine—this too is one of the means of more systematically gathering information and intelligence, a more planned way for the party to survey everything that takes place both in the Soviet machine and under it among the masses and in the entire party as a whole, in order that, on the basis of more complete and systematic information, measures of party leadership may assume a more planned character, with a perspective of long-term, persistent work.

The state machine is bad, we say, very bad. Must we smash up the state machine with a hammer, I ask? Of course we must not and we are not going to. But if we were to smash it up and build it afresh, we *could* build it afresh, because the party exists. The party created the state apparatus and can rebuild it anew, if it really is the party. But if the state machine exists and there is no party, the party can't build a state machine. That is the fundamental idea; from the party you can get the state, but not the party from the state. But the party itself has now to take up the question of approaching the state machine in a new way, embracing and evaluating it as a whole in respect of the most important matters and fundamentally, and along these lines subjecting it to regular influence.

The party must more and more persistently demand and secure from the state, from all its organs, that they learn to work within the framework of a plan and a system, to construct a plan which looks to the future, not staggering from one case to the next, that they learn to train their workers within the framework of this plan, systematically enriching their experience both in the line of specialized Soviet work and in the line of party work, that we may learn, in order to renew the whole state machine, in the machine as a whole and in the departments in particular, to build under the leadership of the party a system of party and Soviet educational institutions where new generations of Soviet experts from the ranks of the workers and peasants may be trained, technicians, functionaries in all spheres, who have grown up into our system from the bottom, who will not look down their noses at an illiterate peasant woman, who will really embody in themselves the demands, feeling and aims of the whole workers' and peasants' state. . . . It is in this sense that the leading role of the party must be raised to a higher level.

Comrades, I must now turn to a question which is of particular importance for the Ukraine, the national question. I have already made the point that the initiative in raising this question is Vladimir Ilyich's. On the eve of his illness he sounded the alarm on this question, fearing that serious mistakes might be committed in this question as in the peasant question. [18] And I felt very acutely the possibility of such mistakes when I read the report in the paper about the Lugansk district conference, where it was said: "Comrade Rakovsky [19] made a report on the national question, but this report found us unprepared and there was no discussion."

I think it was in the same news report, or perhaps it was in another (in *Kommunist* or *Proletary*) that I found the statement that many comrades do not understand why the national question is being brought up again. They think this question is "settled" as far as they are concerned. I must say that I have often met this same mood not only in the Ukraine but also in the north, in Great Russia, especially in Moscow, where some comrades haven't understood how it can be that now, in the sixth year of existence of the workers' and peasants' Soviet state, where all nations are equal, we suddenly put the national question on the congress agenda. After all, haven't we "settled" it long ago? The Ukraine is independent, Georgia, Azerbaidjan, Armenia are independent republics, and so on. What more is there to be done?

Of course, comrades, the national question is not our fundamental aim — our aim is communism. The social question, not the national question, is the basis on which we stand. But then, the peasant economy is not our aim either, but centralized socialist production, high technique and so on. However, the peasant economy is a fact — and not a program or an aim, but a fact, and a fact in many, many millions, tens and hundreds of millions of acres, of farms and of people, and a careless attitude to this basic fact would turn our whole program head over heels. It is the same with the national question. These two questions, the peasant and the national, are very close to each other. They are expressions by and large of the same epoch.

We have, of course, proclaimed the elimination of national slavery, inequality and so on. Of course we have proclaimed the right of each nationality to settle its affairs in its own way, right up to separation from the state—while, naturally, we set above this right our duty of revolutionary self-defense. Wherever any national group links its fate not with the working class but with imperialism, for struggle against the working class, the law of the class war, as was the case in relation to Menshevik Georgia, stands higher than all other laws; but when the task of defending the revolution is accomplished, we say to the peasants, petty bourgeoisie, and backward workers of the nationality concerned: We shall have no differences with you, comrades, on national matters.

We shall not only "allow" you, as it is sometimes inappropriately expressed, no, we shall help you to settle your affairs in the national sense, in the best and most satisfactory way. We shall help you to share through the medium of your own language in the best attainments of human culture, for this is the essence of the matter. Not in our proclaiming "arrange things as you wish," because the peasant is helpless, especially the backward peasant who belongs to a small nation which used to be mercilessly oppressed. He is helpless, and when he sees over him a state machine which may be a workers' and peasants' affair but is inattentive to him, to his national peculiarities, to his language, to his backwardness, he feels himself doubly helpless.

Estrangement of the ruling party and state machine from the bulk of the population in respect to language is a very dangerous kind of estrangement. One cannot have a frivolous attitude to such a political "link" as the national language, the everyday speech of a people. This question is important for the whole of our Union and of tenfold importance for the Ukraine. In Comrade Rakovsky's letter to the Donets provincial conference I found an idea which seems to me exceptionally significant: He combines the peasant question with the national question. If there were to be a split between the proletariat and the peasantry; if the bourgeoisie were to manage, in the person of its political agents, the Social Revolutionaries and Mensheviks—or others, more determined and resolute—to take the leadership of the peasantry, that would mean, Comrade Lenin wrote not long ago, civil war, civil war all along this line until the victory of the proletariat in the West, and we can add that the outcome of this civil war would be doubtful for us.

But, comrades, if a misunderstanding between the proletariat and the peasantry is dangerous it is a hundredfold more dangerous when the peasantry does not belong to the nationality which in old, monarchist Russia was the ruling nationality, that is, when the peasantry, whether Ukrainian, Georgian, Azerbaidjanian or Armenian, is a peasantry which has always seen in the ruling apparatus not only the power of another class over it but also the power of national oppression, so that defensive nationalism led the peasantry to side with its own national bourgeoisie.

Here in the Ukraine— I return to Comrade Rakovsky's letter— where the party consists mostly of town workers and townspeople generally, with only a dash of peasants, where the town workers are to a considerable extent non-Ukrainian, and the national composition of the party has, of course, a definite influence on the composition of the Ukrainian Soviet machine, already in this circumstance alone there is inherent if not a danger then a very serious problem, which it is impossible not to see and which you have to work at solving. There is needed not only an economic bond with the peasant market, not only a general political bond between proletariat and peasantry, you also have to think and think hard about a national bond— about questions of language, schools, culture.

For, comrades, discontent among the peasants, if it were to arise on one basis or another— and it can and will arise because conflicts are inevitable— this discontent will be a hundred times more dangerous when it acquires a coloring of national ideology. National ideology is a factor of enormous importance. National psychology is an explosive force which is in some cases revolutionary and in others counterrevolutionary, but in both cases it is an enormous explosive force. Remember how this dynamite was used by the bourgeoisie during wars when it mobilized the proletariat to defend so-called "national" interests. It was a diabolical experiment and it succeeded, against us. The bourgeoisie showed itself able to utilize the explosive force of nationalism for imperialist aims.

But in the East, in India, in China, hundreds of millions have risen in a national movement directed against imperialism. The national struggle of the East is an enormous explosive force, revolutionary dynamite with a colossal coefficient. The task of the European proletariat is to show itself able to use this force. In our country, comrades, in our constructive work, the national factor is a potential force, it can turn out to be directed this way or that way. If we are not able to approach the peasantry, to study the peasant, his psychology, his language, we may drive him into a second Petlyura[20] movement, and a second Petlyura movement would be more organic, profound, and dangerous than the first.

This second Petlyura movement would be armed with a cultural plan — in the schools, in the cooperatives, in all spheres of life — and every grievance of the Ukrainian peasant would be multiplied by the national factor, and this would be more dangerous than Petlyura's banditry. But if the Ukrainian peasant feels and finds that the Communist Party and the Soviet power deal with him in the sphere of the national question with complete attentiveness and understanding, saying, "We will give you everything we can, we want to help you, our backward brother, to build together with you all the bridges, all the steps by which you will raise yourself up, we want to the utmost of our ability to meet you in your strivings, to help you to share in that language which is your native language, in the benefits of human culture. In all state institutions, on the railways, in the postal service, they must understand you in your own language and speak to you in your own language, because this is your state," then the peasant will grasp and appreciate such an approach.

Even if we cannot give him a well-equipped three-storied school because we are poor, we must provide schools where his sons may learn to read and write in the language understood by their father and mother. If we don't, the peasantry will multiply all its varieties of discontent with the national coefficient, and that will threaten to liquidate the Soviet regime. We have to realize that we have not solved the national question, as we have not solved a single economic or cultural question. We have created only the revolutionary prerequisites for solving the national question. We have smashed the czarist prison-house of peoples, of nationalities. But it is not enough to proclaim national equality, we need to show the oppressed peoples in practice — and they are very mistrustful — that we are with them, that we are for them, that we are serving their national interests not in general phrases but in reality, in work.

People say "better overdone than underdone." An excess of attention and prudence does no harm, but a shortage of it where the national question is concerned will have severe consequences for the party. That is why we have put the national question on the congress agenda. As with all the questions, we have posed this question not only on the plane of principle but also quite concretely, adapting it to the given stage of socialist construction.

What organized expression can we give to national requirements in the state structure? The attitude of the federation to this question was indefinite. In this matter we have during the last few years been completely under the influence of the notion that this stage would not last long, and just as in Czar Peter's time[21] the Old Believers said, "What do we want solidly built houses for, we are expecting the coming of Christ"—so also we were to a certain extent not inclined to busy ourselves with lasting construction work, expecting as we were a rapid development of the revolution.

Then came NEP, and later it turned out that NEP was a long drawn-out business, and we have said to ourselves that we must go over, if not to stone houses—we are a long way off from them!—at least to a more durable even if only temporary form of settlement, and our expression of this awareness is our present state organization of the national question. We began with the formation of the Union of Soviet Republics, and when we formed it we took into account the fact that we had not provided for an organizational machine through which we could correctly sound the specific interests and requirements of the various nations as such. From that we were led to the idea of a special Soviet chamber of nationalities, which at first shocked many comrades.

I must admit that in the beginning I didn't like it much. The very expression "second chamber" seemed unpleasant, with its reminder of old textbooks of state law. But that was not at all the point. The point was that it was necessary to approach the national question in a systematic, organized, and planned way. There is here, if you like, a certain analogy with the Central Control Commission. What is the Central Control Commission? It is not of course a panacea, and it would be absurd to suppose that we have set up an organ which can solve all problems. No, but this is a new organ which more correctly and systematically checks on what is done in our state machine, in the party, and in the working class and thereby facilitates the possibility of a correct solution of problems.

And what is the chamber of nationalities? It is a special organ for more systematically and planfully sounding out where each national corn hurts, how a particular national group will react to this or that measure, and so on. General leadership in national policy remains, of course, wholly and entirely in the hands of our party. But the party cannot solve all these problems out of its own head, by the sole method of inward exercise of party thought; the party needs organized contact with concrete tasks and conditions. To solve old problems the party needs in the national question as well new, more complex, more improved organs, and more systematic and planned methods.

The world situation offers no ground for a change in the foundations of our policy. The internal situation is based on the world situation. The main determining line in the economic and political field is the line of mutual relations between the working class and the peasantry. The fundamental task of the transition period — to ensure relations of alliance with the peasantry — must be carried out from now on by more systematic and planned methods, calculated over a more extended period, in the field of industry, in that of taxation, in that of the state machine, and in that of the national question, which in our country means above all the question of the peasant masses of the formerly oppressed nationalities.

All this work can be accomplished with ever-increasing success if we improve our state machine, and in particular our economic administration, but not in a fragmentary way, not amateurishly — that is inadequate — but according to a broadly conceived plan, calculated over a number of years. It is not possible to improve the state machine from within alone. It can be improved first and foremost through the medium of the ruling party. Our party has guided this state apparatus for five years and it will go on guiding it in the future as well, fully and completely, but it will guide it more and more systematically in accordance with the complex tasks ahead, perfecting and regulating the methods of its own leadership and demanding from the state machine itself the same wide, planned regulation of methods and of selection of personnel.

Comrades, this urgent transfer of our work on to the rails of system and plan will be successful if the basic political prerequisite, the basic condition is present. And the prerequisite of all prerequisites, the condition of all conditions is our party, its clear thinking, its tempered will, its unity, its fighting capacity. Unity not on the basis of mere rallying to action stations in the moment of danger — that is, of course, not sufficient — but the unity which has always been characteristic of our party, unity on the basis of collective courage, firmness, merciless evaluation of all dangers, and foresight into fundamental problems.

The second condition of the party's steadfastness is its increasing influence on the young people. The struggle for the youth, an arena into which our worst enemies, the Mensheviks, are trying to make their way, must be waged unremittingly. In the period immediately ahead, reconnaissance and, so to speak, dangerous political espionage on the part of the counterrevolution can be carried out best through the Mensheviks, on the basis of the wages question, on the basis of the struggle for the youth.

We have hints of this already. In this struggle of Russian and Ukrainian Menshevism, relying on world Menshevism, we see how Menshevism of the Martov shade shakes hands with openly counterrevolutionary Menshevism, that which stood for intervention, for armed uprising, which is represented today by the journal *Zarya* published abroad and which inside Russia is interwoven with Kolchakite and Denikinite counterrevolution. It is not beyond possibility that in this year that lies before us we shall have to wage a struggle against attempts by Menshevism to raise its head, and to wage this struggle, in, so to speak, a more "planned" way, which does not in the least mean a gentler way [*laughter, applause*]. There can be no doubt that we shall succeed in this struggle.

Since the epoch of NEP threatens to be further prolonged, all the dangers which are inherent in it assume a more protracted and menacing character. We know what these dangers are, we have analyzed them more than once. They derive from the market relations which engender of themselves currents of centrifugal force that can distract and rob the state machine in the direction of the interests of private capital, wedge the NEP bourgeoisie into it with their interests and ideas, plunder state industry, turning it inconspicuously into the channels of private accumulation. What we need is socialist primary accumulation, sound even if slow.

These currents of centrifugal force wash our party as well and, of course, cannot but be reflected in the course of long-term development in the party's own influence. Of the fact that our party with its revolutionary keenness is firm and unanimous today there can be no doubt. We saw how it reacted to the two platforms (the "anonymous one" and the "Workers' Truth" one) in which an attempt was made to reconsider the question of leadership of the party. In the past year the party has not weakened in its moral and political self-confidence and awareness, but has grown stronger — and this is not surprising, since it has purged itself of alien elements and added to its proletarian element.

The growth of the party will continue along this path in the future too. On the severe conditions which have been laid down in the conditions of NEP for joining the party, the party can give and is giving a big rebate to workers at the bench. And yesterday's demonstration showed that this rebate will be fully justified — within reasonable limits, of course, and under serious supervision. A change in the ratio of the elements which compose the party's membership, an even bigger shift in favor of purely proletarian elements, workers at the bench, is the fundamental guarantee of the stability of our party and its power of resistance to all harmful influences.

Comrades, as regards the clarity of thought and firmness of will of our party we have had some additional verification during the past year. The verification was a heavy one, because it was provided by a fact which to this day weighs upon the minds of all party members and very wide circles of the working population, or more truly, upon the entire working people of our country and, to a considerable extent, of the whole world. I speak of the illness of Vladimir Ilyich.

When his condition got worse at the beginning of March and the Political Bureau of the Central Committee met to exchange views on what to tell the party and the country about the deterioration in Comrade Lenin's health, I think you can all imagine, comrades, in what mood that session of the Political Bureau took place when we had to issue to the party and the country that first grave and disturbing bulletin. Even at that moment of course, we remained politicians. Nobody will reproach us for that. We were thinking not only about Comrade Lenin's health — of course, first and foremost we *were* concerned at that moment with his pulse rate, his heartbeat, his temperature — we were also thinking of what impression the number of his heartbeats would produce on the political pulse of the working class and of our party.

With alarm and at the same time with the profoundest confidence in the strength of the party, we said that it was necessary — immediately the danger had been revealed — to bring it to the knowledge of the party and the country. Nobody doubts that our foes would endeavor to utilize this news for the purpose of troubling the people, especially the peasants, spreading disturbing rumors, and so on, but none of us doubted for one second that it was necessary immediately to tell the party how matters stood, because to say what is means to enhance the responsibility of every member of the party. Our party is a large party, with half a million members, a great collective with great experience, but among these half-million people Lenin has his own place which, comrades, is beyond comparison with anyone else's.

There has never been in the past such an influence by one man on the destiny not only of one country but of all mankind. There is no yardstick, none has been created, by which we could measure the historical significance of Lenin. And that is why the fact that he has been withdrawn from work for a long period, that his condition is grave, could not but inspire profound political alarm. We know of course, of course, of course, we know for certain that the working class will triumph. We sing: "Nobody will bring us deliverance," including "no heroes. . . ."[22] And this is true, but only in the last analysis of history. That is, in history's last analysis the working class would have triumphed even if there had been no Marx and no Ulyanov-Lenin.[23]

The working class would have worked out the ideas it needed, the methods that were necessary to it, but more slowly. The circumstance that the working class raised up, at two crests of its historical development, two such figures as Marx and Lenin has been of colossal advantage to the revolution. Marx was the prophet with the Tables, and Lenin the greatest fulfiller of the Commandments, teaching not only the labor aristocracy, like Marx, but whole classes and peoples, through experience in the most difficult conditions, acting, maneuvering, and conquering.

This year we had to get through our practical work with only partial participation by Vladimir Ilyich. In the field of ideas we had heard from him not long ago some reminders and indications which will suffice us for several years — on the peasant question, on the state machine, and on the national question. And now it was necessary to announce a worsening in his health. We asked ourselves with natural alarm what conclusions the nonparty masses would draw, the peasants, the Red Army men, because in relation to our state machine the peasants have trust first and foremost in Lenin. Besides everything else, Ilyich represents great moral capital for our state machine in the sphere of mutual relations between the working class and the peasantry. Would not the peasants think, some in our own circle asked themselves, that with a prolonged retirement of Lenin from work, his policy might be changed? How did the party react, the mass of the workers, the country as a whole?

After the appearance of the first alarming bulletin, the party as a whole closed its ranks, braced itself, morally rose to its full height. Comrades, the party consists, of course, of living people, and people have their shortcomings, their defects, and among the Communists there are likewise many who are "human, all too human," as the Germans say. There are and will be conflicts between groups and individuals both serious and trivial, for without such conflicts a great party cannot live. But the political weight, the political specific gravity of the party is determined by the fact that it rises to the surface again whatever tragic shock it has sustained.

The will to unity and discipline, or the secondary and personal, the human, all too human? Comrades, I think we can now draw this conclusion with complete confidence that sensing it would be deprived for a long time of Lenin's leadership, the party closed its ranks, swept aside everything that might threaten the clarity of its thinking, the unity of its will, its fighting capacity.

Before I took my seat in the train to come here to Kharkov I had a talk with our commander of the Moscow military district, Nikolai Ivanovich Muralov, [24] whom many of you know as an old party man, about how the Red Army soldiers were taking the situation in connection with Lenin's illness. Muralov told me that at first the news acted like a lightning stroke, everybody recoiled, but then they began to think more, and more profoundly, about Lenin. Yes, comrades, the nonparty Red Army man has now thought in his own way but very deeply *about the role of the individual in history,* about that which we of the older generation, when we were high-school boys, students, or young workers, studied in little books, in prison, in deportation, and in exile, what we pondered on and disputed about in relation to the "hero" and the "crowd," the subjective factor and objective conditions, and so on and so forth.

And now, in 1923, our young Red Army men have thought about these questions concretely with their hundreds of thousands of minds, and along with them the hundreds of thousands of minds of the peasants of all Russia, the Ukraine and the rest of the Union, about the role of the individual Lenin in history. And how have our political commissars and branch secretaries answered them? They have answered thus: Lenin is a genius, a genius is born once in a century, and world history has seen only two geniuses as leaders of the working class—Marx and Lenin. A genius cannot be created even by order of the mightiest and most disciplined party, but such a party can try to the highest degree attainable to replace it when it is absent, by redoubling its collective efforts.

This is the theory of the individual and the class which our political commissars have been expounding in popular form to the nonparty Red Army men. And this is a correct theory: Lenin is not now at work — we must work twice as hard, be twice as keenly vigilant against dangers, preserve the revolution from them twice as steadfastly, use all opportunities for constructive work twice as persistently. And we are doing all this from the members of the Central Committee to the nonparty Red Army men. . . .

Our work, comrades, is very slow, very partial, even though within the framework of a great plan. Our methods of work are "prosaic": balances and calculations, the food tax and the export of grain — all this we are doing step by step, brick by brick. . . . Isn't there a danger in all this of a sort of hair-splitting degeneration of the party? We cannot permit such a degeneration, any more than a breakup of its unity of action, even to the slightest extent, for even if the present period is going to be prolonged "seriously and for a long time, yet it is not going on forever." And perhaps it won't even last for a long time.

A revolutionary outbreak on a big scale, such as the beginning of revolution in Europe, can occur sooner than many of us now think. And if there is one of Lenin's many teachings on strategy that we ought especially firmly to keep in memory, it is what he has called *the politics of sharp turns:* today on the barricades, tomorrow in the pigsty of the Third State Duma, today the call to world revolution, to the world October, tomorrow negotiations with Kuhlmann and Czernin,[25] signature of the obscene peace of Brest-Litovsk.

The situation changed, or we estimated it afresh in a new way — the western campaign, "We want Warsaw." The situation was estimated afresh — the peace of Riga, also a rather foul peace, as you know. And then — stubborn work, brick by brick, thereafter, reduction in establishments, checking — do we need five telephone operators or only three, if three are enough, don't dare to employ five, for the peasant will have to give several extra bushels of grain to pay for them — petty, everyday, hairsplitting work — and there, look, the flame of revolution blazes up from the Ruhr. What, shall it catch us in a stage of degeneration? No, comrades, no.

We are not degenerating, we are changing our methods and procedures, but the revolutionary conservatism of the party remains higher than anything else for us. We are learning to draw up balance sheets and at the same time we are looking with sharp eyes to West and East, and events won't catch us by surprise. By purging ourselves and enlarging our proletarian base we shall strengthen ourselves.

We go forward in agreement with the peasantry and the petty bourgeoisie, we allow the NEPmen; but in the party we will allow no NEPmanism or petty bourgeois, no — we shall burn it out of the party with sulphuric acid and red-hot irons [*applause*], and at the Twelfth Congress, which will be the first congress held since October without Vladimir Ilyich and one of the few congresses in the history of our party held without him, we shall say to one another that among the basic precepts which we shall inscribe on our minds with a sharp chisel there will be this — don't get ossified, remember the art of sharp turns, maneuver but don't lose yourself, enter into agreements with temporary or long-term allies but don't let them wedge themselves into the party, remain yourselves, the vanguard of the world revolution. And if the signal sounds from the West — and it will sound — though we may be at that moment up to our necks in calculations, balance sheets, and NEP generally, we shall respond without wavering or delay: We are revolutionaries from head to foot, we have been and we shall remain such, we shall be revolutionaries to the end [*stormy applause, all rise and applaud*].

11

For the Internationalist Perspective

By the autumn of 1923 Trotsky realized that the Stalin ma-chine was not going to be stopped or reformed except through a struggle in which the ranks of the party would participate and make the decisions. His hopes that Lenin would recover so that they could act jointly diminished with the worsening of Lenin's condition. His decision was reinforced by the events in Germany that year, when the German Communist Party leadership, advised by Stalin and Zinoviev in Moscow, mis-managed an extraordinary revolutionary situation.

So Trotsky acted at the end of 1923 to form the Left Op-position, also known as the Bolshevik-Leninists, a faction ded-icated to revolutionary internationalism and the restoration of workers' democracy inside the Soviet Union and the Com-munist International. The work of the Left Opposition was the center of Trotsky's political thought and activity for the rest of his life in the Soviet Union.

At the start of this struggle Trotsky was alone in opposi-tion in the Political Bureau and the nature of the issues that he was raising was understood by only a few. So it was rel-atively easy for the Stalin faction to vote him down, censure him, and use party discipline to limit the discussion of the differences. But that did not prevent him then or later from explaining and advocating his revolutionary principles in pub-lic, even when he did not label them as Left Oppositionist or assert that they were being undermined by the bureaucracy.

When he was in the Caucasus recuperating from illness, he was invited to speak to a special session of the Tiflis Soviet in the capital of the Georgian Soviet Republic. He took the opportunity to make a critical analysis of the German defeat in 1923, to clarify the perspectives in the international situ-

ation, and to emphasize the need of a party steeled to meet its revolutionary responsibilities. This speech was made on April 11, 1924.

The translation by George Saunders from a 1924 pamphlet published in Moscow is reprinted from Intercontinental Press, *May 5 and 12, 1969.*

On the Road to the European Revolution

I confess that I am giving my report today under certain handicaps. For two months now I have been in this beautiful land of the Caucasus, which I never before had the chance to visit. I have passed this time in one of the most favored, but at the same time most isolated, corners of the Upper Caucasus, namely, Abkhazia. You know, comrades, Abkhazia is a beautiful country and has fine comrades, but unfortunately this country lags far behind so far as mail and telegraph services go.

Cut off from the center of our Union, Moscow, I have not had access to anything like complete information, what with the long delay in receiving the papers.

Therefore, when some journalist comrades approached me and, according to their unpleasant custom — I may speak frankly, being a journalist myself — asked me for an interview — such is the sorry parliamentary-and-press custom that we have adopted — I actually should have gotten them to inform me of the latest news and reports, rather than enlighten them as interviewers. Allow me then to keep my report in the nature of a general review, summing up certain lessons of the recent past. I will dwell primarily on our international position, which is, however, inseparably linked with the destinies and course of the world revolution and with our internal work, our internal successes.

Comrades, if we take an overall look at the past period, we must say first of all that together with our current successes and failures, we have had one great misfortune, which weighs very heavily in the balance of world forces. That misfortune is the loss of our leader, a loss which is taken into account by our enemies as well as our friends: by our friends as an irreparable loss and by our enemies with malicious glee and high hopes.

All, or nearly all, that could be said on that subject has been said: all measures that, through collective effort, could compensate even in part for this loss, we have taken, are taking and will take. If the sorrow of our friends, the sorrow felt everywhere in the world as well as here among ourselves, cannot be mitigated, at least we will do everything to assure that the malicious hopes of our enemies will not be justified [*stormy applause*].

The world situation from the viewpoint of our Soviet Union and the world revolution remains, as it was before, complex, contradictory, changeable, but generally and on the whole, changing in our favor.

The international situation can be approached of course from various angles. Let me approach it from the angle of a newspaper, today's issue of your paper, *Zarya Vostoka,* one of the best papers of the Soviet Union. Anyone interested may learn from today's issue some of my opinions on international questions. I should say at this point that these opinions are recorded with extreme inaccuracy. This I say with all friendliness toward the correspondent of our paper. I am obliged to speak of this, comrades, both in order to present my views more clearly and precisely, and in order not to cause our friend Chicherin extra difficulties. On the question of Bessarabia, [1] matters are presented in the interview as though I considered war with Rumania likely. This is not so, absolutely not so. The problem is very sharp and important, and ambiguity cannot be permitted here. At issue is not how our complicated relations with Rumania will turn out in general, but to what the breaking off of negotiations, done at Rumania's initiative, will immediately lead. Rumania would not accept the proposals of our government for arranging a plebiscite in Bessarabia. A plebiscite would be the most democratic step to take in this case. On this point the international Mensheviks should come to our support. We propose to poll the population of Bessarabia and to that end to have troops withdrawn and to have the most democratic conditions created for the balloting. It is necessary to state — as we have in vain dinned into the skulls of the representatives of the Second International[2] — that we by no means reject democracy totally and for all situations. No. By comparison with the autocracy, with czarism, democracy was a positive factor. By comparison with the unrestrained, unmitigated reactionary rule of the Black Hundred Rumanian nobility, democracy is of course a plus factor. And it would clearly be a step forward if we created even a temporary democratic regime for polling the population on which country they wish to belong to.

But that was rejected. And so, to the question whether this would mean war, I gave the following answer: We cannot of course take it upon ourselves to guarantee that whatever the circumstances, there will not be war between ourselves and Rumania. Rumania has an army and so do we. Rumania has an army for some reason. We, too, have one for a reason [*applause*]. Comrades, your applause may be taken in Bucharest as a sign that you want to put the army into action . . . [*laughter*].

What does the breaking off of negotiations mean? Let me cite a French proverb that says, "Doors can be either opened or closed." In this case to close the door would mean to recognize de jure, that is, to legalize, the seizure of Bessarabia by Rumania. What would it mean to open the door? Under these conditions it would mean to break it open, but on the international scale what serves for breaking things open is — infantry, cavalry, and artillery. How shall we proceed — shall we open the door or close it? No, we shall leave it *half open*. What does this mean?

We will not recognize the seizure and will openly so declare to the workers of the world and, above all, to the workers of Bessarabia and Rumania. That is the first thing. Then we will wait. Conditions are changing, and many countries that were under feudal landlords or Mensheviks have become good Soviet countries. This may, and should, also be Bessarabia's fate and, thereafter, Rumania's as well. Thus, we have, let us say, an expectant policy, not quite a neutral one, and at any rate not a very "cordial" one.

But Rumania's policy, comrades, is not an independent policy. Behind Rumania stands France, which also stands behind Poland and China, and aims to do the same with Turkey. Right now, when the moment of our detente with France has seemingly come very near — at least the most prominent publicists in the leading organs of the French bourgeoisie have been writing unceasingly to this effect, with Poincare himself exchanging remarks with Chicherin in a very polite tone — this same France has intensified the hostile character of its policies toward us tenfold. In their parliament they have "ratified" the incorporation of Bessarabia into Rumania; as you know, there are some quite complicated words for stealing, thieving, and taking by force, such as annexation, de jure, ratification, and so on.

Simultaneously, France has started a campaign against us in

Trotsky recuperating in the Caucasus in 1924.

Trotsky and Natalia Sedova.

Poland. It has been a long time since the Polish press spoke of us in such hostile terms as it does today. There are also rather serious reports that France is bending its efforts toward worsening our relations with Turkey. Certain organs of the Turkish press that earlier had conducted themselves in a rather amicable fashion toward the Soviet Union have begun to speak a different language. Although the value of the franc has fallen drastically, it nevertheless continues to have a pleasant ring, apparently, in the ears of certain journalists of the Turkish press.

France is also supporting the Little Entente,[3] giving it hundreds of millions for armaments and building it up against us. And at the same time, at home, ruling-class France, in its parliament and press, declares that it has no conflict of interests with the Soviet Union and that a detente with us is entirely possible.

What is the reason for this policy? This is a consummate and graphic expression of the policy of speculators' blackmail. Poincare wants to show us that without France we will have difficulties here, there, and everywhere: the Little Entente is against us; Rumania is against us; in Poland, supposedly, there is a wave of indignation against us; and even in Turkey, it seems, the wheel is turning against us. And France tells us: Just pay what we ask, and all the petty pretensions of the small powers will disappear.

The idea is that France will betray Poland, Rumania, and Turkey as soon as we agree to pay a percentage on all loans and, in general, to bow down before Poincare. And until then, we will have blackmail, a policy of pinpricks. Out of the wolf's coat sticks the tail of a fox: the assurances by the leading organs of France that we have no contradictions with her. It is plain that Poincare miscalculated with this policy. His predecessor on this path was Clemenceau.[4] A more solid and powerful figure. Clemenceau's hatred for us was 24-carat hatred. He surrounded us with barbed wire and tried to strangle us with a blockade. We broke through that barbed wire and we say now: *If Clemenceau failed to destroy us with a barbed-wire blockade, then Poincare doesn't frighten us with his policy of pinpricks.*

As everyone knows, France is one of the countries that have not recognized us, and nonrecognition is one of France's extortionist methods in relation to us. Current French policy is entirely founded on extortion: a platonic and hopeless extortion in regard to us and a real, material extortion in regard to Germany.

That is the difference between the situation of the Soviet Republic and that of the bourgeois German republic. The Menshevik Social Democracy has ruled there for several years, in that archdemocratic republic. And what of it? In international relations this democracy has turned out to be a rug on which General Poincare wipes his boots. But the republic that is crowned by the dictatorship of the proletariat has turned out to be a rock on which the imperialists of the whole world have broken their teeth. There you have a splendid lesson for the working class and for those Mensheviks still capable of learning something.

We lived through the past year under the sign of impending revolution in Germany. During the second half of the year the German revolution grew closer day by day. We saw this as the key factor of world development. If the German revolution had been victorious, this would have radically changed the world relationship of forces. The Soviet Union, with its population of 130 million and its innumerable natural riches, on the one hand, and Germany with its technology, its culture, and its working class, on the other — this bloc, this mighty alliance, would have cut directly across the line of development in Europe and the world. The building of socialism would have acquired an altogether different tempo.

However, contrary to our expectations, the revolution in Germany has not been victorious thus far. Why? It is necessary to think about this question because it can teach us something not only of use to Germany but to ourselves as well.

Under what conditions is a victorious proletarian revolution possible? A certain development of the productive forces is necessary. The proletariat and those intermediate classes of the population that support and follow it must constitute the majority of the population. The vanguard must clearly understand the tasks and methods of proletarian revolution and have the resoluteness to bring it about. And it must lead the majority of the laboring masses with it into decisive battle.

On the other hand, it is necessary that the ruling class, that is, the bourgeoisie, be disorganized and frightened by the whole international and internal situation, that its will be undermined and broken. These are the material, political, and psychological prerequisites for revolution. These are the conditions for the victory of the proletariat. And if we are to ask, Were these conditions present in Germany? — I think we would have to answer with absolute clarity and firmness, Yes, all but one. You recall the period after the middle of last year, the lack of success and the collapse of the passive resistance of bourgeois Germany to the occupation of the Ruhr. This period was characterized by the thorough shaking up of German society. The mark plummeted downward at such a mad pace that our quiet Soviet ruble might have had cause for envy. Prices of basic necessities rose wildly. The dissatisfaction of the working masses was expressed in open clashes with the state. The German bourgeoisie was discouraged and incapable of action.

Ministries rose and fell. French troops stood on the German side of the Rhine. Stresemann,[5] premier of the great coalition, declared: "We are the last bourgeois parliamentary government. After us come either the Communists or the fascists." And the fascists said: "Let the Communists take over; our turn will be next." All this signified the last stage of the crumbling of the foundations of bourgeois society. The workers poured into the Communist Party day after day. To be sure, fairly broad masses were still marking time in the ranks of the Menshevik party. But you remember, when we took power in Petrograd in October, we found Mensheviks still at the head of the unions, because the Petrograd workers, led by our party, had moved forward to the conquest of power so rapidly that they never got around to shaking off the old dust in the trade unions.

Why then in Germany has there been no victory thus far? I think there can be only one answer: because Germany did not have a Bolshevik party, nor did it have a leader such as we had in October. We have here for the first time a tremendous body of historical experience for comparison. Of course, one may say that in Germany, victory is more difficult. The German bourgeoisie is stronger and more clever than ours. But the working class cannot pick and choose its enemies. You comrades here in Georgia fought the Menshevik government that fate had brought you. The German working class is obliged to fight the German bourgeoisie. And one can say with full assurance that history will hardly create objective conditions any more favorable to the German proletariat than those of the latter half of the past year. What was lacking? A party with the tempering that our party has. [*A voice: "Right!"*] This, comrades, is the central question, and all the European parties must learn from this experience, and you and we must learn to understand and value more clearly and profoundly the character, nature, and significance of our own party, which secured victory for the proletariat in October and a whole series of victories since October.

Comrades, I would not want my remarks to be taken in some sort of pessimistic vein — as though, for example, I considered the victory of the proletariat to have been postponed for many years. Not at all. The future favors us. But the past must be analyzed correctly. The turnabout this past year, in October-November, when German fascism and the big bourgeoisie came to the fore, was an enormous defeat. We must record it, evaluate it, and fix it in our memories that way, in order to learn from it. It is an enormous defeat. But from this defeat the German party will learn, become tempered, and grow. And the situation remains, as before, a revolutionary one. But I will return to that point.

On the world scale there have been three occasions when the proletarian revolution reached the point where it required a surgeon's knife. These were October 1917 here; September 1919 in Italy; and the latter half of the past year (July-November) in Germany.

In our country we had a victorious proletarian revolution — *begun, carried through,* and *completed* for the first time in history. In Italy there was a *sabotaged* revolution. The proletariat hurled itself with all its weight against the bourgeoisie, seizing factories, mines, and mills, but the Socialist Party, frightened by the proletariat's pressure on the bourgeoisie, stabbed it in the back, disorganized it, paralyzed its efforts, and handed it over to fascism.

Finally, there is the experience of Germany, where there is a good Communist Party, devoted to the cause of revolution, but lacking as yet in the necessary qualities: a sense of proportion, resoluteness, tempering. And this party at a certain moment let the revolution *slip through its fingers.*

Our entire international and each individual worker should constantly keep these three models in mind, three historical experiences — the October Revolution here, a revolution prepared by history, begun, carried through, and completed by us; the revolution in Italy, prepared by history, lifted up on their backs by the workers, but sabotaged, exploded, by the Socialist Party; and the revolution in Germany, a revolution prepared by history, which the working class was ready to lift onto its back, but which an honest Communist Party lacking the necessary tempering and leadership could not master.

History does not work in such a way that, first, the foundation is laid, then the productive forces grow, the necessary relations between class forces develop, the proletariat becomes revolutionary, then all this is kept in an icebox and preserved while the training of a Communist party proceeds so that it can get itself ready while "conditions" wait and wait; then when it's ready, it can roll up its sleeves and start fighting. No, history doesn't work that way. For a revolution the *coinciding* of necessary conditions is required.

The fact is that if in Germany in the second half of last year our Bolshevik party had been on the scene, with the will that it has now, had before, and will continue to have, with the will that shows itself in action, with a tactical skill that the working class senses, so that it says to itself, "We can trust our fate to this party"; if such a party had been on the scene, it would have carried with it in action and through action the overwhelming majority of the working class.

What do we conclude from all this? The conclusion for our German party is, of course, that a further solidifying of the ranks and closer ties with the masses is necessary, that a careful selection of militant revolutionists and a tempering of the party's will must be accomplished.

But now we must ask? Will the objective conditions for revolution be maintained? This is a very important question for the evaluation of the international situation in general and of that in Germany in particular. During the last few months the situation in Germany has changed sharply. A certain stabilization of the mark, the German monetary unit, has been achieved. Prices in Germany have stopped climbing so rapidly. Industry is now developing there; the economic situation is better than it was last year; unemployment is somewhat less; the situation of the working class has improved a little. These are indisputable facts.

The severity of the situation, then, has somewhat abated. What next? The answer to that question can only be given in its most general outlines now, but this answer will be sufficient nevertheless for an evaluation of the prospects before us.

The development in Europe in the coming period can go along either of two paths, depending on whether the Entente gives Germany a chance to breathe or not. After the experience of last year in Germany, when the red specter of communism barely stopped short of becoming flesh and blood, the bourgeoisie of France, England, and the United States can try to ease Germany's situation a little, grant her some credits and offer such postponements in the payment of reparations as would make economic life in Germany possible.

This would inevitably result in a certain upturn for German industry and a corresponding growth in German exports. German industry is currently working at approximately 50 percent of capacity, and if the economic and financial situation of Germany were slightly eased, there could be a rapid growth of German export. The capacity of the European market, however, is very small, and as a result of German exports we might in a year or less see a catastrophic crisis of English or French industry. The smallest easing of the burden on Germany inevitably increases the crisis in England, where even now there are about a million unemployed.

It is absolutely clear that this would give a mighty impulse to the struggle of the English proletariat. MacDonald,[6] the present English prime minister, about whom we shall have some warm words later on, understands of course that in the present conditions aid to German industry can deal a blow to English industry. Having decided this, he may wash his hands of the matter. He has already refused, after all, to reconsider the Versailles treaty.[7]

Supposing the United States does not come to Germany's assistance and that Poincare continues his policy of stifling Germany. Under such conditions the German mark after a few weeks would begin to fall at a still more frenzied pace than it had before, prices would rise no less frantically, industry would fall off, unemployment increase again, and revolution would develop at a tempo even swifter than that of last year. But the German Communist Party will no longer be the party it was last year. It has already become more experienced, more tempered for the new tests to come, and that increases the chances of victory enormously. There are, then, two perspectives before us: either a temporary easing of the revolutionary situation in Germany at the cost of an inevitable sharpening of revolutionary attitudes in all of Europe, or a postponement of the crisis in England and France at the expense of a furious sharpening of the class relations in Germany. In either case Europe will be traveling the road of great revolutionary upheavals. This, in general and on the whole, is how I evaluate the situation in connection with the course of development in Germany.

We must say a few words at this point about Great Britain with its new experience of a so-called Labour government on parliamentary, "democratic" bases, that is, the most ideal and sacred, so it would seem, for every right-thinking Menshevik.

What has this experience given us thus far? You know that the so-called Labour Party does not have an absolute majority in Parliament. Why? Because a significant section of the English workers to this day tag along at the tail of liberalism. These workers are by far not the most obtuse; they simply don't see much difference between liberalism and MacDonald. They say: "What's the sense of our changing quarters and going to the expense of moving when the only difference is the landlord's last name?"

So none of the parties in Parliament has an absolute majority. The Liberals and Conservatives have stepped back and said to the Labour Party: "Oh sirs, you are the most powerful party. Oh please, come rule and be master over us." The English are great humorists, as you know. This is testified to by Dickens, that great representative of English humor.

And MacDonald took the government. Now we ask: What next? How will the "Labour" government proceed? If it does not have a majority in Parliament, that does not mean its situation is totally hopeless. There is a way out; one need only have the will to find it.

Suppose MacDonald said this: "To our shame, our country has to this day a kind of august dynasty that stands above democracy and that we have no need for." If he added that those sitting in the House of Lords and in other state institutions were all the titled heirs of bloodsuckers and robbers and that it was necessary to take a broom and sweep them out—if he said that, wouldn't the hearts of English workers quicken with joy?

What if he added, "We are going to take their lands, mines, and railroads, and nationalize their banks." And there's surely more to be found in the English banks than we found in ours [*stormy applause*]. If he added: "With the resources freed from the control of the monarchy and the House of Lords we are going to undertake the construction of housing for the workers," he would unleash tremendous enthusiasm.

In England three-quarters of the population is working class. It is pure-proletarian country. It has a small handful of landlords and capitalists—they are very rich and powerful, it is true, but still they are only a handful.

If MacDonald walked into Parliament, laid his program on the table, tapped lightly with his knuckles, and said, "Accept it or I'll drive you all out" (saying it more politely than I've phrased it here)—if he did this, England would be unrecognizable in two weeks. MacDonald would receive an overwhelming majority in any election. The English working class would break out of the shell of conservatism with which it has been so cleverly surrounded; it would discard that slavish reverence for the law of the bourgeoisie, the propertied classes, the church and monarchy.

But MacDonald will not do that. He is afraid to. He is conservative—for the monarchy, for private property, for the church.

You know that the English bourgeoisie has created a variety of churches, religious associations, and sects for the people's needs. As in a big clothing store, everyone can find a church for his own size and shape. This is no accident; it is quite expedient from the ruling-class point of view. This splintering and varied adaptation of the church provides greater flexibility and, consequently, a more successful beclouding of the consciousness of the oppressed class.

In our country the dominant church was the embodiment of the most officious bureaucratism. It did not overly concern itself with the soul. But in England there are subtler methods and devices. In England there is a superflexible, conciliatory, I might even say Menshevik, church. In addition, English Menshevism is thoroughly imbued with the priestly spirit. All this is merely the church's way of adapting to the different groups and layers of the proletariat, a complex division of labor in the service of the bourgeois order.

Comrades, there is no need to mention that even before the "Labour" government I did not have a high opinion either of the Second International or of MacDonald. But you know, and this is something I said earlier today in speaking with some friends, each time you encounter Menshevism in a new situation, you have to conclude that it is even more rotten and worthless than you had supposed.

This so-called Labour government is weighed down totally, to the very limit, with the worst petty-bourgeois prejudices and most disgraceful cowardice in relation to the big bourgeoisie. MacDonald's ministers reek of piety, and make a show of it in every possible way. MacDonald himself is a Puritan; he looks at political questions, if you can call it looking, through the glass of the religion that inspired the revolutionary petty bourgeoisie of the seventeenth century. His colleague, Home Minister Henderson,[8] is the president or vice-president, or something of the sort, of the Christian evangelical societies. Every Sunday the home minister of the Labour government pronounces a devout sermon.

This is not a joke, comrades, not something from the English version of *Krokodil*; this is a fact. And this fact is tied in the most intimate way with the whole English conservative tradition, the clever, skillful, sustained ideological work of the English bourgeoisie. It has created an unbelievable terrorism of public opinion against anyone who dares declare that he is a materialist or atheist. England has a glorious history in science. It gave us Darwin, the Marx of biology. But Darwin did not dare to call himself an atheist.

The English big bourgeoisie is a handful, and no police repressions would help if the political influence of the church did not exist. Lloyd George[9] once said, not without reason, that the church was the central power station of all the parties. To clarify this for you more specifically, let me cite one example that I mentioned in speaking privately with some friends. In 1902, that is, twenty-two years ago, I was in England and, with Vladimir Ilyich, attended a Social Democratic meeting in a church. The meeting proceeded in the following fashion: a worker in the printing trades who had returned from Australia gave a speech that for those times was fairly revolutionary, against the ruling classes, for revolution, etc.; then everyone rose and sang a hymn or psalm on the theme: Merciful God, grant that there be neither rich nor kings nor oppressors [*laughter*]. All this is an important constituent feature of English political mores. The English bourgeoisie is the stronger for it, and the English proletariat weaker.

In recent days I read, I forget in which paper, a speech by MacDonald himself to an evangelical society. He spoke with indignation of the class struggle, preaching that society can save itself only through Christian morality, etc. Isn't it hard to imagine him speaking of the Soviet Republic with indignation? But what happened? This Puritan, pacifist preacher of Christian morality no sooner entered the government than he confirmed a proposal to build five new cruisers. His colleague declared that in the field of military aircraft the plans of the preceding Conservative government would remain unchanged.

Moreover, even after the Labour government came to power in England, the production of light tanks continued at full steam. You see what Christian pacifism looks like in practice. And it is not surprising that the same MacDonald declares that in the field of politics, *continuity* is necessary, that is, whatever the Conservatives did, we will too.

In a letter to Poincare he writes that the alliance between England and France is the basis of European peace and order. Why? How does this follow? Modern-day France is the personification of militarism and reaction. Why should this Labour government of England find itself in alliance with the vile French plutocracy?

Why couldn't a Labour government, an *actual* Labour government, make an alliance with us? Would this be a bad alliance — one between the working class of England and the working class of the Soviet Republic? Between czarist Russia and capitalist England a long struggle went on. Czarist Russia wanted to infringe on England's colonies, above all India, while England denied Russia access to the Dardanelles. Bismarck 10 called this struggle between Russia and England the battle of the elephant and the whale.

But now, with the great new change in history, cannot the whale of Labour England conclude a friendly alliance with the Soviet elephant? Would not such an alliance represent the greatest advantages for both sides? English industry and the English people need our fields, our forests, our bread, our raw materials, and we need their capital and technology. The alliance of Labour England with us would be a strong check on bourgeois France; it would not dare commit further outrages and ravages in Europe.

Together with England we would help Europe reduce the burden of armaments; we would draw closer to the creation of a workers and peasants United States of Europe, without which Europe is threatened with unavoidable economic and political decline.

But what does MacDonald do? This devout pacifist tells Poincare, the most ferocious representative of stock-market France, that he wishes to remain in alliance with him of all people — and consequently in opposition to us and the laboring masses of Europe. There you have real Menshevism, not the pocket edition, like you had here with Zhordania, 11 but Menshevism of world proportions, placed in power in a country that encompasses hundreds of millions of colonial slaves.

In the few weeks of its rule, English Menshevism has become hated in the colonies, in both India and Egypt, where revolutionary nationalist aspirations have won out under the slogan of full separation from England. The Mensheviks will start complaining that English industry can't get along without Indian and Egyptian cotton and colonial raw materials in general. As if that were the question! If MacDonald tried to reach agreement with the Indians and Egyptians on the basis of their full independence, England would have cotton in exchange for machines, would have economic ties, and these ties would develop. But here too MacDonald acts as a Menshevik steward for the English imperialists.

Finally, there is another fact that has a direct symbolic significance for history: it concerns Turkey. Turkey, as you know, has done away with the caliphate. This is a progressive liberal-bourgeois measure. Nationalist Turkey throws off the feudal vestments of the caliph and sultan and becomes a more or less bourgeois-democratic country. This is a step forward.

What does the MacDonald government do, this Menshevik "Labour" government? It crowns a new caliph in Hejaz, the so-called "sheik of Mecca and Medina," in order to have, in his person, a weapon for colonial enslavement.

I read in the *Times*—although it is a Conservative organ, in foreign policy it always expresses the official line of the existing government, whether bourgeois, Liberal, or MacDonaldite—I read there that in Turkey, alas, the age-old, sacred, majestic foundations are cracking and that we have the profound misfortune to see it happening before our eyes. And MacDonald subsidizes this very same newly cooked-up caliph in Hejaz, because for majestic institutions a majestic establishment is necessary, and a corresponding budget.

In particular, the entourage of the caliph is linked with a rather vast harem, which as we have read, was recently expelled from Constantinople. With the unemployment existing in England and the difficulties of the English budget, it is necessary, obviously, for MacDonald to cut unemployment payments slightly in order to cover the additional expenses of the caliph's new harem. This all seems like a humorous anecdote but it is fact, which cannot be erased from history. . . .

Just think! This "humane" and "civilized" England, in the person of Gladstone, [12] threatened Turkey because of its backwardness and barbarity. And now, when Turkey has got on its feet and chased out caliph and sultan, parliamentary England, crowned with the Menshevik government of MacDonald, establishes a caliph under its protectorate. There you have the full measure of the decline of bourgeois democracy!

If in regard to all this you should ask what will be the fate of our further discussions with the new English government regarding possible loans, joint covering of claims, etc., I would find it hard to give even an approximate answer. How can one know what MacDonald will decide to do, and what his Liberal and Conservative controllers will allow him to do?

And here I should correct the second inaccuracy in the interview published in *Zarya Vostoka*. It said there that Trotsky had indicated the possibility that these talks would serve as a lever to overthrow the so-called Labour government of MacDonald. No more, no less! Comrades, if I were to say something like that, comrades Chicherin and Rakovsky would take stern measures against me, and they would be right.

Imagine the situation: we have sent a delegation for talks and at the same time I declare that we have sent this delegation in order, in passing, to overthrow MacDonald. How? What for? To have Baldwin [13] or Lloyd George in his place? Nonsense. I said nothing of the kind. On the contrary, our delegation is one of the levers that may immensely strengthen the English government. Under what conditions? Those of daring and decisive action by that government.

In England there is unemployment; it could be reduced by granting us credits, by increasing our purchasing power. The Soviet Union could serve as a truly vast market for English goods. No colonial plunder could give the English economy the advantages that a solid alliance with us could. Credit is not philanthropy. We pay the going interest rates. There are obvious mutual advantages in such an arrangement.

What are the obstacles? The capitalists demand, by way of MacDonald, that we pay back the czarist debts. When did the victim ever, after breaking free of the ropes that had bound him, pay the robber for the ropes? Well, we broke out of the czarist bonds. And do you think we are going to pay the English stock exchange for them? No, never!

Our own obligations we will rigorously fulfill. We openly and triumphantly avowed in the first Soviet, in 1905, that we would not pay the czarist debts, and we will fulfill that international obligation of ours [*stormy applause*]. If we now deem it necessary to enter into one or another business agreement with the bourgeoisie, we will fulfill our new obligations most rigorously.

Bankers of England, if you give us a loan, then as long as you remain the bankers of England, that is, as long as the English proletariat endures you, we will pay it back promptly and exactly. And when the English proletariat overthrows you, it will disinherit you of our debts to you as well. There you have a clean, businesslike, and irrefutable statement of the situation.

The surest guarantee of our fulfilling international obligations is our own self-interest! If MacDonald would make a broad agreement with us, he would strengthen himself. Of that I have not the slightest doubt. In general, he can win the hearts of millions of workers only by a courageous policy, and then no one could turn him out by parliamentary tricks. As you can see, this is not at all what was ascribed to me in the newspaper interview. It was a hasty conversation, in a railroad coach, before the train pulled out; the comrade was jotting things down quickly with his pencil. I am not trying to reproach him, but merely to *rehabilitate* myself [*laughter*].

That MacDonald will, with all his strength, help to overthrow himself, to me is absolutely clear, as it is to all of you. The Liberals, as I gather from a quick glance at the paper today, left MacDonald in a minority in Parliament on the question of workers' housing, and he felt obliged to accept the Liberal bill. What does this mean? The worker will say, "Why get a Liberal bill via MacDonald when I can get it directly from a Liberal?" From this it is clear not only that the Liberal Party will remove MacDonald as prime minister whenever it wants to; it is also undermining the authority that the Labour Party has in the workers' ranks.

A section of the workers, the more aristocratic, the better off, who voted in the last election for the Labour Party, will probably vote for the Liberals in the next election. They will say, "This is a solid, established firm; why fool around with the middleman?" But the broad mass of workers will make a turn to the left. At what rate I do not know, but there is no doubt that as a result of the temporary splendor of having even a Menshevik government, a very significant strengthening of the left wing in the working class will take place. MacDonald is working for the Communists. Yes, from the viewpoint of the international revolution, he is working for us.

However, I certainly don't intend to send him a note of thanks for that. He is working in this direction not only unselfishly but even unconsciously. Pushed by the Liberals and Conservatives, who intentionally compromise him, revealing that he is only a toy in their hands, MacDonald in turn pushes the English workers toward the revolutionary road. Such will be the final result of this historical experiment, the advent to power of the English Labour Party.

Because of insufficient time I will not pause on Italy. Moreover, the situation there is clear. Italian fascism, continuing its desperate gamble, is preparing the greatest revolutionary vengeance by the Italian proletariat— of that we cannot have the slightest doubt.

Such are the basic elements of the European situation as I understand them. How is this reflected in our international stance? It seems to me the answer is clear from all that has been said. We have grown stronger. We have been recognized by several countries. [14] The price placed as a condition for such recognition we all know. We are revolutionists not jurists, but we do not deny the weight of de jure. Recognition has significance. What kind? It makes it difficult for the bourgeoisie to open up a new struggle against us by military means. It does not, of course, make war impossible—it's ridiculous even to speak of that—there will be wars. But surprise attacks, as in 1918 and 1919, when expeditions were landing everywhere, when open support for insurrections went on, that kind of thing has now become much more difficult.

As a result of being recognized by both great and small, sudden war does not threaten us; which is to say, our international position has become more secure. This is a big plus factor, and we will enter this plus in our book in the credit column. But no more than that. For the rest, the struggle of the capitalist states against us continues full force, and the bourgeoisie's hatred of us, like wine, grows stronger with time, becomes more restrained, cautious, and shrewd.

Moreover, not all of the bourgeoisie by far have reached the point of granting us legal recognition. France still has not recognized us, and France is the strongest military power in Europe; it has the mightiest army. Also not recognizing us is the United States of America. This is no small country, and it has concentrated in its hands the wealth of the entire world.

I spoke yesterday with some Red Army men of the Sukhum regiment and reminded them of the well-known verses, "I'll buy everything, says gold./I'll seize everything, says dagger." In the United States the richest gold of the bourgeoisie is gathered; and in France, there is the strongest capitalist dagger; and these two countries have not recognized us.

In her relations with us France carries on furious blackmail, putting its hangers-on, such as Rumania and Poland, up to no good, and trying to do the same with Turkey. It is true that in France, as a result of the upcoming elections one may expect the advent to power of the so-called Left Front. [15] Its foreign policy, however, will differ from that of Poincare hardly more than MacDonald's has from the policy of Baldwin. At the same time, France's insoluble financial difficulties are preparing a revolutionary denouement.

The United States continues to digest in its enormous belly the riches it stole from Europe during the imperialist war. The United States, too, is an archdemocratic country. Its intervention in the recent imperialist war arose out of purely idealistic motives—to help democracy against militarism. We remember all that. Having robbed Europe, weakened it, bled it dry, the United States has become a colossal tower of babel of bourgeois might.

While digesting what it has stolen, it is staying out of European affairs. But at the same time, it is diligently preparing for the war of the future. Aviation and poison gas have first priority. The United States, that enormous world factory, becomes more and more the world poison gas factory. These preparations are not only meant for weakened Japan, but for Europe as well. You see reports in the press to the effect that the enlightened Americans consider the old methods of war too barbaric, outdated, and medieval, and feel it is necessary to apply new methods, more subtle, chemical, and humane, which will not cause death but merely induce sleep, and even inspire pleasant dreams.

You comrades know the importance of laughing gas in certain operations; as far as I know, dentists frequently pull teeth with the aid of such gas. But when American capital prepares laughing gas in order to pull the revolutionary teeth of Europe, should the need arise, we have to be very, very much on guard.

For the time being, enlightened America is trying out its gases only on its own criminals, who are no longer electrocuted there—a backward method!—but are subjected to the action of "laughing" gas. It's the latest thing in technology and Quaker humaneness! The Americans promise to subject whole cities, regions, and provinces to the action of their gases. Imagine the prospect: rich and sated America sends hungry, revolutionary Europe squadrons of planes and spills its laughing gas on our heads. This is not something out of a fantasy!

Poison gas was even used on a large scale in the past imperialist war. The old methods of extermination are no longer adequate. Military chemistry is now divided into two spheres: explosives and poisons. I would find it hard to say which is more humane.

In Leningrad we have a museum of military chemistry, an unavoidable military institution. But I read yesterday that there is a poster in this museum to the effect that the thing to do is not to destroy the enemy's forces but to paralyze them with gas. Here it seems we are beginning to echo the bourgeois hypocrites. This doesn't suit us! It's not true that gas is more "humane."

If some country tomorrow discovered a gas capable of destroying entire armies, it would immediately put this into action against its enemies. War in general is a shameful and repulsive barbarity; we know this well, and we will not occupy ourselves with vile phrases about humane methods of warfare. This

suits Quakers and Puritans but not us! We take facts in their
natural aspect, without deceiving ourselves or others.

The thing to do is not to humanize warfare but to abolish
it. How? By abolishing capitalist society. There is no other
way. For that reason we have been and shall remain mortal
foes of the bourgeois system. We shall maintain, as before,
and with more conviction than ever, our course toward social
revolution.

"You've made a mistake," cry the reformists. "Hadn't you
hoped the war would pass directly over into revolution?" Yes,
we hoped that. And in fact a mortal danger did threaten the
European bourgeoisie at the end of the war. But the revolution
was accomplished only here. In Germany and Austro-Hungary
it stopped half-way. France was deeply shaken; in England
mighty strikes unfolded. But matters never went so far as
revolution.

In 1918 and 1919 we did in fact expect the rapid and victorious development of the European revolution. Regarding
tempo we miscalculated. What was the heart of our error?
Despite all our experience, we underestimated the importance
of the revolutionary party. A revolutionary situation existed.
Europe was rocked to its foundations. The workers and peasants came out of the trenches gnashing their teeth.

What was lacking in Europe? A Bolshevik party, that is
all. We hoped that the party would be built rapidly, under
fire. However, it has become clear that a certain period of
time is necessary for its establishment, the inner process of selection, its becoming matured and tempered. Not so long a
time as our party required for its preparation but not so short
a time as we had hoped, either. Thus, in 1918-1919, everything was ready for the proletarian revolution — except the
proletarian party.

Nevertheless, in this first postwar hour, capitalist Europe
underwent its first epileptic attack. It withstood the attack, righted itself, and is trying, after the fact, to give the appearance
of almost total health. But we know well that it is only enjoying a historic interval — between the first and the second
attack.

Last year we expected the victory of the German proletariat,
which would of course have been reflected throughout Europe
and the world. It turned out that, this time too, we underestimated the importance of the party's preparedness. Although
the Communist Party in Germany is an honest revolutionary
party, it was still not prepared in actuality; it did not know
how to maneuver actively, as our party did, nor how to decide

at the crucial hour to put all its cards on the table, to dispel all doubt and all doubters, to hurl itself forward and see things through to the end [*stormy applause*]. That is why the second attack, the fatal one, has not yet come.

The German bourgeoisie is trying to right itself, to change the political relation of forces in its own favor. We are living in an intermediate period between the first and second revolutionary attacks, which should put an end to the European bourgeoisie. How long this period of time will last we do not know.

The capitalist organism is still a powerful one, even in its death agony: in the convulsions that precede death it is capable of dealing the most savage blows. And at whom will those blows be dealt if not at the Soviet Union? That is why, even after all those who have "recognized" us, we must be on our guard.

The basic condition for our security and military preparedness is the successful development of our economy, that is, above all the development of our industry in adaptation to the needs of the peasant masses, influencing of the village economy through industry, raising the level of the village economy, strengthening the ties between industry and agriculture, and thereby strengthening our financial stability during the transition to a stable paper currency. My report is not devoted to these complex questions, which I will just mention in passing.

We have achieved a great success in the economic field by the very fact that we have moved the economic body of our country off dead center. The level of the productive forces is rising. But it is rising in two directions at once: socialist and capitalist. Everything depends on the relation between these. Our basic efforts are aimed at making socialist accumulation take place more rapidly than capitalist accumulation, which has its place under NEP. The international struggle that we are conducting has its direct continuation in the economic struggle within the bounds of our Soviet Union. The predominance of the accumulations of the state sector over those of the private sector is the basic determinant of our stability, both within and without.

This issue has not yet been resolved. But if we have succeeded in spite of everything in creating conditions in which the imperialist bourgeoisie has "recognized" us, that is, has been forced to reckon with our long-term existence; if we continue to preserve the political conditions internally whereby we are free to decide for ourselves up to what line or point we will permit private capital and what concessions we will make to it; if we keep in mind withal that over the past seven years we have accumulated a vast experience unrivaled in history — then we can have no reason at all to doubt that we will cope with the basic task of economic construction as well.

The political condition for this is the unbroken tie between the party and the class. And we have had in the recent period the most favorable and, moreover, indisputable proofs that this exists. The most important fact of recent weeks and months has been the influx of workers from the plant floors into the ranks of our party. [16] This is the best way for the fundamental revolutionary class in our country to show its will: by raising its hand and saying, we vote our confidence in the RKP, [17] it is pursuing the straightforward line of struggle against the bourgeoisie; it knows when it is necessary to yield and how much to yield, but it will never yield anything essential. This vote is a reliable, sure, and unerring verification, by comparison with which parliamentary votes seem phantomlike, superficial, and, most of all, simply charlatanistic. This free vote of proletarian confidence is the basic political guarantee not only of our existence but of our further success. On this base we can and should build.

On this base, above all, our further military development shall also rest. We should raise the level of military technique, creating a close tie between it and industry. We need a solid and powerful air force, going hand in hand with civil aviation. If we wish to protect our cities from the bourgeoisie's laughing-gas and poison-gas showers, we should have squadrons of our own reconnaissance aircraft and fighter planes along the Soviet borders.

With the present technology and methods of warfare, air power becomes an effective threat only if it is multiplied by chemistry. They have chemistry, and we too shall have military chemistry. The chemistry of explosives and of poisons should become central concerns of the Soviet worker and peasant, both man and woman, for it is a matter of defending the revolution. We want to be independent; we want to live; and we will defend ourselves and make ourselves secure. We need an air force. We are building it. And we will complete it.

We have a Society of Friends of the Air Force. Now we need to build, through combined private, governmental, party, and professional initiative, a Society of Friends of Military Chemistry. We are poor, but we have a will to live, a will to struggle and to win [*stormy applause*]. They are stronger technologically, but the outcome of a war is decided not by bare technology but by the strength of morale multiplied by technology. The power of morale in a war is on our side.

Here is a fresh example. Recently by a voluntary agreement we extended the borders of Soviet Byelorussia to include twice as much. There had been one and a half million people in it, and now there are four million. What does this mean? That we have basically carried out an elementary duty: the Byelorussian has the right to live in his own Byelorussia. But from the military point of view this is equivalent to three new Red Army corps [*stormy applause*]. You may rebuke me for speaking openly of this, because Poland might learn our "secrets." Let it learn and let it try to follow our example; let it give its Byelorussians autonomy; let it try to weaken us that way!

More and more these days we are going over to a territorial militia system. Who else could afford this kind of thing? Only a country that has no contradiction or hatred between the ruling class and the people, between the commanders and the ranks of its army. Not a single bourgeois country can adopt a militia system. But we can! There you have the Red Army's strength of morale. How will the soldier of this or that country behave in the event of a European conflict? No ruling class of any bourgeois country knows the answer. But how our Red Army men and sailors will conduct themselves we know very well [*stormy applause*].

Comrades, every one of us today is doing some kind of personal or private work. We often say that we have to learn to trade. If someone from Mars or the moon were to read our papers they might think, Here is a race of petty traders. But no! We are learning to trade, but we will never barter away our revolutionary spirit. We will remain what we were on the night of October 24-25, 1917 [*stormy applause*].

In our economic work, in our cultural work, in our military work, we will conduct ourselves in such a way as to prepare for the eventuality that the bourgeoisie will maintain itself for a number of years to come. But if tomorrow or the day after, Europe is seized by a new revolutionary fever and the proletariat of Germany or France look to us for the support and aid of the Soviet Union, it makes no difference whether they look to Moscow or to Tiflis [*voices: "Makes no difference!"*] or to other centers of our Union, they will find us the same iron-and-steel Bolsheviks, students and heirs of Lenin's work, strengthened by stern discipline, ready to fight to the end wherever the revolution requires. [*Stormy applause. The "International."*]

Less than two weeks later, on April 21, Trotsky spoke in Moscow at the Communist University of the Toilers of the East on the occasion of the third anniversary of this institution for the education of revolutionaries from the Orient and the Asian parts of the Soviet Union.

Here we find him giving a popular introduction to the theory of the permanent revolution and dealing with the prospects for socialist revolution in the colonial countries, especially in the Far East. In explaining why Bolshevism finds its greatest response among the most oppressed, he saw women in the forefront of the struggle for liberation.

The Chinese revolution of 1925-27 soon confirmed the perspective of socialist revolution: it also became one of the issues further dividing the Left Opposition from the bureaucracy.

The speech is reprinted from Fourth International, *December 1942.*

Prospects and Tasks in the East

Comrades! Although it is not customary at anniversary celebrations to take up time with theoretical discussions, permit me nevertheless to make a few observations of a general character to bear out my statement that your university is not an ordinary, revolutionary, educational institution, but a lever of world historic significance.

The political and cultural movement of today rests on capitalism. It is an outcome of capitalism; it has grown out of it and has finally outgrown it. But, roughly speaking, there are two types of capitalism — the capitalism of the imperialist countries and colonial capitalism. The most striking example of the first kind of capitalism is — Great Britain. At present it has at its head the so-called "Labour" government of Ramsay MacDonald.

Great Britain is the seat of classical capitalism. Marx wrote his work *Capital* in London where he had the opportunity of being in direct touch with and to observe the development of the foremost country in the world. In the colonies capitalism is not a product of local conditions and development but is fostered by the penetration of foreign capital. This is the reason for the existence of two types of capitalism. The question arises, to speak not exactly in scientific, but nevertheless in correct terms: Why is MacDonald so conservative, so narrow in his outlook, and so dull? The answer is — because Great Britain is the classical land of capitalism, because there the development of capitalism was organic, from handicraft through manufacture to present-day industrialism, and because it was gradual and "evolutionary." That is why, if you were to open MacDonald's skull, you would find an accumulation not only of the prejudices of yesterday and the day before yesterday, but an accumulation of the intellectual dust and prejudices of the last few centuries.

At first sight there seems to be a historic contradiction in the fact that Marx was a child of backward Germany, the most backward of the great European countries in the first half of the nineteenth century (excepting Russia, of course). Why, during the nineteenth and the opening years of the twentieth century, did Germany produce Marx and Russia, Lenin? This seems to be an obvious anomaly! But it is an anomaly which is explained in the so-called dialectics of historical development. In British machinery and British textiles, history provided the most revolutionary factor of development. But machinery and textiles went through a slow process of development in Great Britain, and on the whole the human mind and consciousness are extremely conservative. When economic development is slow and systematic, enlightenment is slow in penetrating into the thick skulls of ordinary human beings.

Subjectivists and idealists generally say that human consciousness and critical thought, etc., etc., take history in tow, just like tugs take barges in tow. This is not so. We, here, are Marxists and therefore know that the driving power in history are the productive forces which have hitherto developed, so to speak, behind the backs of the people, and which find it very difficult to penetrate into the conservative thick skulls of ordinary human beings and to kindle in them a spark of new political ideas. I repeat that this is very difficult when the development is slow, organic, and evolutionary. But when the productive forces of the metropolis, of a country of classical capitalism, such as Great Britain, find ingress into more backward countries, like Germany in the first half of the nineteenth century, and Russia at the merging of the nineteenth and twentieth centuries, and in the present day in Asia; when the economic factors burst in a revolutionary manner, breaking up the old order; when development is no longer gradual and "organic," but assumes the form of terrible convulsions and drastic changes of former social conceptions, then it becomes easier for critical thought to find revolutionary expression, provided that the necessary theoretical prerequisites exist in the given country.

That is why Marx made his appearance in Germany in

the first half of the nineteenth century, that is why Lenin made his appearance here in Russia and why we observe what looks at first sight like a paradox, that the country of the oldest, most developed, and most successful European capitalism, I mean Great Britain, is the home of the most conservative "Labour" Party. On the other hand, in our Soviet Union, in a country with a very backward economic and cultural development, we have (we can say it frankly, for it is a fact) the best Communist Party in the world.

It must be said that, according to its economic development, Russia is midway between a classical metropolis, such as Great Britain, and a colonial country, like India or China. Moreover, that which constitutes the difference between our Soviet Union and Great Britain, as far as methods and forms of development are concerned, is still more noticeable in the development of the countries of the East. Into the latter, capitalism penetrates in the form of foreign finance capital. It introduces machinery into these countries, it destroys their old economic basis and erects on its ruins strongholds of capitalist economic development. The progress of capitalism in the countries of the East is not gradual and slow and is by no means "evolutionary," but drastic and catastrophic, frequently much more catastrophic than here, in former czarist Russia.

Comrades, it is from this fundamental viewpoint that we must study events in the East during the next few years, or rather decades. If you will take the trouble to study such prosaic books as the reports of British and American banks for 1921-22-23, you will find in the figures of the balance sheets of the banks of London and New York a forecast of imminent revolutionary events in the East.

Great Britain has once more assumed the role of world usurer. The U. S. A. has accumulated enormous quantities of gold; the vaults of the banks contain three billion dollars. This is a drag on the economic system of the U. S. A. You will ask: To whom do the U. S. and England lend their money? You of course know that they do not give any to us, to Soviet Russia. Nor has Germany received anything, and France managed to get but a few crumbs to save the franc. To whom, then, do they give loans? They give them chiefly to the colonial countries, for they finance the industrial development of Asia, South America, and South Africa. I will not take up your time by quoting the figures which I have before me. Suffice it to say that, previous to the recent imperialist war, colonial and semicolonial countries received from the U. S. A. and Great Britain probably only about half as much as capitalistically developed countries, whereas now the financial investments in colonial countries exceed to a considerable extent the investments in old capitalist countries. Why? There are many reasons for this, but the two main reasons are: lack of confidence in bankrupt and emasculated old Europe, with rabid French militarism in the very heart of it, a militarism which foreshadows more convulsions; and on the other hand—the need of colonial countries as providers of raw material and consumers of machinery and other British and American manufactured goods.

During the war and at the present day we witness a feverish industrialization of colonial, semicolonial and, generally speaking, of all backward countries: Japan, India, South America, and South Africa. There is no doubt whatever that if the Kuomintang Party [18] in China succeeds in uniting China under a national-democratic regime, the capitalist development of China will make enormous strides forward. And all this leads to the mobilization of countless proletarian masses which will immediately emerge from a prehistoric, semibarbarian state and will be thrust into the whirlpool of industrialism. Therefore, in these countries there will be no time for the refuse of past centuries to accumulate in the minds of the workers. A guillotine, as it were, will be set to work in their minds which will sever the past from the future at one stroke, and compel them to look for new ideas, new forms, and new ways of life and struggle. And this will be the time for Marxist-Leninist parties to make their first appearance in some countries, and to pursue a bold course of development in others. I mean, of course, the Japanese, Chinese, Turkish, and Indian Communist parties.

Comrades and workers of the East, in 1883 there came into being in Switzerland the Russian group of "Emancipation of Labor." [19] Is that so long ago? From 1883 to 1900—seventeen years, and from 1900 to 1917—also seventeen years, together thirty-four years—a third of a century—a generation: only a third of a century has intervened between the organization of the first theoretical propagandist group of Marxists in the reign of Alexander III [20] and the conquest of czarist Russia by the proletariat. Those who lived through it know it to have been a long and difficult period. But from the viewpoint of historical development, the speed with which events developed was most rapid. And in the countries of the East, the pace of development will be (as we have every reason to believe) still more rapid. Looking at things in this aspect, what is the role of the Communist University of the Toilers of the East? It is the seedbed of "Emancipation of Labor" groups for the countries of the East.

It is true, of course, that the dangers confronting the young Marxists of the East are great, and we must not shut our eyes to this fact. We know, and you know it as well as we do, that the Bolshevik Party was formed under circumstances of hard internal as well as external struggle. You know that in the nineties of the nineteenth century a kind of emasculated and falsified Marxism formed a prominent part of the political education of the bourgeois intellectuals—the followers of Struve, [21] who subsequently became a political lackey of the bourgeoisie, joined the Cadets, later went over to the Octobrists, and veered even more to the right.

Russia was backward, not only economically, but also politically. Marxism preached the inevitability of capitalism, and those bourgeois-progressive elements which wanted capitalism for its own sake and not for the sake of socialism, accepted Marxism, having previously deprived it of its revolutionary sting. Such temporary exploitations of Marxism in the interests of a bourgeois-progressive policy were typical of the southeastern Balkan countries as well as of our own country. Let us consider now if Marxism runs the same risks in the East. To a certain extent, it does. And why? Because the national movement in the East is a progressive factor in world history. The struggle for independence in India is a highly progressive movement, but we all know that it is at the same time a struggle for strictly limited national-bourgeois aims. The struggle for the liberation of China, the ideology of Sun Yat-sen, [22] is a democratic struggle with a progressive ideology, but bourgeois nevertheless. We approve of Communist support to the Kuomintang Party in China, which we are endeavoring to revolutionize. This is inevitable, but here too there is a risk of a national-democratic revival. Such is the case in all the countries of the East in which the national struggle for liberation from colonial slavery is going on. The young proletariat of the East must rely on this progressive movement for support. But it is as clear as daylight that the young Marxists of the East run the risk of being torn out of the "Emancipation of Labor" group and of becoming permeated with nationalist ideology.

But you have the advantage over the older generations of Russian, Rumanian, and other Marxists in that you live and work not only in the post-Marxian, but even in the post-Lenin epoch. Your advantage consists in having sprung directly from the epoch which will be known in history as the Lenin epoch. Both Marx and Lenin were revolutionary politicians with whom theory and practice went hand in hand. As a general proposition, this is of course correct and incontrovertible. But there is nevertheless a distinction, and a signal distinction, between these two historic figures, which originated not only in the difference in the individuality of the two men, but also in the difference between epochs.

Marxism, of course, is not an academic science, but a lever of revolutionary action. This is borne out by Marx's saying: "The world has been sufficiently explained by philosophers, it is time to remodel it." But was it possible to make a full use of Marxism through the working-class movement during Marx's life, in the epoch of the First and subsequently of the Second Internationals? Was Marxism put into practice at that time? Of course not. Did Marx have the opportunity and the supreme happiness to apply his revolutionary theory to decisive historic action: the conquest of power by the proletariat? The answer is in the negative. Marxist teaching has of course nothing academic about it, for Marx himself is entirely a product of revolution and of a correct and critical appreciation of the downfall of bourgeois democracy. He published his *Manifesto* in 1847. He went through the revolution of 1848 as a left-winger of bourgeois democracy, estimating all the events of this revolution in a Marxist way or Marxist spirit. He wrote his work *Capital* in London, and was at the same time the founder of the First International and the inspiration of the policy of the most advanced groups of the working class of all countries. But he was not at the head of a party which decided the destiny of the world or even the destiny of one country. Whenever we want to give a concise answer to the question: Who is Marx? we say: "Marx . . . is the author of *Capital*." And when we ask ourselves — who is Lenin? we say: "Lenin is the author of the October Revolution." Lenin, more than anyone else, was emphatic in saying that he did not intend to revise, remodel, or alter the teachings of Marx. Lenin came, to use the words of the Bible, not to change the law of Marx but to fulfill it.

I repeat, no one was more emphatic than Lenin in asserting this. But at the same time he had to free Marx from the misinterpretations of his teachings introduced by the generations which separated Lenin from Marx — from the Kautskyism, [23] MacDonaldism, and the conservatism of the upper strata of the working class, of the reformist and nationalist bureaucracy.

He had to apply to the full the weapon of true Marxism
(cleansed from misinterpretation and falsification) to the
greatest event in world history. Although Marx himself was
able to embody in his theory the trend of events of decades
and centuries, yet his teaching was subsequently subdivided
into separate elements and in the everyday struggle
was frequently assimilated in a mutilated and incorrect form.
But Lenin came upon the scene. Under totally new conditions,
he collected all the teachings of Marx and demonstrated them
in a historic action on a world scale. You have seen this action
and you are associated with it. This places you under an obligation, and on this obligation the Communist University
of the Toilers of the East is founded.

There is every reason to believe that the Communist University of the Toilers of the East will furnish a nucleus of
workers which will act as a class-conscious, Marxist, and Leninist leaven in the movement of the proletariat of the East.

Comrades, you will be in great demand, and as I said before this will not happen gradually, but all at once, and, so
to speak, "catastrophically." I advise you to read once more
one of Lenin's most recent articles: "Better Less, but Better."
The main theme of this article is the question of organization,
but it deals also with the prospective development in the countries of the East in connection with European development.
The main and fundamental idea of this article is that a setback in the development of the Western revolution is possible.
This setback can be caused by MacDonaldism, which is the
most conservative force in Europe. We have before us the spectacle of Turkey abolishing the caliphate, and MacDonald re-
establishing it. Is not this a striking example of the counterrevolutionary Menshevism of the West and of the progressive
national-bourgeois democratism of the East? Afghanistan is at
present the scene of truly dramatic events: the Great Britain
of Ramsay MacDonald is fighting there against the left national-
bourgeois wing, which aims at the Europeanization of an independent Afghanistan. It endeavors to place in power in that
country the most unenlightened and reactionary elements, imbued with the worst prejudices of pan-Islamism, of the caliphate,
etc. A correct appreciation of these two colliding forces will
enable you to understand why the East will be drawn more
and more to us — the Soviet Union and the Third International.

We witness in Europe, the past development of which caused
the monstrous conservatism of the upper strata of the working
class, an ever-growing economic deterioration and disintegra-

tion. There is no way out for the old continent. This is shown partly by the reluctance of the U. S. A. to lend money to Europe, based on the well-founded assumption that economically Europe is played out. At the same time we see that the U. S. A. and Great Britain are compelled to finance the economic development of the colonial countries, driving them with whirlwind rapidity onto the path of revolution. And if Europe is going to be kept in the present state of decomposition by this narrow-minded, aristocratic MacDonaldism of the upper strata of the working class, the center of gravity of the revolutionary movement will be transferred to the East. And then it will become evident that if it required several decades of capitalist development in Great Britain, with the assistance of this revolutionary factor, to rouse our old Russia and the old East out of their slumber, it will require a revolution in the East, which, sweeping back to Great Britain, will break (if necessary) a number of thick skulls and thus give an impetus to the revolution of the European proletariat [*applause*]. This is *one* of the historic possibilities which we must never lose sight of.

I read in the material you sent me about the overwhelming impression produced in Kazan by one of the women students of your university — a Turkish woman, when she addressed the women of that city, including the illiterate and the old. This might seem an insignificant episode, but it is nevertheless of considerable historical importance. The strength and meaning of Bolshevism consist in the fact that it appeals to the oppressed and exploited masses and not to the upper strata of the working class. That is why Bolshevism is being assimilated by the countries of the East, not because of its theories, which are far away from being fully understood, but because of its spirit of freedom and liberty. Your own paper tells us over and over again that the name of Lenin is known not only in the villages of the Caucasus, but even in the remotest parts of India. We know that the workers of China, who probably never read anything written by Lenin, are irresistibly drawn toward Bolshevism. Such is the powerful influence of this great historic movement! They feel in their innermost hearts that it is a teaching for the oppressed and exploited, for hundreds of millions to whom it is the only possible salvation. That is why Leninism meets with a passionate response among workingwomen who are the most oppressed section of society. When I read about the success of one of your female students in Kazan among the illiterate Tatar women, I was reminded of my recent short visit to Baku where I heard for the first time a Turkomen Communist woman, and had an opportunity to observe in the hall the enthusiasm of hundreds of such women, who having heard our message of liberation had awakened to a new life. I realized then for the first time that women will play a more important role in the liberation movement of the East than in Europe and here in Russia [*applause*]. This will be the case for the simple reason that Eastern women are even more oppressed and entangled in agelong prejudices than men.

It is for this reason that the new spirit, which is now animating the popular movements, has a stronger effect on women than on men. Although the East is still under the influence of Islam and of old creeds, prejudices, and customs, there are signs that this influence is waning rapidly. We can liken the present state of the East to a piece of cloth which has perished. When you look at it at a distance, its texture and design seem to be perfect and its folds are as graceful as before. But a slight touch, a zephyr breeze is enough to make this beautiful material fall to pieces. Thus we have in the East old creeds which seem to be deeply rooted, but which are in reality only a shadow of the past. For instance, the caliphate was abolished in Turkey and nothing happened to those who made this bold attempt on an agelong institution. This shows that old Eastern creeds have lost their power, and that in the imminent historic movement of the revolutionary working masses, these creeds will not be a serious obstacle. But this also means that Eastern women, who under present conditions are enslaved and thwarted in all their desires and ambitions, will, with the removal of the veil, see themselves deprived of all spiritual support because of the newly arisen economic conditions. They will thirst for new ideas and a new consciousness capable of allotting them their proper place in society. Believe me, there will be no better comrade in the East and no better champion of the ideas of revolution and communism than the awakened workingwoman [*applause*].

Comrades, that is why your university has such a worldwide historic significance. Profiting by the ideological and political experience of the West, it produces the revolutionary leaven which will permeate the East. For you the time for action is imminent. British and American finance capital is destroying the economic foundation of the East. It is creating new conditions. It destroys the old and creates the need for something new. You will sow the seed of communism, and you will reap a far richer revolutionary harvest than the old Marxist generations of Europe.

But, comrades, I should not like my complimentary remarks to rouse in you a spirit of Eastern conceit [*laughter*]. I see that none of you have interpreted my remarks in that way. For if anyone has become imbued with such overbearance and contempt for the West, it will prove a shortcut to national-democratic ideology. No, comrades, the Communist revolutionary students of this university must learn to look upon our world movement as a whole, and to utilize the forces of East and West for the attainment of our one great aim. You must learn to coordinate the rising of Hindu peasants, the strike of bourgeois democrats of the Kuomintang, the Korean struggle for independence, the bourgeois-democratic regeneration of Turkey, and the educational and economic work in the Soviet Republic of Transcaucasia.

All this must be taken into account in connection with the work and struggle of the Communist International in Europe, and especially in Great Britain where slowly (much more slowly than we should wish) but irresistibly, British communism is undermining MacDonald's conservative strongholds [*applause*]. I repeat that your advantage over the older generation consists in the fact that you are learning the alphabet of Marxism, not in emigrant circles (far removed from the actualities of life) in countries where capitalism holds its sway, which was our fate, but in an atmosphere conquered and permeated by Leninism. We cannot tell if the last chapter of the revolutionary struggle with imperialism will be unfolded in one, two, three, or even five years' time. But we know that every year a fresh class of graduates will leave the Communist University of the East. Every year will produce a new nucleus of Communists who have thoroughly learned the alphabet of Leninism, and who with their own eyes have seen the application of this alphabet. If the decisive events take place in twelve months' time, we shall have at our disposal one class of graduates. If two years will have to elapse, we shall have two classes of graduates, and so on. When the moment for decisive action is upon us, the students of the Communist University of the Toilers of the East will say: "We are ready. We have not spent our time here in vain. We have not only learned to translate the ideas of Marxism and Leninism into the language of China, India, Turkey, and Korea; we have also learned to translate into the language of Marxism the sufferings, aspirations, demands, and hopes of the working masses of the East." When these masses ask you who taught you this, your answer will be: "The Communist University of the Toilers of the East." And thereupon they will say what I am saying now on the day of your third anniversary: "All honor and glory to the Communist University of the East." [*Enthusiastic ovation and singing of the "International."*]

12

The War Danger — The Defense Policy and the Opposition

A victory of the German revolution would have strengthened the Left Opposition in the Soviet Union: its defeat reinforced the conservative views and practices of the Soviet bureaucracy. At the end of 1924 Stalin proclaimed the theory of "socialism in one country," which was a negation of the internationalist perspectives of Lenin and the Bolsheviks. It served to transform the Communist parties of all countries into pawns of Soviet diplomacy and led ultimately to collaboration with imperialism.

The death of Lenin allowed the retreat from internationalism to proceed under the guise of a struggle against "Trotskyism." The spurious idea of socialism in one country was presented as orthodox Marxism-Leninism, counterposed to Trotsky's concept of permanent revolution. Old differences between Lenin and Trotsky were revived or distorted, new ones were invented.

This ideological struggle against Trotsky was supplemented by organizational measures. In 1925 he was removed as commissar of war and reassigned to a post on the Supreme Council of National Economy where the bureaucracy sought to bury him in routine tasks. Instead, Trotsky plunged into the work, attempting to reorganize and strengthen the economy and in the process confronting the bureaucrats at every turn.

Zinoviev and Kamenev, who had broken with Stalin and his policies in 1925, joined with Trotsky's Left Opposition in 1926 in a bloc known as the United Opposition. The program of this bloc was: more rapid industrialization based on democratic planning; collectivization of farming as a long-term

Leaders of the Opposition after their expulsion from the party in 1927. Standing from left to right: Rakovsky, Drobnis, Beloborodov, Sosnovsky. Sitting: Serebryakov, Radek, Trotsky, Boguslavsky, Preobrazhensky.

policy; upgrading of wages; defense of the workers and poor peasants against NEPmen, bureaucrats, and wealthy peasants; and inner-party democracy in the Russian party and the Comintern.

The struggle soon came to a climax. Trotsky was expelled from the Political Bureau at the end of 1926. Stalin then set out to expel him from the Central Committee and from the party before the Fifteenth Party Congress, scheduled for 1927. Stalin succeeded, after several attempts, in securing Trotsky's expulsion from the committee in October and from the party in November. The Fifteenth Congress, delayed, met in December when party membership was declared incompatible with the expression of Opposition views.

Zinoviev and Kamenev recanted in order to remain in the party. But thousands of Oppositionists were driven out of the party, many soon to be banished to exile colonies and concentration camps.

On January 17, 1928, Trotsky was banished from Moscow to Alma-Ata, a town in Turkestan near the Chinese border. He was accompanied by Natalia Sedova and their older son and coworker Leon Sedov. Their stay in Alma-Ata lasted a year. In January 1929, Trotsky was exiled to Turkey.

It is difficult to present Left Opposition speeches by Trotsky which are fully satisfactory as expositions of the struggle. He continued to make important public speeches on cultural, literary, scientific subjects. But there were not many occasions when he could speak freely in public as an Oppositionist without running the risk of punitive measures, including possible expulsion from the party, which he was anxious for tactical reasons to postpone as long as possible. Most of his speeches connected directly with the struggle were made behind closed doors and, if transcribed, remain locked away in the Kremlin archives.

As a result, most Left Opposition material after 1923 was produced in written form — at first as pamphlets and articles in the Soviet press, as long as that was possible, and later, when these avenues were closed, in mimeographed and typewritten copies, similar to the samizdat *(self-publication) methods used by Soviet dissidents today. Those who want to understand the ideas and evolution of the Left Opposition are urged to read such works as* The New Course, Lessons of October, The Real Situation in Russia, The Third International After Lenin, Problems of the Chinese Revolution, My Life, *and* The Stalin School of Falsification.

This speech, which is representative of the fight in its final phase, was made at a joint plenary session of the Central Committee and the Central Control Commission on August 1, 1927. A danger of war had recently developed in connection with a break in relations between Britain and the Soviet Union, and Stalin thought this was a favorable moment to get Trotsky expelled. Trotsky, however, responded by taking the offensive with an annihilating criticism of Stalinist policies that had produced catastrophic defeats in Britain and in China.

The translation by John G. Wright is from The Stalin School of Falsification, *published in 1937.*

Trotsky: You have allotted me forty-five minutes. I will summarize as concisely as possible in view of the very wide scope of the subject under consideration. Your theses assert that the Opposition allegedly holds some sort of Trotskyist formulation on the questions of war and defeatism. New fictions! Paragraph 13 of your theses is entirely devoted to this twaddle. So far as the Opposition as a whole is concerned, it can in no way be held accountable for my former differences with Lenin, differences which, upon these questions, were altogether secondary in character. So far as I am personally concerned, I can make a brief reply to the silly insinuations. Back in the time of the imperialist war, the appeals to the international proletariat — all of them dealing with war and the struggle against war — were written by me in the name of the first Council of People's Commissars and in the name of the Central Committee of the party. I wrote the war section of our party program, the main resolution of the Eighth Party Congress and the resolution of a number of Soviet congresses, the manifesto of the First World Congress of the Comintern, a considerable portion of which is devoted to war, and the programmatic manifesto of the Second World Congress of the Comintern which devotes considerable space to the evaluation of war, its consequences, and future perspectives. I wrote the theses of the Third World Congress of the Comintern on the question of the international situation and the perspectives of war and revolution. At the Fourth World Congress I was assigned by the Central Committee of the party to give the report on the perspectives of the international revolution and war. At the

Fifth World Congress (1924) I wrote the manifesto on the occasion of the tenth anniversary of the imperialist war.[1] There were no disputes whatever in the Central Committee over these documents, and they were adopted not only without any controversy, but virtually without any corrections. I ask: How is it that my "deviation" failed to manifest itself throughout my entire long and rather intensive activity in the Communist International?

Now it suddenly appears after my rejection of "economic defeatism" in 1926 — an absurd and illiterate slogan advanced by Molotov[2] for the English workers — that I had presumably parted company with Leninism. Why then did Molotov hide his silly slogan in his back pocket after my criticism of it?

Molotov: There was no slogan at all.

Trotsky: That's what I say. There was nonsense, but no slogan. That's just what I say. [*Laughter.*] Why then was it deemed necessary to exaggerate grossly old differences which, moreover, were liquidated long ago? For what purpose? For the purpose of covering up and camouflaging the actual palpable and current differences. Is it possible to pose seriously the question of a revolutionary struggle against war and of the genuine defense of the USSR while at the same time orienting toward the Anglo-Russian Committee? Is it possible to orient the working-class masses toward a general strike and an armed insurrection in the course of a war while simultaneously orienting towards a bloc with Purcell, Hicks, and other traitors?[3] I ask: *Will our defensism be Bolshevik or trade-unionist?* That is the crux of the question!

Let me first of all remind you of what the present leadership has taught the Moscow proletariat during the whole of the last year. Everything centers round this point. I read you the verbatim directives of the Moscow Committee: "The Anglo-Russian Committee can, must, and undoubtedly will play a tremendous role in the struggle against all types of intervention directed at the USSR. It [the Anglo-Russian Committee!] will become the organizing center for the international forces of the proletariat in the struggle against all attempts of the international bourgeoisie to start a new war."

Molotov has made here the remark that "through the Anglo-Russian Committee we disintegrated Amsterdam."[4] It is as clear as noonday that even now he has grasped nothing. We disintegrated the Moscow workers together with the workers of the entire world, deceiving them as to where their enemies were, and where their friends.

Skrypnik: What a tone!

Trotsky: The tone is suited to the seriousness of the question. You consolidated Amsterdam, and you weakened yourselves. The General Council is now more unanimously against us than ever before.

It must be said, however, that the scandalous directive I just read expresses much more fully, clearly, and honestly the actual standpoint of those who favored the preservation of the Anglo-Russian Committee than does the scholastic hocus-pocus of Bukharin.[5] The Moscow Committee taught the Moscow workers and the Political Bureau taught the workers of the entire Soviet Union that in the event of a war danger our working class would be able to seize hold of the rope of the Anglo-Russian Committee. That is how the question stood politically. But this rope proved rotten. Saturday's issue of *Pravda,* in a leading article, speaks of the "united front of traitors" in the General Council. Even Arthur Cook, Tomsky's own beloved Benjamin, keeps silent. "An utterly incomprehensible silence!" cries *Pravda.* That is your eternal refrain: "This is utterly incomprehensible!" First you staked everything on the group of Chiang Kai-shek; I mean to say Purcell and Hicks, and then you pinned your hopes on "loyal" Wang Chin-wei, that is, Arthur Cook. But Cook betrayed even as Wang Chin-wei betrayed two days after he had been enrolled by Bukharin among the loyal ones. You turned over the Minority Movement bound hand and foot to the gentlemen of the General Council. And in the Minority Movement itself you like-wise refuse to counterpose and are incapable of counterposing genuine revolutionists to the oily reformists. You rejected a small but sturdier rope for a bigger and an utterly rotten one. In passing across a narrow and unreliable bridge, a small but reliable prop may prove one's salvation. But woe to him who clutches at a rotten prop that crumbles at a touch— for, in that case, a plunge into the abyss is inevitable. Your present policy is a policy of rotten props on an international scale. You successively clutched at Chiang Kai-shek, Feng Yu-hsiang, Tang Cheng-chih, Wang Chin-wei, Purcell, Hicks, and Cook.[6] Each of these ropes broke at the moment when it was most sorely needed. Thereupon, first you said, as does the leading article in *Pravda* in reference to Cook, "This is utterly incomprehensible!" in order to add on the very next day, "We always foresaw this."

Let us take the entire tactical, or rather strategical line in China as a whole. The Kuomintang is the party of the liberal bourgeoisie in the period of revolution—the liberal bourgeoisie which draws behind it, deceives, and betrays the workers and peasants.

The Communist Party, in accordance with your directives, remains throughout all the betrayals within the Kuomintang and submits to its bourgeois discipline.

The Kuomintang as a whole enters into the Comintern and does not submit to its discipline, but merely utilizes the name and the authority of the Comintern to dupe the Chinese workers and peasants.

The Kuomintang serves as a shield for the landlord-generals who hold in their grip the soldier-peasants.

Moscow — at the end of last October — demands that the agrarian revolution be kept from developing so as not to scare away the landlords in command of the armies. The armies become mutual insurance societies for the landlords, large and small alike.

The landlords do not raise any objection to their military expeditions being called national revolutionary, so long as the power and the land remain in their hands. The proletariat, which composes a young revolutionary force in no wise inferior to our own proletariat in 1905, is driven under the command of the Kuomintang.

Moscow offers counsel to the Chinese liberals: "Issue a law for the organization of a *minimum* of workers' detachments." This, in March 1927! Why the counsel to the tops — Arm yourselves to the minimum? and why not a slogan to the rank and file — Arm yourselves to the maximum? Why the minimum and not the maximum? In order not to "scare away" the bourgeoisie, so as not to "provoke" a civil war. But the civil war came inevitably, and proved far more cruel, catching the workers unarmed and drowning them in blood.

Moscow came out against the building of soviets in the "army's rear" — as if the revolution is the rump of an army! — in order not to disorganize the rear of the very same generals who two days later crushed the workers and peasants in their rear.

Did we reenforce the bourgeoisie and the landlords by compelling the Communists to submit to the Kuomintang and by covering the Kuomintang with the authority of the Comintern? Yes, we did.

Did we weaken the peasantry by retarding the development of the agrarian revolution and of the soviets? Yes, we did.

Did we weaken the workers with the slogan of "minimum arming" — nay, not the slogan but the polite counsel to the bourgeois tops: "Minimum arming," and "No need for soviets"?

Yes, we did. Is it to be wondered that we suffered a defeat, having done everything that could have made victory difficult?

Voroshilov[7] gave the most correct, conscientious, and candid explanation for this entire policy. "The peasant revolution," he says, "might have interfered with the northern expedition of the generals." You put a brake on the revolution for the sake of a military expedition. That is exactly how Chiang Kai-shek viewed the matter. The development of the revolution might, you see, make an expedition difficult for a "national" general. But, after all, the revolution itself is indeed an actual and a real expedition of the oppressed against the oppressors. To help the expedition of the generals, you put a brake on the revolution and disorganized it. Thereby the expedition of the generals was turned into a spearhead not only against the workers and the peasants but also — precisely because of that — against the national revolution.

Had we duly secured the complete independence of the Communist Party, assisted it to arm itself with its press and with correct tactics; had we given it the slogans "Maximum arming of the workers!" "Extend the peasant war in the villages!" the Communist Party would have grown, not from day to day, but from hour to hour, and its cadres would have been tempered in the fires of revolutionary struggle. The slogan of soviets should have been raised from the very first days of the mass movement. Everywhere, wherever the slightest possibility existed, steps for the actual realization of soviets should have been taken. Soldiers should have been drawn into the soviets. The agrarian revolution would have disorganized the pseudorevolutionary armies but it would have likewise transmitted the infection to the counterrevolutionary armies of the enemy. Only on this foundation could it have been possible to forge gradually a real revolutionary, i.e., workers' and peasants' army.

Comrades! We have heard here a speech made not by Voroshilov, the people's commissar for army and navy, but by Voroshilov, a member of the Political Bureau. This speech, I say, is in itself a catastrophe. It is equivalent to a lost battle. [*Shouts from the Opposition benches: "Correct!"*]

Last May, during the plenum of the Executive Committee of the Communist International,[8] when after finally assigning Chiang Kai-shek to the camp of reaction, you put your stakes on Wang Chin-wei, and then on Tang Cheng-chih, I wrote a letter to the ECCI. It was on May 28. "The shipwreck of this policy is absolutely inevitable." What did I propose? Here is literally what I wrote. On May 28, I wrote: "The plenum would do the right thing if it buried Bukharin's resolution, and replaced it with a resolution of a few lines. In the first place, peasants and workers should place no faith in the leaders of the Left Kuomintang but they should, instead, build their soviets jointly with the soldiers. In the second place, the soviets should arm the workers and the advanced peasants. In the third place, the Communist Party must assure its complete independence, create a daily press, and assume the leadership of creating the soviets. Fourth, the land must be immediately taken away from the landlords. Fifth, the reactionary bureaucracy must be immediately dismissed. Sixth, perfidious generals and counterrevolutionists generally must be summarily dealt with. And finally, the general course must be towards the establishment of a revolutionary dictatorship through the soviets of workers' and peasants' deputies." Now, compare this with: "There is no need for a civil war in the villages," "Do not alarm the fellow travelers," "Do not irritate the generals," "Minimum arming of the workers," and so on. This is Bolshevism! While our position is called in the Political Bureau . . . Menshevism. Having turned yourselves inside out, you have firmly resolved to call white, black. But your misfortune is that international Menshevism — from Berlin to New York — approves of the Chinese policy of Stalin-Bukharin, and being fully cognizant of the issue, solidarizes with your political line on the Chinese question.

Please try to understand that in question here is not the individual betrayals of the Chinese members of the Kuomintang, or of the right and left Chinese army commanders, or English trade unionists, and Chinese or English Communists. When one rides in the train, it is the earth that appears to be in motion. The whole trouble lies in the fact that you placed hopes on those who were not to be relied upon; you underestimated the revolutionary training of the masses, the principal requirement for which is inoculating the masses with mistrust towards reformists, vague "left" centrists, and all vacillators in general. The fullest measure of this mistrust is the supreme virtue of Bolshevism. Young parties have still to acquire and assimilate this quality. Yet you have acted and are acting in a diametrically opposite direction. You inoculate young parties with the hopes that the liberal bourgeoisie and the liberal labor politicians from the trade unions will move to the left. You hinder the education of the English and Chinese Bolsheviks. That is the source whence come these "betrayals" which each time catch you unaware.

The Opposition warned that the Chinese Communist Party under your leadership would inevitably come to Menshevist policies—for which the Opposition was at the time mercilessly condemned. It is with certainty that we now warn you that the British Communist Party, under the influence of the policies that you are foisting on it, is becoming inevitably poisoned by centrism and conciliationism. If you do not turn the helm sharply, the consequences with respect to the British Communist Party will not be any better than those with respect to the Chinese party. The same thing applies to the Comintern as a whole.

It is high time to understand that the centrism of Bukharin-Stalin is unable to withstand the test of events. [9] The greatest events in the history of mankind are revolution and war. We have put the centrist policy to the test on the Chinese revolution. The revolution demanded decisive conclusions from vacillating directives. The Chinese Communist Party found itself compelled to draw these conclusions. That is why it has arrived—and it could not have failed to do so—at Menshevism. The unprecedented collapse of your leadership in China demands that you finally repudiate the policy which compelled you under the most difficult conditions to clutch at rotten ropes.

Next to the revolution the greatest historical test is war. We say beforehand: There will be no room during the events of war for the Stalinist and Bukharinist policy of zigzags, side-stepping, and subterfuges—the policy of centrism. This applies to the entire leadership of the Comintern. Today, the only test put to the leaders of the foreign Communist parties is the question: Are you ready to vote night and day against "Trotskyism"? But war will confront them with far weightier demands. Meanwhile, the policy with respect to the Kuomintang and the Anglo-Russian Committee has obviously made them turn their eyes towards the Amsterdam and Social Democratic tops. No matter how you squirm—the line of the Anglo-Russian Committee was the line of relying upon the rotten rope of the Amsterdam bureaucracy, whose worst section at the present time is the General Council. In the event of war you will have to stumble time and again over "surprises." The rotten ropes will fall apart in your hands. War will cause a sharp differentiation among the present tops of the Comintern. A certain section will go over to the Amsterdam position under the slogan: "We want to defend the USSR seriously—we do not wish to be a handful of fanatics." Another section of the European Communists—we firmly believe they will be in the majority—will stand on the position of Lenin, on the position of Liebknecht[10] that we are defending. There will be no room for the intermediate position of Stalin. That is why, permit me to say this frankly, all this talk of a handful of Oppositionists, of generals without an army, and so forth and so on, seem utterly ludicrous to us. The Bolsheviks have heard all this more than once — both in 1914 and in 1917. We foresee tomorrow all too clearly, and we are preparing for it. Never before did the heart of the Opposition beat with such an immutable conviction of its correctness. Never before was there such unanimity as now prevails.

Zinoviev and Kamenev:[11] Absolutely correct!*

Trotsky: Nor will there be any room for the gradual centrist backsliding with respect to *internal policies* under the conditions of war. All the controversies will congeal, the class contradictions will become aggravated, the issues will be posed point-blank. It will be necessary to give clear and precise answers.

Which do we need during wartime: *"Revolutionary unity"* or *"union sacree"*? The bourgeoisie has devised for the period of war and war danger a special political condition under the name of "civil peace" or *"union sacree."* The meaning of this purely bourgeois concept is this, that the differences and squabbles of all bourgeois parties, including the Social Democracy, as well as internal disagreements within all parties must, you see, be silenced for the duration of the war — in the aim of the best possible befuddlement and deception of the masses. *"Union sacree"* is the highest form of the conspiracy of the rulers against the ruled. Needless to say, if our party has nothing to hide in the political sense from the working class during peacetime, then this is all the more true during wartime when the purity and clarity of the political line, the profundity of the ties with the masses are life-and-death questions. That is why, under the incomparably greater centralization of our party, as compared with any bourgeois party, we permitted ourselves in the heat of the civil war to discuss in the sharpest possible way and to resolve in a democratic party way, all the fundamental questions of political leadership. This was the inevitable overhead expense by means of which the party worked out and reenforced a correct line, and fortified its revolutionary unity. There are — or rather it would

---

* Zinoviev and Kamenev, as is well known, did not hold out for long. — L. T.

be more correct to say, only yesterday we still had—comrades who thought that after the death of Lenin, the absolute correctness of the leadership among us was assured to such an extent that it no longer required to be checked upon by the party. We, on the other hand, think just the contrary: today the leadership requires a checkup and a change more than ever before in the entire history of our party. What we need is not a hypocritical "*union sacree*" but honest revolutionary unity.

The shilly-shallying centrist policy cannot hold its own during wartime. It must turn either to the right or to the left, i.e., take either the Thermidorian road[12] or the road of the Opposition. [*Commotion in the hall.*]

Is victory in war possible on a Thermidorian path? Generally speaking, such a victory is not excluded. As the first step, repeal the monopoly of foreign trade. Give the kulak the opportunity of doubling the export and the import. Enable the kulak to squeeze the middle peasant. Compel the poor peasant to understand that without the kulak there is no other road. Raise and reenforce the importance of the bureaucracy, of the administration. Cast aside the demands of the workers as so much "guildism." Restrict the workers politically in the Soviets, reestablish last year's election decree and gradually extend it in favor of the property owners. That would be the road of Thermidor. Its name is—*capitalism on the installment plan.* Then at the head of the army would stand the lower commanding staff of kulaks, and the high commanding staff of intellectuals and bourgeoisie. On this road victory would signify the acceleration of the switch to the bourgeois rails.

Is victory possible on the revolutionary proletarian path? Yes, it is possible. Nor is that all. The entire world situation bespeaks the fact that victory is most assured in the event of war precisely on this path. But for that, we must first dispel the political twilight in which all cats appear to be gray. The kulak on the right—is an enemy. The agricultural laborers and poor peasants on the left—are friends. Through the poor peasant lies the road to the middle peasant. We must create a political environment which makes it impossible for the bourgeoisie and the bureaucracy to give free play to their elbows and to push the workers aside, while saying, "This is not the year 1918, my boy!" It is necessary that the working class itself be able to say: "In 1927, we are not only better fed, but politically we are greater masters of the state than in 1919." Along this road, victory is not only possible, but is most surely secured, for only on this road will we have the support of the lower classes among the people of Poland, Rumania, and the whole of Europe. . . .

Can the Stalinist centrist course give victory? The course which vacillates between both camps, which promises first to comfort the kulak, to adopt his son and to cherish his grandson, and then irresolutely passes to the creation of the groups of poor peasants; which alters the electoral decrees from year to year, i.e., the Soviet constitution, first to the side of the kulak, and then against him, and then once again in his favor as was done in Northern Caucasus; which orients itself toward Chiang Kai-shek and Wang Chin-wei, Purcell and Cook, the perfidious tops, while confusing the rank and file — can this course give victory? This course has dictated to our Political Bureau the unbelievable decree of October 29, 1926, in relation to China which made it prohibitory to introduce the civil war into the Chinese village, which made it binding not to drive away the fellow travelers or the bourgeoisie, the landlords and the generals; or that other directive with the appeal to the liberal bourgeoisie to give the workers a minimum (!!!) of arms. This course irritates or dampens the ardor of some while it fails to win over the others; it loses the "friend" Wang Chin-wei and confuses the Communists. This course signifies constant clutching at rotten ropes. During peacetime such a course might persist for an indefinite period of time. Under the conditions of war and revolution, centrism must turn the helm sharply either to the right or to the left. It is already splitting into a right and a left wing, both of which are incessantly growing at the expense of the center. This process will be inevitably speeded up; and the war, if it is thrust upon us, will invest the process with a feverish character. The Stalinist center will inevitably melt away. Under these conditions the Opposition will be needed by the party more than ever before, in order to aid the party in rectifying the line, and at the same time preventing the disruption of revolutionary unity, and preserving the party cadres, its basic capital, from being dismembered. Because the overwhelming majority of the genuinely Bolshevik proletarian cadres — with a correct policy, with a clear line, and under the compulsion of objective conditions — will be able to reconstitute the policies, and steer a firm revolutionary course, not out of fear, but from conviction. It is this, and this alone, that we are striving to achieve. The lie of conditional defensism, the lie of the two parties, and the most despicable lie of an uprising — these lies we fling back into the faces of the calumniators. [*A voice from the Opposition benches: "Hear! Hear!"*]

But does not the criticism of the Opposition reflect upon the authority of the USSR in the international labor movement?

We would never think of even posing such a question. This very posing of the question of authority is worthy of the papal church, or feudal generals. The Catholic Church demands an unquestioning recognition of its authority on the part of the faithful. The revolutionist gives his support, while criticizing, and the more undeniable is his right to criticize, all the greater is his devotion in struggling for the creation and strengthening of that in which he is a direct participant. The criticism of the Stalinist mistakes may, of course, lower the "indisputable" and puffed-up Stalinist authority. But that is not the mainstay of the revolution and of the republic. Open criticism and actual correction of mistakes will give evidence to the entire international proletariat of the inner strength of the regime, which under the most adverse conditions is able to find internal guarantees for the assurance of the correct road. In this sense, the criticism of the Opposition, and the consequences already arising from it, and which will arise to a greater degree on the morrow, in the last analysis, raises the authority of the October Revolution and strengthens it not with a blind but with a revolutionary trust of the international proletariat— and thereby raises our capacity for defense on an international scale.

The draft resolution of the Political Bureau says: "The preparation for war against the USSR signifies nothing else but the reproduction on an extended base of the class struggle between the imperialist bourgeoisie and the victorious proletariat."

Is that correct? Absolutely correct. But the resolution goes on to add: "Everyone who, like the Opposition in our party, casts doubt on this character of the war . . . etc." Does the Opposition cast doubt on this general class significance of the war? Nonsense! It does not. There is not even a hint of it. Only those can assert the contrary who have themselves become completely lost in a maze, and seek to entangle others. Does this mean, however, that the general class meaning, undeniable to all of us, should serve as a cover for any and every blunder, and backsliding? No, it does not mean this. It provides no such cover. If we take for granted a priori and forevermore that the given leadership is the only conceivable and born leadership, then every criticism of the incorrect leadership will appear as a denial of the defense of the socialist fatherland, and a call to an uprising. But such a position is a pure and simple denial of the party. According to you, in the event of war, the party will serve only for the purpose of defense. But how the defense should be carried out, will be told the party by somebody else. Or again, to put it more succinctly and plainly: Do we, the Opposition, cast any doubts on the defense of the socialist fatherland? Not in the slightest degree. It is our hope not only to participate in the defense, but to be able to teach others a few things. Do we cast doubts on Stalin's ability to sketch a correct line for defense of the socialist fatherland? We do so and, indeed, to the highest possible degree.

In his recent article in *Pravda,* Stalin poses the following question: "Is the Opposition really opposed to the victory of the USSR in the coming battles with imperialism?" Allow me to repeat this: "Is the Opposition really opposed to the victory of the USSR in the coming battles with imperialism?" We leave aside the brazen impudence of the question. We do not intend to dwell now on Lenin's carefully weighed characterization of Stalinist methods — of Stalin's rudeness and disloyalty. We will take the question as it has been posed, and give an answer to it. Only White Guards can be "opposed to the victory of the USSR in the impending battles with imperialism." The Opposition is *for* the victory of the USSR; it has proved this and will continue to prove this in action, in a manner inferior to none. But Stalin is not concerned with that. Stalin has essentially a different question in mind, which he does not dare express, namely, "Does the Opposition really think that the leadership of Stalin is incapable of assuring victory to the USSR?" Yes, we think so.

Zinoviev: Correct!

Trotsky: The Opposition thinks that the leadership of Stalin makes victory more difficult.

Molotov: And what about the party?

Trotsky: The party has been strangled by you. The Opposition thinks that the leadership of Stalin makes the victory more difficult. The Opposition insisted on that with regard to the Chinese revolution. Its warnings have been confirmed by events, to a frightful extent. It is necessary to effect a change in policy without waiting for a similar catastrophic test from within. Every Oppositionist, if he is a genuine Oppositionist and not a fraud, will assume in the event of war whatever post, at the front or behind the lines, that the party will intrust to him, and carry out his duty to the end. But not a single Oppositionist will renounce his right and his duty, on the eve of war or during the war, to fight for the correction of the party's

course—as has always been the case in our party—because
therein lies the most important condition for victory. To sum
up. For the socialist fatherland? Yes! For the Stalinist course?
No!

PART THREE

Preparing Anew

begins in 1929 and follows the exiled revolutionary through Turkey, France, Norway, and Mexico as he explains the causes of the degeneration of the October Revolution; establishes the movement that becomes the Fourth International; seeks to mobilize a revolutionary struggle against war and fascism; refutes the charges leveled against him in the Moscow trials and offers to turn himself over to the GPU if an independent commission of inquiry finds him guilty; and concludes with the testament he writes in 1940, half a year before he is assassinated by an agent of Stalin.

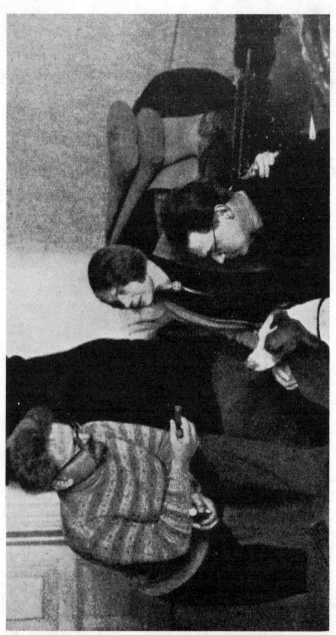

Trotsky, Natalia, and Leon Sedov in Alma-Ata.

13

Open Letter to the Workers of the USSR

To tell the world for the first time his version of the bitter struggle inside the Soviet Union and his expulsion from that country, Trotsky wrote a series of articles soon after he reached Turkey and sold them to major newspapers and magazines throughout the world. In the United States they were translated in The New York Times *and* The New Republic. *They were also published in Russian in Paris as a pamphlet under the title of* What Happened and How. *The Soviet press immediately began a furious campaign against Trotsky, pointing to the publication of the articles in the capitalist press as evidence that Trotsky had "sold himself to the world bourgeoisie and [was] conspiring against the Soviet Union." Soviet cartoons showed "Mr. Trotsky" receiving sacks of dollars. Trotsky made a reply to the slanders in an open letter to the workers in the Soviet Union.*

It is reprinted here from The Militant, *May 1-15, 1929.*

Dear Comrades:

I write to you in order to tell you again that Stalin, Yaroslavsky,[1] et al. are deceiving you. They say that I made use of the bourgeois press in order to carry on a struggle against the Soviet Republic, in whose creation and defense I worked hand in hand with Lenin. They are deceiving you. I used the bourgeois press in order to defend the interests of the Soviet Republic against the lies, trickery, and perfidy of Stalin and Company.

They ask you to condemn my articles. Have you read them? No, you have not read them. They are giving you a false translation of separate fragments. My articles have been published in the Russian language in a special booklet in exactly the form in which I wrote them. Demand that Stalin reprint them without abbreviations or falsifications. He dare not do it. He fears the truth more than anything else. Here I want to summarize the contents of my articles.

1. In the resolution of the GPU [2] as to my banishment it states that I am conducting "preparations for an armed struggle against the Soviet Republic." In *Pravda* (No. 41, February 19, 1929) the statement about armed struggle was omitted. Why? Why did Stalin not dare repeat in *Pravda* what was said in the resolution of the GPU? Because he knew that no one would believe him. After the history of the Wrangel officer, [3] after the exposure of the agent provocateur sent by Stalin to the Oppositionists with the proposal of a military plot, no one will believe that the Bolshevik-Leninists, desiring to convince the party of the correctness of their views, are preparing an armed struggle. That is why Stalin did not dare print in *Pravda* what was stated in the resolution of the GPU of January 18.

But if that is true, why introduce this obvious lie into the resolution of the GPU? Not for the USSR but for Europe, and for the whole outside world. Through the Tass agency Stalin systematically and daily cooperates with the bourgeois press of the whole world, propagating his slander against the Bolshevik-Leninists. Stalin can in no other way explain this banishment and his innumerable arrests, except by accusing the Opposition of preparing an armed struggle. With this monstrous lie he has done enormous harm to the Soviet Republic. The whole bourgeois press has discussed the fact that Trotsky, Rakovsky, Smilga, Radek, I. N. Smirnov, Beloborodov, Muralov, Mrachkovsky, [4] and many others who built the Soviet Republic and defended it, are now preparing an armed struggle against the Soviet power. It is obvious how such an idea must weaken the Soviet Republic in the eyes of the whole world. In order to justify his repressions, Stalin is compelled to compose these monstrous legends, doing incalculable harm to the Soviet power. That is why I considered it necessary to appear in the bourgeois press and say to the whole world: It is not true that the Opposition intends to wage an armed struggle against the Soviet power. The Opposition has waged and will wage a ruthless struggle *for* the Soviet power against all its enemies. This declaration of mine has been printed in newspapers with a circulation of tens of millions in all the languages of the world. It will serve to strengthen the Soviet Republic. Stalin wants to strengthen his position at the expense of the Soviet Republic. I want to strengthen the Soviet Republic by exposing the lies of the Stalinists.

2. Stalin and his press have for a long time been propagating the statement all over the world that I declare the Soviet Republic has become a bourgeois state, that the proletarian power is wrecked, etc. In Russia, many workers know that this is a vicious slander, that it is founded on falsified quotations. I have exposed these falsifications dozens of times in letters which have been circulated from hand to hand. But the outside bourgeois press believes them, or pretends to believe them. All these counterfeit Stalinist quotations appear in the columns of the newspapers of the world as a demonstration of the assertion that Trotsky considers the fall of the Soviet power inevitable. Thanks to the enormous interest of international public opinion, and especially that of the broad popular masses, in what is being created in the Soviet Republic, the bourgeois press, impelled by its business interests, its desire for circulation, the demands of its readers, was compelled to print my articles. In those articles I said to the whole world that the Soviet power, in spite of the misleading policies of the Stalin leadership, is deeply rooted in the masses, is very powerful, and will outlive its enemies.

You must not forget that the overwhelming majority of the workers in Europe, and especially in America, still read the bourgeois press. I made it a condition that my articles should be printed without the slightest change. It is true that certain papers in a few countries violated this condition, but the majority fulfilled it. In any case all the papers were compelled to publish the fact that, in spite of the lies and slanders of the Stalinists, Trotsky is convinced of the deep inner power of the Soviet regime, and firmly believes that the workers will succeed by peaceful measures in changing the present false policy of the Central Committee.

In the spring of 1917, Lenin, imprisoned inside Switzerland, employed a "sealed train"[5] of the Hohenzollerns in order to get to the Russian workers. The chauvinist press attacked Lenin, going so far as to call him a German agent, and address him as Herr Lenin. Imprisoned by the Thermidorians in Constantinople I employed the bourgeois press as a sealed train in order to speak the truth to the whole world. The attacks of the Stalinists against "Mr. Trotsky," stupid in their intemperance, are nothing but a repetition of the bourgeois

and Social Revolutionary attacks upon "Herr Lenin." Like
Lenin I regard with tranquil contempt the public opinion of
the philistines and bureaucrats whose spirit Stalin represents.

3. I told in my articles, distorted and falsified by Yaroslavsky, how, why, and under what circumstances I was banished
from the USSR. The Stalinists are propagating rumors in
the European press to the effect that I was permitted to leave
Russia at my own request. I exposed this lie. I told how I
was sent over the border forcibly after a preliminary agreement between Stalin and the Turkish police. And here I acted
not only in the interests of my own personal defense against
slander, but first of all in the interests of the Soviet Republic.
If the Oppositionists really desired to leave the borders of
the Soviet Union, that would be understood by the whole world
as a sign that they considered the situation of the Soviet government hopeless. We have not the shadow of such a thought.
The Stalinist policies have dealt a terrible blow not only to
the Chinese revolution, the English working-class movement,
and the whole Comintern, but also to the inner stability of
the Soviet regime. That is indisputable. However, the situation is not in the least hopeless. The Opposition in no case
intends to fly from Soviet Russia. I categorically refused to
cross the border, proposing instead that they should imprison
me. The Stalinists did not dare resort to that measure; they
were afraid that the workers would insistently demand my
liberation. They preferred to make a bargain with the Turkish police, and they transported me to Constantinople by main
force. This I explained to the whole world. Every thinking
worker will say that if Stalin through Tass daily feeds the
bourgeois press with slanders against the Opposition, then
I was obliged to publish a refutation of these slanders.

4. In tens of millions of newspapers I told the whole world
that it was not the Russian workers who exiled me, nor the
Russian peasants, nor the Soviet Red Guards, nor those with
whom we conquered power and fought shoulder to shoulder
on all fronts in the civil war. It was the bureaucrats who exiled me, people who have got the power into their hands and
converted themselves into a bureaucratic caste bound together
by a solidarity of privilege. In order to defend the October
Revolution, the Soviet Republic, and the revolutionary name
of the Bolshevik-Leninists, I told the whole world the truth
about Stalin and the Stalinists. I reminded them again that
Lenin in his maturely considered testament[6] described Stalin
as *disloyal.* That word is understood in all the languages
of the world. It means an untrustworthy or dishonest man

who is guided in his activities by bad motives, a man whom you cannot trust. That is how Lenin characterized Stalin, and we see again how correct Lenin's warning was. There is no worse crime for a revolutionist than to deceive his party, to poison with lies the mind of the working class. And that is at present Stalin's chief occupation. He is deceiving the Comintern and the international working class, attributing to the Opposition counterrevolutionary intentions and activities in relation to Soviet power. Exactly because of his inward inclination to that kind of activity, Lenin called Stalin disloyal. Exactly for that reason, Lenin proposed to the party that Stalin be removed from his post. So much the more necessary now, after all that has happened, to explain to the whole world what Stalin's disloyalty consists of—that is, his perfidy and dishonesty in relation to the Opposition.

5. The slanderers (Yaroslavsky and the other agents of Stalin) are raising a hullabaloo on the subject of American dollars. Otherwise it would hardly be worthwhile to stoop to this rubbish. But the most vicious bourgeois newspapers take satisfaction in spreading Yaroslavsky's dirt. In order to leave nothing unclear I will therefore tell you about the dollars.

I gave my articles to an American press agency in Paris. Lenin and I, dozens of times, have given interviews and written expositions of our views on one question or another to such agencies. Thanks to my banishment and the mysterious circumstances of it, the interest in this matter throughout the world was colossal. The agency counted on a good profit. It offered me half the income. I answered that I personally would not take a cent, but that the agency should deliver, at my direction, a half of its income from my articles, and that with this money I will publish in the Russian language and in foreign languages a whole series of Lenin's writings (his speeches, articles, letters) which are suppressed in the Soviet Republic by the Stalinist censorship. I will also use this money to publish a whole series of important party documents (reports of conferences, congresses, letters, articles, etc.) which are concealed from the party because they clearly demonstrate the theoretical and political bankruptcy of Stalin. This is the "counterrevolutionary" (according to Stalin and Yaroslavsky) literature which I intend to publish. An accurate account of the sums expended in this way will be published when the time comes. Every worker will say that it is infinitely better to publish the writings of Lenin with money received in the form of an accidental contribution from the bourgeoisie than to propagate slanders against the Bolshevik-Leninists with money collected from the Russian workers and peasants.

Do not forget, comrades: the testament of Lenin remains as before in Russia a counterrevolutionary document, for the circulation of which you are arrested and exiled. And that is not accidental. Stalin is waging a struggle against Leninism on an international scale. There remains hardly one country in the world where at the head of the Communist Party today stand those revolutionists who led the party in the days of Lenin. They are almost all expelled from the Communist International. Lenin guided the first four congresses of the Comintern. Together with Lenin I drew up all the fundamental documents of the Comintern. At the Fourth Congress, in 1922, Lenin divided equally with me the fundamental report on the New Economic Policy and the Perspectives of the International Revolution. After the death of Lenin, almost all the participants, at any rate all without exception of the influential participants of the first four congresses, were expelled from the Comintern. Everywhere in the world at the heads of the Communist parties stand new, accidental people, who arrived yesterday from the camp of our opponents and enemies. In order to adopt an anti-Leninist policy, it was necessary first to overthrow the Leninist leadership. Stalin has done this, relying upon the bureaucracy, upon new petty-bourgeois circles, upon the state apparatus, upon the GPU, and upon the financial resources of the state. This has been carried through not only in the USSR, but also in Germany, in France, in Italy, in Belgium, in the United States, in the Scandinavian countries — in a word, in almost every country in the world.

Only a blind man could fail to understand the meaning of the fact that the closest colleagues and comrades-in-arms of Lenin in the Russian Communist Party and the whole Comintern, all the leaders of the Communist parties in the first hard years, all the participants and leaders of the first four congresses, almost to a man, have been removed from their posts, slandered and expelled. This mad struggle with the Leninist leadership was necessary to the Stalinists in order to carry through an anti-Leninist policy.

When they were hounding the Bolshevik-Leninists, they reassured the party by saying that it would now be monolithic. You know that the party is now more divided than ever. And this is not the end. There is no salvation on the Stalinist road. You can adopt either an Ustrialovist[7] — that is a consistently Thermidorian policy — or a Leninist policy. The centrist position of Stalin inevitably leads to an accumulation of enormous economic and political difficulties and to the continual decimation and destruction of the party.

It is still not too late to alter the course. It is necessary abruptly to change the policy and the party regime in the spirit of the Opposition platform. It is necessary to put an end to the shameful persecution of the best revolutionary Leninists in the Communist Party of the Soviet Union and in the whole world. It is necessary to restore the Leninist leadership. It is necessary to condemn and root out the disloyal, that is, untrustworthy and dishonest, methods of the Stalin apparatus. The Opposition is ready with all its might to help the proletarian kernel of the party to fulfill this vital task. Rabid persecution, dishonest slanders, and governmental repressions cannot dim our loyalty to the October Revolution or to the international party of Lenin. We will remain true to them both to the end — in the Stalinist prisons, in exile, and in banishment.

With Bolshevik greetings,
Leon Trotsky

Constantinople
March 27, 1929

14

Interview from Prinkipo

The Trotskys sought asylum in several European countries but none would grant them visas so they remained in Turkey, finding refuge on the island of Prinkipo in the sea of Marmora, one and a half hours by boat from Constantinople. They lived in Turkey for four and a half years.

In 1929 Trotsky began to publish the Russian-language Bulletin of the Opposition, *which printed all of his principal shorter writings until his death, and to write several of his most important books. He made contact with supporters of the Left Opposition in several European countries, the United States, Canada, China, and parts of Latin America. By 1930 they were able to unite as the International Left Opposition, which regarded itself as a faction of the Communist International fighting for the regeneration of the Comintern on a Leninist basis.*

Many visitors crossed the sea of Marmora to see Trotsky, including journalists seeking interviews. One of these, representing the British publication Manchester Guardian, *came to Prinkipo in 1931, when Trotsky was writing* The History of the Russian Revolution.

Trotsky was out fishing and the journalist waited until his return. "He wears waterproof boots to his knees and a Sherlock Holmes cap, with the flaps meeting under his chin, to ward off the spray. It is now nearly two o'clock and he has been fishing since five this morning. Though he is over fifty years old, he springs ashore lightly and leads us to the house. . . . We agree that the best way to avoid distortion is to decide beforehand what questions will be of chief interest to our readers, and then to write down Trotsky's replies as a continuous narrative. Soon he sets to work, dictating in a musical mixture of French and German."

The interview was run in two parts, "The Five-Year Plan and the World" and "America Discovers the World," in the Manchester Guardian *of February 27 and 28, 1931.*

Fishing was Trotsky's chief form of recreation on Prinkipo.

World opinion on the Five-Year Plan[1] has consisted until recently of two fundamental assertions that are absolutely contradictory: first, that the Five-Year Plan is utopian and that the Soviet state is on the verge of economic failure; secondly, that Soviet export trade involves dumping, which threatens to upset the pillars of the capitalist order. Either of these two assertions can be used as a weapon with which to belabor the Soviet state, but together they have the great disadvantage of being radically opposed to one another. To upset capitalist economy by offering goods at low prices would require an unprecedented development of productive forces. If the Five-Year Plan has suffered a check and Soviet economy is gradually disintegrating, on what economic battlefield can the Soviet Union marshal its ranks to open a dumping offensive against the most powerful capitalistic states in the world?

Which, then, of these two contradictory assertions is correct? Both of them are false. The Five-Year Plan has not suffered a check; this is demonstrated by the efforts to transform it into a Four-Year Plan. Personally I regard this attempt at acceleration as premature and ill-judged. But the mere fact that it is possible, the fact that hundreds of Soviet economists, engineers, works directors, and trade unionists have admitted the possibility of such a transformation, shows that the plan is far from being the failure it is declared to be by those observers in Paris, London, and New York who are accustomed to study Russian affairs through a telescope.

But suppose we admit that this gigantic plan may become a reality, should we not, then, admit the possibility of dumping in the near future? Let us consult statistics. Industrialization in the USSR is increasing at the rate of 20 to 30 percent per annum — a phenomenon unparalleled in economic history. But these percentages indicate a rise from the economic level that the Soviet Union inherited from the former owning class, a level of appalling backwardness. In the most important branches of its economy the Soviet Union will remain, even after the realization of the Five-Year Plan, far behind the more advanced capitalist states. For instance, the average consumption of coal per person in the USSR will be eight times less than it is in the U. S. A. today. Other figures are more or less analogous. At the present time — that is, during the third year of the Five-Year Plan — Soviet exports represent about 1 1/2 percent of the world's export trade. What percentage would suffice, in the opinion of those who fear dumping, to upset the balance of world trade? Fifty percent, perhaps, 25 percent, 10 percent? To attain even the last figure Soviet exports would

have to increase seven- or eightfold, thereby instantly causing
the ruin of Russian domestic economy. This consideration
alone, based as it is on undisputed statistics, demonstrates
the falseness of the philippics of such men as the Locker-
Lampsons in England and Representative Fish in America.[2]
It matters not whether such philippics are the product of bad
faith or of sincere panic; in either case, they are deceiving
the public when they assert that Soviet economy is failing
and at the same time claim that enough Russian goods can
be sold abroad below cost price to menace the world market.

The most recent form of attack called forth by the Five-Year
Plan appeared in the French newspaper, *Le Temps,* which
pursues the same aims as the British diehards and may without exaggeration be described as one of the most reactionary
papers in the world. Not long ago this journal drew attention
to the rapid advance being made in the industrialization of
the USSR, and called on all the Western states to coordinate
their economies for the purpose of boycotting Soviet trade.
In this instance there was no question of dumping; the rapidity
with which economic development is occurring was in itself
considered a menace to be opposed by vigorous measures.
One point should be emphasized: in order to remain effective, an economic blockade would have to become more and
more stringent, and this would eventually lead to war. But
even if a blockade were established and war ensued, and even
if the Soviet system were overthrown by such a war—which
I do not for a moment consider possible—even then the new
economic principle of state planning that has proved its efficacy
in the Soviet system would not be destroyed. Such a course
would merely result in sacrificing many lives and arresting
the development of Europe for decades.

But to return to our former question: Will the Five-Year
Plan be realized? First we must know just what we mean by
"realization," and this is not a matter that can be determined
with minute precision, like a sporting record. I see the Five-
Year Plan as a working hypothesis used as the basis of a
gigantic experiment whose results cannot be expected to coincide exactly with the hypothesis. The relations between the
various ramifications of an economy over a period of years
cannot be established a priori with any exactitude. Compensa-
tory corrections must be made during the progress of the work
itself. However, I am certainly of the opinion that, allowing
for necessary corrections and alterations, the Five-Year Plan
is realizable.

You ask wherein my opinion on this matter differs from

that of the present Soviet government. Let us set aside entirely the political question and the question of the Communist International, since these matters have no bearing on the use of large-scale hypothetical perspectives in economic planning. On the contrary, for several years I defended this method against those who now apply it. I am of the opinion that the Five-Year Plan should have been undertaken earlier. It should be mentioned here that the first projects for the plan envisaged an annual increase starting at 9 percent and gradually dropping to 4 percent. It was against the diminution, which was then sponsored by the Stalin-Rykov group,[3] that the Opposition raised a vehement protest. That is why it was accused of super-industrialization. As a result of our criticism, the second project, elaborated in 1927, provided for an average annual increase of 9 percent. The Opposition found this figure wholly inadequate in view of the possibilities inherent in a nationalized economy. Capitalist industry in czarist Russia yielded nearly a mean 12 percent of profit, of which one-half was consumed by the owners while the other half was used to increase production. Now, under nationalization, almost the entire 12 percent can be used to increase production. To this must be added the savings effected by the absence of competition, the centralization of works according to a unified plan, unity of financing, and other factors. If a well organized trust enjoys an enormous advantage over isolated industrial enterprises, what must be the advantage of a nationalized industry, a veritable trust of trusts? This is why, from 1922 on, I based the possible yearly increase of industry at over 20 percent. This percentage, indeed, finally became accepted as the basis of the Five-Year Plan, and experience has not only proved the soundness of this hypothetical calculation, but shown that it is likely to be exceeded.

Under the influence of this success, for which the present leadership itself was unprepared, there has been a tendency to go to the opposite extreme. Though Russia is not sufficiently prepared for it, the realization of the plan in four years is being attempted, and the task is pursued almost as a problem in sport. I am wholly opposed to this excess of bureaucratic maximalism, which imperils the large-scale increase of nationalized industry. In the course of the last year I have several times issued a warning against speeding up the collectivization of agriculture too much. Thus the roles now seem to be exchanged: the Left Opposition, which for years struggled for industrialization and collectivization, now feels itself duty-bound to apply the brakes. Moreover, I consider the attitude of those

officials who talk as if Russia had already entered into socialism with the third year of the Five-Year Plan as false and
likely to prejudice their reputations. No, Russian economy is
still in a transitional stage, and conceals within itself wide
contradictions that may possibly lead to economic crises and
temporary setbacks. To shut one's eyes to this would be un-
forgivable. I cannot here go more closely into this complex
question, but it should be recognized that all these contradictions, difficulties, possible crises, and setbacks in no degree
minimize the epoch-making significance of this gigantic experiment in economic planning, which already has proved
that a nationalized industry, even in a backward country, can
increase at a tempo that none of the old civilized nations could
possibly attempt. This alone transforms the lesson of the past
and opens up an entirely new perspective.

As an illustration of what I mean, let us take a hypothetical
example. In England Mr. Lloyd George is promoting a plan
of public undertakings worked out by Liberal economists with
the double object of liquidating unemployment and of
reorganizing and rationalizing industry. Now let us suppose,
for purposes of demonstration, that the British government
were to sit at a round table with the government of the USSR
in order to work out a plan of economic cooperation over a
series of years. Let us suppose that this plan embraced all
the most important branches of the economy of the
two countries and that the conference, unlike many others,
resulted in concrete, cut-and-dried mutual agreements and undertakings: for such and such a number of tractors, electro-technical
units, textile machines, and so forth, England would receive
an equivalent quantity of grain, timber, perhaps later, raw
cotton — all, naturally, according to the prices current on the
world market. This plan would begin modestly but would
develop like an inverse cone, coming in the course of the years
to include an ever-larger number of undertakings so that
ultimately the most important economic branches in both
countries would dovetail into one another like the bones of the
skull. Can one doubt for a moment that, on the one hand,
the coefficient of increase now contemplated by the Soviet government would, with the help of British technique, be vastly
increased; and that, on the other, the Soviet Union would
enable Great Britain to satisfy her most vital importing needs
under the most favorable conditions? It is impossible to say
under what political auspices such collaboration would be
possible. But when I take the principle of a centralized economic
plan as it is being carried out today in a poor and backward

country and apply it in imagination to the mutual relations of the advanced nations with the Soviet Union and with one another, I see therein a spacious outlook for mankind.

The most striking feature of American life during the last quarter century has been the unprecedented growth of economic power and the equally unprecedented weakening of the political mechanism in the face of that power. Two episodes — one from the past, the other from the present — will illustrate what I mean. Perhaps the most important, and certainly the most vigorous activity of Theodore Roosevelt,[4] who ranks as the most noteworthy of recent presidents, was his struggle against the trusts. What remains of that activity today? Vague memories among the older generation. The struggles of Roosevelt and the enactment of restrictive legislation were followed by the present formidable expansion of the trusts.

Now consider President Hoover.[5] To him the trusts form almost as natural a part of the social system as material production itself. Hoover, who is credited with the possession of an engineering mind, believed that the powerful trusts, on the one hand, and the standardization of production, on the other, would be instruments capable of assuring uninterrupted economic development, free from any crisis. His spirit of engineering optimism pervaded, as is well known, the Hoover Commission's investigation of recent economic changes in the United States. The report of the commission, which was signed by seventeen apparently competent American economists, including Hoover himself, appeared in 1929. But a few months before the greatest crisis in American history Hoover's report painted a picture of untroubled economic progress.

Roosevelt sought to dominate the trusts; Hoover sought to dominate the crisis by giving rein to the trusts, which he considered the highest expression of American individualism. The significance of these two failures differs, but both the engineering prudence of Hoover and the obstreperous impulsiveness of Roosevelt reveal a helpless empiricism in the fundamental problems of social life.

The approach of an acute crisis was for long easily perceptible. The Hoover Commission might have found weighty economic advice in the Russian press had it not been so laden with self-sufficiency. I myself wrote in the summer of 1928: "We cannot help but believe that a crisis will follow the present world swing of American capitalism, and that this crisis may be both deep and acute. But to assume that this approaching crisis will result in a weakening of the North American hegemony would be altogether foolish and could lead only to the grossest errors in political strategy. Exactly the opposite will occur: in a time of crisis the hegemony of the United States will prove more complete, more brutal, more merciless than in a time of upward swing. The United States will conquer her difficulties at the expense of Europe." [6]

It must be admitted that only that part of this forecast has been fulfilled which deals with the imminence of a crisis, and not that part which prophesies an aggressive economic policy toward Europe on the part of the United States. In regard to this I can only say that the transatlantic empire is reacting more slowly than I anticipated in 1928. I remember, during a meeting of the Soviet for Work and Defense in July 1924, exchanging some short notes with the late Leonid Krassin, [7] who had just then returned from England. I wrote him that in no case should I have confidence in so-called Anglo-Saxon solidarity, which was merely a verbal remnant of war coop- eration, and would shortly be torn to shreds by economic reality. He answered me as follows (I have the note still — a leaf torn out of a notebook): "I regard increasing friction be- tween England and America in the immediate future as improbable. You cannot imagine how provincial the Americans are in regard to world politics. Not for years yet will they dare to quarrel with England." I replied: "With a checkbook in his pocket even a provincial will soon enough find occasion to behave like a man of the world."

Certainly it cannot be disputed that the Americans have no experience or training in "Weltpolitik"; they have grown too quickly, and their views have not kept up with their bank accounts. But the history of humanity, and especially English history, has amply illustrated how world hegemony is at- tained. The provincial visits the capitals of the Old World, and he reflects. Now the material basis of the United States is on a scale heretofore unknown. The potential preponderance of the United States in the world market is far greater than was the actual preponderance of Great Britain in the most flourishing days of her world hegemony — let us say the third quarter of the nineteenth century. This potential strength must inevitably transfer itself into kinetic form, and the world will one day witness a great outburst of Yankee truculence in every sector of our planet. The historian of the future will inscribe in his books: "The famous crisis of 1930-3-? was a turning point in the whole history of the United States in that it evoked such a reorientation of spiritual and political aims that the old Monroe Doctrine, 'America for the Americans,' came to be superseded by a new doctrine, 'The Whole World for the Americans.'"

The blustering militarism of the German Hohenzollerns at the end of the nineteenth and the beginning of the twentieth centuries, which rose with the yeast of the rapid development of capitalism, will appear as child's play before that accompanying the growing capitalist activity of the United States. Of Wilson's Fourteen Points,[8] which even at the moment of their formulation possessed no real content, there will remain still less, if that be possible, than remains of Roosevelt's fight against the trusts. Today dominant America has not yet extricated herself from the perplexing situation caused by the crisis, but this state of affairs will pass. It will be followed by an effort on her part to safeguard in every corner of the world positions that will act as safety valves against a new crisis. The chapter of her economic expansion may, perhaps, begin with China, but this will in no way hinder her from expanding in other directions.

The so-called "limitation of armaments" stands in no sort of contradiction to the forecasts outlined above, certainly not in contradiction to the direct interests of America. It is entirely obvious that a reduction of armaments prior to a conflict between two nations benefits the stronger far more than the weaker. The last war showed that hostilities between industrial nations last not months but years, and that war is waged not so much with weapons prepared beforehand as with those forged during the combat. Consequently, the economically stronger of two nations has an interest in limiting the military preparedness of its prospective opponent. The preponderance of standardized and "trustified" industry in the United States is capable, when deflected to war production, of endowing that country during a war with such a preeminence as we can today scarcely imagine.

From this standpoint parity of navies is in fact no parity. It is a predominance assured beforehand to the one backed by the stronger industry. Quite apart from all possible doctrines, political programs, sympathies, and antipathies, I believe that the naked facts and cold logic keep us from considering accords over parity of fleets or any agreements of a like kind as guarantees of peace or, indeed, as even any lessening of war danger. If a pair of duelists or their seconds agree beforehand on the caliber of the revolvers, it in no way prevents one of them from being killed.

Mr. MacDonald esteems the results achieved on his American journey as the loftiest triumph of peace politics. As I am speaking here in an interview, wherein one does not so much explain one's opinion as proclaim it, I shall allow myself to turn to a speech that I made in 1924 about the relations between America and Europe. At that time, if I remember aright, Curzon was foreign minister[9] and was engaging in saber-rattling against Soviet Russia. In a polemic against Lord Curzon (which now, of course, has lost all political interest) I observed that he was only treading on Russia's heels in consequence of the unsatisfactory position in which England was being placed by the growing power of the United States and by the world situation generally. His protests against Soviet Russia were to be interpreted as the result of his dissatisfaction at having to negotiate accords with the United States that were not of equal advantage to both parties. "When it comes to the point," I said, "it will not be Lord Curzon who will execute this unpleasant task; he is too spirited. No, it will be entrusted to MacDonald. All the pious eloquence of MacDonald, Henderson, and the Fabians will be needed to make that capitulation acceptable."[10]

You ask me what my conclusions are? But I do not feel obliged to draw any in this interview. Conclusions are a matter of practical politics and therefore depend upon one's program and the social interests behind it. In these respects your newspaper and I differ very much. That is why I have confined myself scrupulously to facts and processes, which, since they are indisputable, must be taken into account by any and every program that is realistic and not fantastical. These facts and processes tell us that the next epoch will develop beneath the shadow of powerful capitalist aggression on the part of the United States. In the third quarter of the fifteenth century Europe discovered America; in the second quarter of the twentieth century America will discover the world. Her policy will be that of the open door, which, as is well known, opens not inward but only outward in America.

15

In Defense of the Russian Revolution

In the autumn of 1932 a Danish Social Democratic student group invited Trotsky to speak in Copenhagen on the fifteenth anniversary of the Russian Revolution. Trotsky welcomed the opportunity to go abroad although he and Natalia were in Copenhagen for only a little over a week, and the entire trip away from Prinkipo fell short of a month.

The speech was given on November 27, 1932, before an audience of around two thousand, his only speech before a large audience in the eleven years of his last exile.

Isaac Deutscher reports in The Prophet Outcast: *"As the authorities had allowed the lecture on the condition that he would avoid controversy, he spoke in a somewhat professorial manner, giving the audience the quintessence of the three volumes of his just concluded* History. *His restraint did not conceal the depth and force of his conviction; the address was a vindication of the October Revolution, all the more effective because free of apologetics and frankly acknowledging partial failures and mistakes. Nearly twenty-five years later members of the audience still recalled the lecture with vivid appreciation as an oratorical feat."*

The translation is from a Pioneer Publishers' pamphlet of the same title published in 1933.

Permit me to begin by expressing my sincere regrets over my inability to speak before a Copenhagen audience in the Danish tongue. Let us not ask whether the listeners lose by it. As to the speaker, his ignorance of the Danish language deprives him of the possibility of familiarizing himself with Scandinavian life and Scandinavian literature immediately, at first hand and in the original. And that is a great loss.

The German language, to which I have had to take recourse, is rich and powerful. My German, however, is fairly limited. To discuss complicated questions with the necessary freedom, moreover, is possible only in one's own language. I must therefore beg the indulgence of the audience in advance.

The first time that I was in Copenhagen was at the International Socialist Congress, and I took away with me the kindest recollections of your city. But that was over a quarter of a century ago. Since then, the water in the Ore Sund and in the fjords has changed over and over again. And not the water alone. The war broke the backbone of the old European continent. The rivers and seas of Europe have washed down not a little blood. Mankind, and particularly European mankind, has gone through severe trials, has become more somber and more brutal. Every kind of conflict has become more bitter. The world has entered into the period of the great change. Its most extreme expressions are *war* and *revolution*.

Before I pass on to the theme of my lecture, the revolution, I consider it my duty to express my thanks to the organizers of this meeting, the Copenhagen organization of the Social Democratic student body. I do this as a political opponent. My lecture, it is true, pursues historico-scientific and not political aims. I want to emphasize this right from the beginning. But it is impossible to speak of a revolution, out of which the Soviet Republic arose, without taking up a political position. As a lecturer I stand under the same banner as I did when I participated in the events of the revolution.

Up to the war, the Bolshevik Party belonged to the International Social Democracy. On August 4, 1914, the vote of the German Social Democracy for the war credits put an end to this connection once and for all, and opened the period of uninterrupted and irreconcilable struggle of Bolshevism against Social Democracy. Does this mean that the organizers of this assembly made a mistake in inviting me as a lecturer? On this point the audience will be able to judge only after my lecture. To justify my acceptance of the kind invitation to present a report on the Russian Revolution, permit me to point to the fact that during the thirty-five years of my political life the question of the Russian Revolution has been the practical and theoretical axis of my interests and of my actions. The four years of my stay in Turkey were principally devoted to the historical elaboration of the problems of the Russian Revolution. Perhaps this fact gives me a certain right to hope that I will succeed, in part at least, in helping not only friends and sympathizers, but also opponents, better to understand many features of the revolution which had escaped their attention before. At all events, the purpose of my lecture is: *to help to understand.* I do not intend to conduct propaganda for the revolution nor to call upon you to join the revolution. I intend to explain the revolution.

I do not know if in the Scandinavian Olympus there was a special goddess of rebellion. Scarcely! In any case, we shall not call upon her favor today. We shall place our lecture under the sign of Snotra, the old goddess of knowledge. Despite the passionate drama of the revolution as a living event, we shall endeavor to treat it as dispassionately as an anatomist. If the lecturer is drier because of it, the listeners will, let us hope, take it into the bargain.

Let us begin with some elementary sociological principles, which are doubtless familiar to you all, but as to which we must refresh our memory in approaching so complicated a phenomenon as the revolution.

Human society is an historically originated collaboration in the struggle for existence and the assurance of the maintenance of the generations. The character of a society is determined by the character of its economy. The character of its economy is determined by its means of productive labor.

For every great epoch in the development of the productive forces there is a definite corresponding social regime. Every social regime until now has secured enormous advantages to the ruling class.

Out of what has been said, it is clear that social regimes are not eternal. They arise historically, and then become fetters on further progress. "All that arises deserves to be destroyed."

But no ruling class has ever voluntarily and peacefully abdicated. In questions of life and death arguments based on reason have never replaced the argument of force. This may be sad, but it is so. It is not we that have made this world. We can do nothing but take it as it is.

Revolution means a change of the social order. It transfers the power from the hands of a class which has exhausted itself into those of another class which is on the rise. The insurrection is the sharpest and most critical moment in the struggle of two classes for power. The insurrection can lead to the real victory of the revolution and to the establishment of a new order only when it is based on a progressive class, which is able to rally around it the overwhelming majority of the people.

As distinguished from the processes of nature, a revolution is made by human beings and through human beings. But in the course of revolution, too, men act under the influence of social conditions which are not freely chosen by them, but are handed down from the past and imperatively point out the road which they must follow. For this reason, and only for this reason, a revolution follows certain laws.

But human consciousness does not merely passively reflect its objective conditions. It is accustomed to react to them actively. At certain times this reaction assumes a tense, passionate, mass character. The barriers of right and might are broken down. The active intervention of the masses in historical events is in fact the most indispensable element of a revolution.

But even the stormiest activity can remain in the stage of demonstration or rebellion, without rising to the height of revolution. The uprising of the masses must lead to the overthrow of the domination of one class and to the establishment of the domination of another. Only then have we a whole revolution. A mass uprising is no isolated undertaking, which can be conjured up any time one pleases. It represents an objectively conditioned element in the development of a revolution, as a revolution represents an objectively conditioned process in the development of society. But if the necessary conditions for the uprising exist, one must not simply wait passively, with open mouth. As Shakespeare says, "There is a tide in the affairs of men which, taken at the flood, leads on to fortune."

To sweep away the outlived social order, the progressive class must understand that its hour has struck, and set before itself the task of conquering power. Here opens the field of conscious revolutionary action, where foresight and calculation combine with will and courage. In other words: here opens the field of action of the party.

The revolutionary party unites within itself the flower of the progressive class. Without a party which is able to orientate itself in its environment, evaluate the progress and rhythm of events, and early win the confidence of the masses, the victory of the proletarian revolution is impossible. These are the reciprocal relations of the objective and the subjective factors in insurrection and in revolution.

In disputations, particularly theological ones, it is customary, as you know, for the opponents to discredit scientific truth by driving it to an absurdity. This method is called in logic "reductio ad absurdum." We shall try to pursue the opposite method: that is, we shall start from an absurdity so as to approach the truth with all the greater safety. In any case, we cannot complain of lack of absurdities. Let us take one of the freshest and crassest.

The Italian writer, Malaparte, who is something in the nature of a fascist theoretician—there are such, too—not long ago launched a book on the technique of the coup d'etat. Naturally, the author devotes not an inconsiderable number of pages of his "investigation" to the October upheaval.

In contradistinction to the "strategy" of Lenin, which remained tied up with the social and political conditions of Russia in 1917, "the tactics of Trotsky," in Malaparte's words, "were, on the contrary, not tied up with the general conditions of the country." This is the main idea of the book! Malaparte compels Lenin and Trotsky, in the pages of his book, to carry on numerous dialogues in which both participants together show as much profundity as nature put at the disposal of Malaparte alone. In answer to Lenin's considerations on the social and political prerequisites of the upheaval, Malaparte has his alleged Trotsky say, literally, "Your strategy requires far too many favorable circumstances; the insurrection needs nothing, it suffices to itself." You hear: "The insurrection needs nothing!" There it is, my dear listeners, the absurdity which must help us to approach the truth. The author repeats persistently, that in the October Revolution, not the strategy of Lenin but the tactics of Trotsky won the victory. These tactics threaten, according to his words, even now the repose of the states of Europe. "The strategy of Lenin," I quote word for word, "is no immediate danger for the governments of Europe. But their present and, moreover, permanent danger is constituted by the tactics of Trotsky." Still more concretely, "Put Poincare in the place of Kerensky and the Bolshevik coup d'etat of October 1917 would succeed just as well." It is hard to believe that such a book has been translated into several languages and is taken seriously.

We seek in vain to discover what is the necessity altogether of the historically conditioned strategy of Lenin, if "Trotsky's tactics" can fulfill the same tasks in every situation. And why are successful revolutions so rare, if only a few technical recipes suffice for their success?

The dialogue between Lenin and Trotsky presented by the fascist author is in content, as well as form, an insipid invention from beginning to end. Of such inventions, there are not a few floating around the world. So, for example, in Madrid there has been printed a book, *La Vida del Lenin (The Life of Lenin),* for which I am as little responsible as for the tactical recipes of Malaparte. The Madrid weekly, *Estampa,* published in advance whole chapters of this alleged book of Trotsky's on Lenin, which contain horrible desecrations of the memory of that man whom I valued and still value incomparably higher than anyone else among my contemporaries.

But let us leave the forgers to their fate. Old Wilhelm Liebknecht,[1] the father of the unforgettable fighter and hero, Karl Liebknecht, liked to say, "A revolutionary politician must provide himself with a thick skin." Doctor Stockmann[2] even more expressively recommended that anyone who proposed to act in a manner contrary to the opinion of society should refrain from putting on new trousers. We will take note of the two good pieces of advice, and go on to the order of the day.

What questions does the October Revolution raise in the mind of a thinking man?

1. Why and how did this revolution take place? More concretely, why did the proletarian revolution conquer in one of the most backward countries of Europe?

2. What have been the results of the October Revolution? and finally,

3. Has the October Revolution stood the test?

The first question, as to the causes, can now be answered more or less exhaustively. I have attempted to do this in great detail in my *History of the Russian Revolution.* Here I can formulate only the most important conclusions.

The fact that the proletariat reached power for the first time in such a backward country as the former czarist Russia seems mysterious only at first glance; in reality, it is fully in accord with historical law. It could have been predicted and it was predicted. Still more, on the basis of the prediction of this fact the revolutionary Marxists built up their strategy long before the decisive events.

The first and most general explanation is: Russia is a backward country, but only a part of world economy, only an element of the capitalist world system. In this sense Lenin exhausted the riddle of the Russian Revolution with the lapidary formula, "The chain broke at its weakest link."

A crude illustration: the Great War, the result of the contradictions of world imperialism, drew into its maelstrom countries of *different* stages of development, but made the *same claims* on all the participants. It is clear that the burdens of the war had to be particularly intolerable for the most backward countries. Russia was the first to be compelled to leave the field. But to tear itself away from the war, the Russian people had to overthrow the ruling classes. In this way the chain of war broke at its weakest link.

Still, war is not a catastrophe coming from outside, like an earthquake, but as old Clausewitz[3] said, the continuation of politics by other means. In the last war, the main tendencies of the imperialistic system of "peacetime" only expressed themselves more crudely. The higher the general forces of production, the tenser the competition on the world markets, the sharper the antagonisms, and the madder the race for armaments, in that measure the more difficult it became for the weaker participants. For precisely this reason the backward countries assumed the first places in the succession of collapses. The chain of world capitalism always tends to break at its weakest link.

If, as a result of exceptional or exceptionally unfavorable circumstances — let us say, a successful military intervention from the outside or irreparable mistakes on the part of the Soviet government itself — capitalism should arise again on the immeasurably wide Soviet territory, together with it would inevitably arise also its historical inadequacy, and such capitalism would in turn soon become the victim of the same contradictions which caused its explosion in 1917. No tactical recipes could have called the October Revolution into being, if Russia had not carried it within its body. The revolutionary party in the last analysis can claim only the role of an obstetrician, who is compelled to resort to a Caesarean operation.

One might say in answer to this: "Your general considerations may adequately explain why old Russia had to suffer shipwreck, that country where backward capitalism and an impoverished peasantry were crowned by a parasitic nobility and a rotten monarchy. But in the simile of the chain and its weakest link there is still missing the key to the real riddle: How could the *socialist* revolution conquer in a *backward country*? History knows of more than a few illustrations of the decay of countries and civilizations accompanied by the collapse of the old classes for which no progressive successors had been found. The breakdown of old Russia should, at first sight, rather have changed the country into a capitalist colony than into a socialist state."

This objection is very interesting. It leads us directly to the kernel of the whole problem. And yet, this objection is erroneous; I might say, it lacks internal symmetry. On the one hand, it starts from an exaggerated conception of the backwardness of Russia; on the other, from a false theoretical conception of the phenomenon of historical backwardness in general.

Living beings, including man, of course, go through similar stages of development in accordance with their ages. In a normal five-year-old child, we find a certain correspondence between the weight, and the size of the parts of the body and the internal organs. But when we deal with human consciousness, the situation is different. In contrast with anatomy and physiology, psychology, both individual and collective, is distinguished by an exceptional ability of absorption, flexibility, and elasticity; therein consists the aristocratic advantage of man over his nearest zoological relatives, the apes. The absorptive and flexible psyche, as a necessary condition for historical progress, confers on the so-called social "organisms," as distinguished from the real, that is, biological organisms, an exceptional variability of internal structure. In the development of nations and states, particularly capitalist ones, there is neither similarity nor regularity. Different stages of civilization, even polar opposites, approach and intermingle with one another in the life of one and the same country.

Let us not forget, my esteemed listeners, that historical backwardness is a *relative* concept. There being both backward and progressive countries, there is also a reciprocal influencing of one by the other: there is the pressure of the progressive countries on the backward ones; there is the necessity for the backward countries to catch up with the progressive ones, to borrow their technology and science, etc. In this way arises the *combined type of development:* features of backwardness are combined with the last word in world technology and in world thinking. Finally, the historically backward countries, in order to escape from their backwardness, are often compelled to rush ahead of the others.

The flexibility of the collective consciousness makes it possible under certain conditions to achieve the result, in the social arena, which in individual psychology is called "overcoming the consciousness of inferiority." In this sense we can say that the October Revolution was an heroic means whereby the people of Russia were able to overcome their own economic and cultural inferiority.

But let us pass over from these historico-philosophic, perhaps somewhat too abstract, generalizations and put the same question in concrete form, that is, within the cross section of living economic facts. The backwardness of Russia expressed itself most clearly at the beginning of the twentieth century in the fact that industry occupied a small place in that country in comparison with agriculture, the city in comparison with the village, the proletariat in comparison with the peasantry. Taken as a whole, this meant a low productivity of the national labor. Suffice it to say that on the eve of the war, when czarist Russia had reached the peak of its well-being, the national income was eight to ten times lower than in the United States. This is expressed in figures, the "amplitude" of its backwardness, if the word "amplitude" can be used at all in connection with backwardness.

At the same time, however, the law of combined development expresses itself in the economic field at every step, in simple as well as in complex phenomena. Almost without highways, Russia was compelled to build railroads. Without having gone through the stage of European artisanry and manufacture, Russia passed on directly to mechanized production. To jump over intermediate stages is the fate of backward countries.

While peasant agriculture often remained at the level of the seventeenth century, Russia's industry, if not in scope, at least in type, stood at the level of the progressive countries and rushed ahead of them in some respects. It suffices to say that the giant enterprises, with over a thousand employees each, employed, in the United States, less than 18 percent of the total number of industrial workers, in Russia over 41 percent. This fact is hard to reconcile with the conventional conception of the economic backwardness of Russia. It does not, on the other hand, refute this backwardness, but complements it dialectically.

The same contradictory character was shown by the class structure of the country. The finance capital of Europe industrialized Russian economy at an accelerated tempo. Thereby the industrial bourgeoisie assumed a large-scale capitalistic and antipopular character. The foreign stockholders, moreover, lived outside of the country. The workers, on the other hand, were naturally Russians. Against a numerically weak Russian bourgeoisie, which had no national roots, stood therefore a relatively strong proletariat, with strong roots in the depths of the people.

The revolutionary character of the proletariat was furthered by the fact that Russia in particular, as a backward country, under the compulsion of catching up with its opponents, had not been able to work out its own conservatism, either social or political. The most conservative country of Europe, in fact of the entire world, is considered, and correctly, to be the oldest capitalist country— England. The European country freest of conservatism would in all probability be Russia.

But the young, fresh, determined proletariat of Russia still constituted only a tiny minority of the nation. The reserves of its revolutionary power lay outside of the proletariat itself — in the peasantry, living in half-serfdom, and in the oppressed nationalities.

The subsoil of the revolution was the agrarian question. The old feudal-monarchic system became doubly intolerable under the conditions of the new capitalist exploitation. The peasant communal areas amounted to some 140 million dessiatines.[4] But thirty thousand large landowners, whose average holdings were over two thousand dessiatines, owned altogether 70 million dessiatines, that is, as much as some 10 million peasant families or 50 millions of peasant population. *These statistics of land tenure constituted a ready-made program of agrarian revolt.*

The nobleman, Bokorkin, wrote in 1917 to the dignitary, Rodzianko, the chairman of the last municipal Duma, "I am a landowner and I cannot get it into my head that I must lose my land, and for an unbelievable purpose to boot, for the experiment of the socialist doctrine." But it is precisely the task of revolutions to accomplish that which the ruling classes cannot get into their heads.

In autumn 1917 almost the whole country was the scene of peasant revolts. Of the 624 departments of old Russia, 482, that is, 77 percent, were affected by the movement! The reflection of the burning villages lit up the arena of the insurrections in the cities.

But the war of the peasants against the landowners — you will reply to me — is one of the classic elements of the bourgeois, by no means of the proletarian revolution!

Perfectly right, I reply — so it was in the past. But the inability of capitalist society to survive in an historically backward country was expressed precisely in the fact that the peasant insurrections did not drive the bourgeois classes of Russia forward, but on the contrary drove them back for good into the camp of the reaction. If the peasantry did not want to be completely ruined, there was nothing else left for it but to join the industrial proletariat. This revolutionary joining of the two oppressed classes was foreseen with genius by Lenin and prepared by him long ahead of time.

Had the bourgeoisie courageously solved the agrarian question, the proletariat of Russia would not, obviously, have been able to take the power in 1917. But the greedy and cowardly Russian bourgeoisie, too late on the scene, prematurely a victim of senility, did not dare to lift its hand against feudal property. But thereby it delivered the power to the proletariat and together with it the right to dispose of the destinies of bourgeois society.

In order for the Soviet state to come into existence, therefore, it was necessary for two factors of different historical nature to collaborate: the peasant war, that is, a movement which is characteristic of the dawn of bourgeois development, and the proletarian insurrection, that is, a movement which announces the decline of the bourgeois movement. Precisely therein consists the *combined* character of the Russian Revolution.

Once the peasant bear stands up on his hind feet, he becomes terrible in his wrath. But he is unable to give conscious expression to his indignation. He needs a leader. For the first time in the history of the world, the insurrectionary peasantry found a faithful leader in the person of the proletariat.

Four million industrial and transportation workers led a hundred million peasants. That was the natural and inevitable reciprocal relation between proletariat and peasantry in the revolution.

The second revolutionary reserve of the proletariat was constituted by the oppressed nationalities, who moreover were also predominantly made up of peasants. Closely tied up with the historical backwardness of the country is the extensive character of the development of the state, which spread out like a grease spot from the center at Moscow to the circumference. In the East, it subjugated the still more backward peoples, basing itself upon them, in order to stifle the more developed nationalities of the West. To the seventy million Great Russians, who constituted the main mass of the population, were added gradually some ninety millions of "other races."

In this way arose the empire, in whose composition the ruling nationality made up only 43 percent of the population, while the remaining 57 percent consisted of nationalities of varying degrees of civilization and legal deprivation. The national pressure was incomparably cruder in Russia than in the neighboring states, and not only those beyond the western boundary but beyond the eastern one, too. This conferred on the national problem a gigantic explosive force.

The Russian liberal bourgeoisie, in the national as well as in the agrarian question, would not go beyond certain ameliorations of the regime of oppression and violence. The "democratic" governments of Miliukov and Kerensky, which reflected the interests of the Great Russian bourgeoisie and bureaucracy, actually hastened to impress upon the discontented nationalities, in the course of the eight months of their existence, "You will obtain only what you tear away by force."

The inevitability of the development of the centrifugal national movement had been early taken into consideration by Lenin. The Bolshevik Party struggled obstinately for years for the right of self-determination for nations, that is, for the right of full secession. Only through this courageous position on the national question could the Russian proletariat gradually win the confidence of the oppressed peoples. The national independence movement, as well as the agrarian movement, necessarily turned against the official democracy, strengthened the proletariat, and poured into the stream of the October upheaval.

In these ways the riddle of the proletarian upheaval in an historically backward country loses its veil of mystery.

Marxist revolutionaries predicted, long before the events, the march of the revolution and the historical role of the young Russian proletariat. I may be permitted to repeat here passages from a work of my own in 1905:

"In an economically backward country the proletariat can arrive at power earlier than in a capitalistically advanced one. . . .

"The Russian revolution creates the conditions under which the power can (and in the event of a successful revolution must) be transferred to the proletariat, even before the policy of bourgeois liberalism receives the opportunity of unfolding its talent for government to its full extent."

"The fate of the most elementary revolutionary interests of the peasantry . . . is bound up with the fate of the whole revolution, that is, with the fate of the proletariat. The proletariat, once arrived at power, will appear before the peasantry as the liberating class."

"The proletariat enters into the government as the revolutionary representative of the nation, as the acknowledged leader of the people in the struggle with absolutism and the barbarism of serfdom."

"The proletarian regime will have to stand from the very beginning for the solution of the agrarian question, with which the question of the destiny of tremendous masses of the population of Russia is bound up."[5]

I have taken the liberty of quoting these passages as evidence that the theory of the October Revolution which I am presenting today is no casual improvisation, and was not constructed ex post facto under the pressure of events. No, in the form of a political prognosis it preceded the October upheaval by a long time. You will agree that a theory is in general valuable only insofar as it helps to foresee the course of development and influences it purposively. Therein, in general terms, is the invaluable importance of Marxism as a weapon of social and historical orientation. I am sorry that the narrow limits of the lecture do not permit me to enlarge the above quotation materially. I will therefore content myself with a brief resume of the whole work which dates from 1905.

In accordance with its immediate tasks, the Russian revolution is a bourgeois revolution. But the Russian bourgeoisie is antirevolutionary. The victory of the revolution is therefore possible only as a victory of the proletariat. But the victorious proletariat will not stop at the program of bourgeois democracy; it will go on to the program of socialism. The Russian revolution will become the first stage of the socialist world revolution.

This was the theory of the *permanent revolution* formulated by me in 1905 and since then exposed to the severest criticism under the name of "Trotskyism."

To be more exact, it is only a part of this theory. The other part, which is particularly timely now, states:

The present productive forces have long outgrown their national limits. A socialist society is not feasible within national boundaries. Significant as the economic successes of an isolated workers' state may be, the program of "socialism in one country" is a petty-bourgeois utopia. Only a European and then a world federation of socialist republics can be the real arena for a harmonious socialist society.

Today, after the test of events, I see less reason than ever to dissociate myself from this theory.

After all that has been said above, is it still worthwhile to recall the fascist writer, Malaparte, who ascribes to me tactics which are independent of strategy and amount to a series of technical recipes for insurrection, applicable in all latitudes and longitudes? It is a good thing that the name of the luckless theoretician of the coup d'etat makes it easy to distinguish him from the victorious practitioner of the coup d'etat; no one therefore runs the risk of confusing Malaparte with Bonaparte.[6]

Without the armed insurrection of November 7, 1917, the Soviet state would not be in existence. But the insurrection itself did not drop from heaven. A series of historical prerequisites was necessary for the October Revolution.

1. The rotting away of the old ruling classes — the nobility, the monarchy, the bureaucracy.

2. The political weakness of the bourgeoisie, which had no roots in the masses of the people.

3. The revolutionary character of the peasant question.

4. The revolutionary character of the problem of the oppressed nations.

5. The significant social weight of the proletariat.

To these organic preconditions we must add certain conjunctural conditions of the highest importance:

6. The revolution of 1905 was the great school, or in Lenin's words, the "dress rehearsal" of the revolution of 1917. The soviets, as the irreplaceable organizational form of the proletarian united front in the revolution, were created for the first time in the year 1905.

7. The imperialist war sharpened all the contradictions, tore the backward masses out of their immobility and thereby prepared the grandiose scale of the catastrophe.

But all these conditions, which fully sufficed for the *outbreak of the revolution,* were insufficient to assure the *victory of the proletariat* in the revolution. For this victory one condition more was needed:

8. The Bolshevik Party.

When I enumerate this condition as the last in the series, I do it only because it follows the necessities of the logical order, and not because I assign the party the last place in the order of importance.

No, I am far from such a thought. The liberal bourgeoisie — yes, it can seize the power and has seized it more than once as the result of struggles in which it took no part; it possesses organs of seizure which are admirably adapted to the purpose. But the working masses are in a different position; they have long been accustomed to give, and not to take. They work, are patient as long as they can be, hope, lose their patience, rise up and struggle, die, bring victory to the others, are betrayed, fall into despondency, again bow their necks, again work. This is the history of the masses of the people under all regimes. In order to take the power firmly and surely into its hands the proletariat needs a party, which far surpasses the other parties in the clarity of its thought and in its revolutionary determination.

The party of the Bolsheviks, which has been described more than once and with complete justification as the most revolutionary party in the history of mankind, was the living condensation of the modern history of Russia, of all that was dynamic in it. The overthrow of czarism had long since become the necessary condition for the development of economy and culture. But for the solution of this task, the forces were insufficient. The bourgeoisie feared the revolution. The intelligentsia tried to bring the peasant to his feet. The muzhik, incapable of generalizing his own miseries and his aims, left this appeal unanswered. The intelligentsia armed itself with dynamite. A whole generation was burned up in this struggle.

On March 1, 1887, Alexander Ulyanov[7] carried out the last of the great terrorist plots. The attempted assassination of Alexander III failed. Ulyanov and the other participants were executed. The attempt to substitute a chemical preparation for the revolutionary class suffered shipwreck. Even the most heroic intelligentsia is nothing without the masses. Under the immediate impression of these facts and conclusions grew up Ulyanov's younger brother Vladimir, the later Lenin, the greatest figure of Russian history. Even in his early youth he placed himself on the foundations of Marxism, and turned his face toward the proletariat. Without losing sight of the village for a moment, he sought the way to the peasantry through the workers. Having inherited from his revolutionary predecessors their determination, their capacity for self-sacrifice, and their willingness to go to the limit, Lenin at an early age became the teacher of the new generation of the intelligentsia and of the advanced workers. In strikes and street fights, in prisons and in exile, the workers received the necessary tempering. They needed the searchlight of Marxism to light up their historical road in the darkness of absolutism.

In the year 1883 there arose among the emigres the first Marxist group. In the year 1898, at a secret meeting, the foundation of the Russian Social Democratic Workers' Party was proclaimed (we all called ourselves Social Democrats in those days). In the year 1903 occurred the split between Bolsheviks and Mensheviks. In the year 1912 the Bolshevik faction finally became an independent party.

It learned to recognize the class mechanics of society in struggle, in the grandiose events of twelve years (1905-1917). It educated cadres equally capable of initiative and subordination. The discipline of its revolutionary action was based on the unity of its doctrine, on the tradition of common struggles, and on confidence in its tested leadership.

Thus stood the party in the year 1917. Despised by the official "public opinion" and the paper thunder of the intelligentsia press, it adapted itself to the movement of the masses. Firmly it kept in hand the control of factories and regiments. More and more the peasant masses turned toward it. If we understand by "nation" not the privileged heads but the majority of the people, that is, the workers and peasants, then Bolshevism became in the course of the year 1917 a truly national Russian party.

In September 1917, Lenin, who was compelled to keep in hiding, gave the signal, "The crisis is ripe, the hour of the insurrection has approached." He was right. The ruling classes had landed in a blind alley before the problems of the war, the land, and national liberation. The bourgeoisie finally lost its head. The democratic parties, the Mensheviks and Social Revolutionaries, wasted the remains of the confidence of the masses in them by their support of the imperialist war, by their policy of ineffectual compromise and concession to the bourgeois and feudal property owners. The awakened army no longer wanted to fight for the alien aims of imperialism. Disregarding democratic advice, the peasantry smoked the landowners out of their estates. The oppressed nationalities at the periphery rose up against the bureaucracy of Petrograd. In the most important workers' and soldiers' soviets the Bolsheviks were dominant. The workers and soldiers demanded action. The ulcer was ripe. It needed a cut of the lancet.

Only under these social and political conditions was the insurrection possible. And thus it also became inevitable. But there is no playing around with the insurrection. Woe to the surgeon who is careless in the use of the lancet! Insurrection is an art. It has its laws and its rules.

The party carried through the October insurrection with cold calculation and with flaming determination. Thanks to this, it conquered almost without victims. Through the victorious soviets the Bolsheviks placed themselves at the head of a country which occupies one-sixth of the surface of the globe.

The majority of my present listeners, it is to be presumed, did not occupy themselves at all with politics in the year 1917. So much the better. Before the young generation lies much that is interesting, if not always easy. But the representatives of the older generation in this hall will surely well remember how the seizure of power by the Bolsheviks was received: as a curiosity, as a misunderstanding, as a scandal; most often as a nightmare which was bound to disappear with the first rays of dawn. The Bolsheviks would last twenty-four hours, a week, a month, a year. The period had to be constantly

lengthened. The rulers of the whole world armed themselves
against the first workers' state: civil war was stirred up, inter-
ventions again and again, blockade. So passed year after
year. Meantime history has recorded fifteen years of existence
of the Soviet power.

"Yes," some opponent will say, "the adventure of October
has shown itself to be much more substantial than many of
us thought. Perhaps it was not even quite an 'adventure.' Nevertheless, the question retains its full force: What was achieved
at this high cost? Were then those dazzling tasks fulfilled which
the Bolsheviks proclaimed on the eve of the revolution?"

Before we answer the hypothetical opponent, let us note that
the question in and of itself is not new. On the contrary, it
followed right at the heels of the October Revolution, since
the day of its birth.

The French journalist, Claude Anet, who was in Petrograd
during the revolution, wrote as early as October 27, 1917:

"The maximalists (which was what the French called the
Bolsheviks at that time) have seized the power and the great
day has come. At last, I say to myself, I shall behold the
realization of the socialist Eden which has been promised us
for so many years. . . . Admirable adventure! A privileged
position!" And so on and so forth. What sincere hatred behind
the ironical salutation! The very morning after the capture
of the Winter Palace, the reactionary journalist hurried to register his claim for a ticket of admission to Eden. Fifteen years
have passed since the revolution. With all the greater absence
of ceremony our enemies reveal their malicious joy over the
fact that the land of the Soviets, even today, bears but little
resemblance to a realm of general well-being. Why then the
revolution and why the sacrifices?

Worthy listeners—permit me to think that the contradictions,
difficulties, mistakes, and want of the Soviet regime are no
less familiar to me than to anyone else. I personally have never concealed them, whether in speech or in writing. I have
believed and I still believe that revolutionary politics, as distinguished from conservative, cannot be built up on concealment. "To speak out that which is" must be the highest principle of the workers' state.

But in criticism, as well as in creative activity, perspective
is necessary. Subjectivism is a poor adviser, particularly in
great questions. Periods of time must be commensurate with
the tasks, and not with individual caprices. Fifteen years! How
much that is in the life of one man! Within that period not

a few of our generation were borne to their graves and those who remain have added innumerable gray hairs. But these same fifteen years — what an insignificant period in the life of a people! Only a minute on the clock of history.

Capitalism required centuries to maintain itself in the struggle against the Middle Ages, to raise the level of science and technology, to build railroads, to stretch electric wires. And then? Then humanity was thrust by capitalism into the hell of wars and crises! But socialism is allowed by its enemies, that is, by the adherents of capitalism, only a decade and a half to install paradise on earth with all modern improvements. No, such obligations were never assumed by us. Such periods of time were never set forth.

The processes of great changes must be measured by scales which are commensurate with them. I do not know if the socialist society will resemble the biblical paradise. I doubt it. But in the Soviet Union there is no socialism as yet. The situation that prevails there is one of transition, full of contradictions, burdened with the heavy inheritance of the past, and in addition under the hostile pressure of the capitalistic states. The October Revolution has proclaimed the principle of the new society. The Soviet Republic has shown only the first stage of its realization. Edison's first lamp was very bad. We must know how to distinguish the future from among the mistakes and faults of the first socialist construction.

But the unhappiness that rains on living men! Do the results of the revolution justify the sacrifice which it has caused? A fruitless question, rhetorical through and through; as if the processes of history admitted of an accounting balance sheet! We might just as well ask, in view of the difficulties and miseries of human existence, "Does it pay to be born altogether?" To which Heine wrote, "And the fool expects an answer." Such melancholy reflections have not hindered mankind from being born and from giving birth. Suicides, even in these days of unexampled world crisis, fortunately constitute an unimportant percentage. But peoples never resort to suicide. When their burdens are intolerable, they seek a way out through revolution.

Besides, who becomes indignant over the victims of the socialist upheaval? Most often those who have paved the way for the victims of the imperialist war, and have glorified or, at least, easily accommodated themselves to it. It is now our turn to ask, "Has the war justified itself? What has it given us? What has it taught?"

The reactionary historian, Hippolyte Taine, in his eleven-volume pamphlet against the Great French Revolution describes, not without malicious joy, the sufferings of the French people in the years of the dictatorship of the Jacobins [8] and afterward. The worst off were the lower classes of the cities, the plebeians, who as "sansculottes" had given up the best of their souls for the revolution. Now they or their wives stood in line through cold nights to return empty-handed to the extinguished family hearth. In the tenth year of the revolution Paris was poorer than before it began. Carefully selected, artificially pieced-out facts serve Taine as justification for his annihilating verdict against the revolution. Look, the plebeians wanted to be dictators and have precipitated themselves into misery!

It is hard to conceive of a more uninspired piece of moralizing. First of all, if the revolution precipitated the country into misery, the blame lay principally on the ruling classes who drove the people to revolution. Second, the Great French Revolution did not exhaust itself in hungry lines before bakeries. The whole of modern France, in many respects the whole of modern civilization, arose out of the bath of the French Revolution!

In the course of the Civil War in the United States in the sixties of the last century, five hundred thousand men were killed. Can these sacrifices be justified?

From the standpoint of the American slaveholder and the ruling classes of Great Britain who marched with them — no! From the standpoint of the Negro or of the British workingman — absolutely! And from the standpoint of the development of humanity as a whole — there can be no doubt whatever. Out of the Civil War of the sixties came the present United States with its unbounded practical initiative, its rationalized technology, its economic energy. On these achievements of America, humanity will build the new society.

The October Revolution penetrated deeper than any of its predecessors into the holy of holies of society — into its property relations. So much the longer time is necessary to reveal the creative consequences of the revolution in all the spheres of life. But the general direction of the upheaval is already clear: the Soviet Republic has no reason whatever to hang its head before its capitalist accusers and speak the language of apology.

To evaluate the new regime from the standpoint of human development, one must first answer the question, "How does social progress express itself and how can it be measured?"

The deepest, the most objective, and the most indisputable criterion says — progress can be measured by the growth of the productivity of social labor. The evaluation of the October Revolution from this point of view is already given by experience. The principle of socialistic organization has for the first time in history shown its ability to record unheard-of results in production in a short space of time.

The curve of the industrial development of Russia, expressed in crude index numbers, is as follows, taking 1913, the last year before the war, as 100. The year 1920, the highest point of the civil war, is also the lowest point in industry—only 25, that is to say, a quarter of the prewar production. In 1925 it rose to 75, that is, three-quarters of the prewar production; in 1929 about 200, in 1932, 300, that is to say, three times as much as on the eve of the war.

The picture becomes even more striking in the light of the international index. From 1925 to 1932 the industrial production of Germany has declined one and a half times, in America twice; in the Soviet Union it has increased fourfold. These figures speak for themselves.

I have no intention of denying or concealing the seamy side of Soviet economy. The results of the industrial index are extraordinarily influenced by the unfavorable development of agriculture, that is to say, of that field which has essentially not yet risen to socialist methods, but at the same time has been led on the road to collectivization with insufficient preparation, bureaucratically rather than technically and economically. This is a great question, which however goes beyond the limits of my lecture.

The index numbers cited require another important reservation. The indisputable and, in their way, splendid results of Soviet industrialization demand a further economic checking-up from the standpoint of the mutual adaptation of the various elements of economy, their dynamic equilibrium, and consequently their productive capacity. Here great difficulties and even setbacks are inevitable. Socialism does not arise in its perfected form from the Five-Year Plan, like Minerva from the head of Jupiter, or Venus from the foam of the sea. Before it are decades of persistent work, of mistakes, corrections, and reorganization. Moreover, let us not forget that socialist construction in accordance with its very nature can only reach perfection on the international arena. But even the most unfavorable economic balance sheet of the results obtained so far could reveal only the incorrectness of the preliminary calculations, the errors of the plan, and the mistakes of the leadership, but could in no way refute the empirically firmly established fact—the possibility, with the aid of socialist methods, of raising the productivity of collective labor to an unheard-of height. This conquest, of world historical importance, cannot be taken away from us by anybody or anything.

After what has been said, it is scarcely worthwhile to spend time on the complaints, that the October Revolution has brought Russia to the downfall of its civilization. That is the voice of the disquieted ruling houses and the salons. The feudal-bourgeois "civilization" overthrown by the proletarian upheaval was only barbarism with decorations a la Talmi. While it remained inaccessible to the Russian people, it brought little that was new to the treasury of mankind.

But even with respect to this civilization, which is so bemoaned by the White emigres, we must put the question more precisely — in what sense is it ruined? Only in one sense; the monopoly of a small minority in the treasures of civilization has been destroyed. But everything of cultural value in the old Russian civilization has remained untouched. The Huns of Bolshevism have shattered neither the conquests of the mind nor the creations of art. On the contrary, they carefully collected the monuments of human creativeness and arranged them in model order. The culture of the monarchy, the nobility, and the bourgeoisie has now become the culture of the museums.

The people visit these museums eagerly. But they do not live in them. They learn. They build. The fact alone that the October Revolution taught the Russian people, the dozens of peoples of czarist Russia, to read and write, stands immeasurably higher than the whole former hothouse Russian civilization.

The October Revolution has laid the foundations for a new civilization, which is designed, not for a select few, but for all. This is felt by the masses of the whole world. Hence their sympathy for the Soviet Union, which is as passionate as once was their hatred for czarist Russia.

Worthy listeners — you know that human language is an irreplaceable tool, not only for giving names to events but also for evaluating them. By filtering out that which is accidental, episodic, artificial, it absorbs that which is essential, characteristic, of full weight. Notice with what nicety the languages of civilized nations have distinguished two epochs in the development of Russia. The culture of the nobility brought into world currency such barbarisms as *czar, Cossack, pogrom, nagaika.* You know these words and what they mean. The October Revolution introduced into the language of the

Trotsky at the podium in Copenhagen,
November 27, 1932.

world such words as *Bolshevik, Soviet, kolkhoz, Gosplan, Piatiletka.* [9]   Here practical linguistics holds its historical supreme court!

The profoundest significance, but the hardest to submit to immediate measurement, of that great revolution consists in the fact that it forms and tempers the character of the people. The conception of the Russian people as slow, passive, melancholy, mystical, is widely spread and not accidental. It has its roots in the past. But in Western countries up to the present time those far-reaching changes have not been sufficiently considered which have been introduced into the character of the people by the revolution. Could it have been otherwise?

Every man with experience of life can recall the picture of some youth that he has known, receptive, lyrical, all too susceptible, who later, all at once, under the influence of a powerful moral impetus, became hardened and unrecognizable. In the development of a whole nation, such moral transformations are wrought by the revolution.

The February insurrection against the autocracy, the struggle against the nobility, against the imperialist war, for peace, for land, for national equality, the October insurrection, the overthrow of the bourgeoisie, and of those parties which sought agreements with the bourgeoisie, three years of civil war on a front of five thousand miles, the years of blockade, hunger, misery, and epidemics, the years of tense economic reconstruction, of new difficulties and renunciations—these make a hard but a good school. A heavy hammer smashes glass, but forges steel. The hammer of the revolution forged the steel of the people's character.

"Who will believe," wrote a czarist general, Zalessky, with indignation, shortly after the upheaval, "that a porter or a watchman suddenly becomes a chief justice; a hospital attendant, the director of a hospital; a barber, an officeholder; a corporal, a commander-in-chief; a day worker, a mayor; a locksmith, the director of a factory?"

"Who will believe it?" They had to believe it. They could do nothing else but believe it, when the corporals defeated generals, when the mayor—the former day worker—broke the resistance of the old bureaucracy, the wagon-greaser put the transportation system in order, the locksmith as director put the industrial equipment into working condition. "Who will believe it?" Let them only try and not believe it.

For an explanation of the extraordinary persistence which the masses of the people of the Soviet Union are showing throughout the years of the revolution, many foreign observers rely, in accord with ancient habit, on the "passivity" of the Russian character. Gross anachronism! The revolutionary masses endure their privations patiently but not passively. With their own hands they are creating a better future and they want to create it, at any cost. Let the class enemy only attempt to impose his will from the outside on these patient masses! No, he would do better not to try it!

Let us now in closing attempt to ascertain the place of the October Revolution, not only in the history of Russia but in the history of the world. During the year 1917, in a period of eight months, two historical curves intersect. The February upheaval—that belated echo of the great struggles which had been carried out in past centuries on the territories of Holland, England, France, almost all of Continental Europe—takes its place in the series of bourgeois revolutions. The October Revolution proclaims and opens the domination of the proletariat. It was world capitalism that suffered its first great defeat on the territory of Russia. The chain broke at its weakest link. But it was the chain that broke, and not only the link.

Capitalism has outlived itself as a world system. It has ceased to fulfill its essential mission, the increase of human power and human wealth. Humanity cannot stand still at the level which it has reached. Only a powerful increase in productive forces and a sound, planned, that is, socialist organization of production and distribution can assure humanity—all humanity—of a decent standard of life and at the same time give it the precious feeling of freedom with respect to its own economy. Freedom in two senses—first of all, man will no longer be compelled to devote the greater part of his life to physical labor. Second, he will no longer be dependent on the laws of the market, that is, on the blind and dark forces which have grown up behind his back. He will build up his economy freely, that is, according to a plan, with compass in hand. This time it is a question of subjecting the anatomy of society to the X ray through and through, of disclosing all its secrets and subjecting all its functions to the reason and the will of collective humanity. In this sense, socialism must become a new step in the historical advance of mankind. To our ancestor, who first armed himself with a stone axe, the whole of *nature* represented a conspiracy of secret and hostile forces. Since then, the natural sciences, hand in hand with practical technology, have illuminated nature down to its most secret depths. By means of electrical energy, the physicist passes judgment on the nucleus of the atom. The hour is not far when science will easily solve the task of the alchemists, and turn manure into gold and gold into manure. Where the demons and furies of nature once raged, now rules ever more courageously the industrial will of man.

But while he wrestled victoriously with nature, man built up his relations to other men blindly, almost like the bee or the ant. Belatedly and most undecidedly he approached the problems of human society. He began with religion, and passed on to politics. The Reformation represented the first victory of bourgeois individualism and rationalism in a domain which had been ruled by dead tradition. From the church, critical thought went on to the state. Born in the struggle with absolutism and the medieval estates, the doctrine of the sovereignty of the people and of the rights of man and the citizen grew stronger. Thus arose the system of parliamentarism. Critical thought penetrated into the domain of government administration. The political rationalism of democracy was the highest achievement of the revolutionary bourgeoisie.

But between nature and the state stands economic life. Technology liberated man from the tyranny of the old elements — earth, water, fire, and air — only to subject him to its own tyranny. Man ceased to be a slave to nature, to become a slave to the machine, and, still worse, a slave to supply and demand. The present world crisis testifies in especially tragic fashion how man, who dives to the bottom of the ocean, who rises up to the stratosphere, who converses on invisible waves with the antipodes, how this proud and daring ruler of nature remains a slave to the blind forces of his own economy. The historical task of our epoch consists in replacing the uncontrolled play of the market by reasonable planning, in disciplining the forces of production, compelling them to work together in harmony and obediently serve the needs of mankind. Only on this new social basis will man be able to stretch his weary limbs and — every man and every woman, not only a selected few — become a full citizen in the realm of thought.

But this is not yet the end of the road. No, it is only the beginning. Man calls himself the crown of creation. He has a certain right to that claim. But who has asserted that present-day man is the last and highest representative of the species homo sapiens? No, physically as well as spiritually he is very far from perfection, prematurely born biologically, feeble in thought, and without any new organic equilibrium.

It is true that humanity has more than once brought forth giants of thought and action, who tower over their contemporaries like summits in a chain of mountains. The human race has a right to be proud of its Aristotle, Shakespeare, Darwin, Beethoven, Goethe, Marx, Edison, and Lenin. But why are they so rare? Above all because, almost without exception, they came out of the upper and middle classes. Apart from rare exceptions, the sparks of genius in the suppressed depths of the people are choked before they can burst into flame. But also because the processes of creating, developing, and educating a human being have been and remain essentially a matter of chance, not illuminated by theory and practice, not subjected to consciousness and will.

Anthropology, biology, physiology, and psychology have accumulated mountains of material to raise up before mankind in their full scope the tasks of perfecting and developing body and spirit. Psychoanalysis, with the inspired hand of Sigmund Freud, has lifted the cover of the well which is poetically called the "soul." And what has been revealed? Our conscious thought is only a small part of the work of the dark psychic forces. Learned divers descend to the bottom of the ocean and there take photographs of mysterious fishes. Human thought, descending to the bottom of its own psychic sources, must shed light on the most mysterious driving forces of the soul and subject them to reason and to will.

Once he has done with the anarchic forces of his own society, man will set to work on himself, in the pestle and the retort of the chemist. For the first time mankind will regard itself as raw material, or at best as a physical and psychic semi-finished product. Socialism will mean a leap from the realm of necessity into the realm of freedom in this sense too, that the man of today, with all his contradictions and lack of harmony, will open the road for a new and happier race.

16

Farewell to Prinkipo

During Trotsky's stay in Prinkipo the most important de-
velopment in world politics was the rise of fascism in Ger-
many, and the failure of the powerful German Communist
Party to stop the Nazis, thanks to the false and ultraleftist
policy imposed on it by Moscow. The story of Trotsky's in-
terventions, appeals, and warnings will be found in the collection of his writings from this period, The Struggle Against
Fascism in Germany. *But the Stalinists capitulated to Hitler*
without firing a single shot.

When this happened early in 1933, and the Comintern later
proclaimed that its policy in Germany had been correct from
start to finish, and not a single Communist Party anywhere
in the world raised a question about the German catastrophe,
Trotsky and the Left Opposition decided that the Comintern
was finished as a revolutionary force—that is, it could no
longer be reformed—and that it was necessary now to work
for the creation of a new International and new revolutionary
parties throughout the world. This momentous decision coin-
cided with the granting of a visa by the French government
in the summer of 1933, which enabled Trotsky to move closer
to the center of world politics.

On July 15, 1933, Trotsky completed his first article urging
the Left Opposition to discontinue its efforts to reform the Com-
munist International, a radical change in perspective that
opened up many new problems and possibilities. In addition,
Trotsky was to leave in a few days for France. Despite his
excitement about both the coming sea voyage and the new
political challenge, Trotsky's thoughts also turned back to the
years he had spent on Prinkipo. So he kept on writing, this
time in his diary, and produced a short reminiscence that was
as much a part of Trotsky as his purely political essays and
speeches.

In a translation by Max Eastman it first appeared in The
Modern Monthly, *March 1934.*

So! Distinct and incontestable French visas have been affixed to our passports. In two days we depart from Turkey. When I arrived here with my wife and son—four and a half years ago—the light of "prosperity" was shining brightly in America. Today, those times seem prehistoric, almost legendary.

Prinkipo is an island of peace and forgetfulness. The life of the world reaches here after long delays and hushed down. But the crisis found its way here too. From year to year fewer people come from Stamboul, and those who do come have less and less money. Of what use is the superabundance of fish, when there is no demand for it?

Prinkipo is a fine place to work with a pen, particularly during autumn and winter when the island becomes completely deserted and woodcocks appear in the park. Not only are there no theaters here, but no movies. Automobiles are forbidden. Are there many such places in the world? In our house we have no telephone. The braying of the donkey acts soothingly upon the nerves. One cannot forget for a minute that Prinkipo is an island, for the sea is under the window, and there is no hiding from the sea at any point on the island. Ten meters away from the stone fence we catch fish, at fifty meters—lobsters. For weeks at a time the sea is as calm as a lake.

But we are in close connection with the world outside, for we get mail. That is the climax of the day. The post brings fresh newspapers, new books, letters from friends, and letters from foes. This pile of printed and written paper holds much that is unexpected, especially from America. I find it difficult to believe that so many people exist in this world who are urgently concerned with the salvation of my soul. In the course of these years I have received such a quantity of religious literature as would suffice for the salvation not of a single person, but of a brigade of confirmed sinners. All the pertinent places in the devout books are considerately scored on the margins. However, no fewer people are interested in my soul's perdition, and they express their corresponding wishes with a laudable frankness, even though anonymously. Graphologists demand that I forward my handwriting to have my character analyzed. Astrologists request to be told the day and hour of my birth to draw my horoscope. Autograph collectors wheedle for my signature to add to those of two American presidents, three heavyweight champions, Albert Einstein, Colonel Lindbergh, and of course Charlie Chaplin. Such letters arrive almost exclusively from America. Gradually I have learned to guess from the envelope whether the request will be for a cane toward the home museum, or whether a desire will be expressed to recruit me as a Methodist preacher, or a prophecy forthcoming of eternal tortures on one of the vacant spits in hell. As the crisis sharpened, the proportion of these letters swung decidedly in favor of the infernal regions.

The post brings much that is unexpected. A few days ago it brought the French visa. The skeptics — and there were such in our house too — were put to shame. We are leaving Prinkipo. Our house is already almost empty; wooden boxes stand below, and young hands are busy hammering nails. In our old and neglected villa, the floors this spring were decorated with paint of a composition so mysterious that tables, chairs, and even feet, stick lightly to the floor even now, four months later. It is strange, but it seems to me that during these years my feet have grown a little into the soil of Prinkipo as well.

I have had few ties, really, with the island itself, the circumference of which can be covered on foot in two hours. But for that reason I made more ties with the waters that wash it. During these fifty-three months, with the help of my invaluable tutor, I have become very intimate with the sea of Marmora. His name is Charolambos, and his universe is described by a radius of approximately four kilometers around Prinkipo. But Charolambos knows his universe. To an undiscerning eye the sea seems identical throughout its whole extent. Yet the bottom of the sea enfolds an immeasurable variety of physical organisms, minerals, flora, and fauna. Charolambos, alas, is illiterate, but he reads with artistry the beautiful book of the sea of Marmora. His father and grandfather and great-grandfather, and the grandfather of his great-grandfather, were fishermen. His father still fishes even now. The old man's specialty is lobsters. In summer he catches them not with nets as other fishermen do — as his son and I do — but he hunts them. It is the most enthralling spectacle. The old man discerns the lobster's hiding place under a rock through the water at a depth of five or eight meters and more. With a very long pole tipped with iron he pushes the rock over and the exposed lobster flees. The old man gives an order to the oarsman, pursues the lobster, and with a second long pole to which is attached a small reticular bag upon a square frame, he overhauls the lobster, covers it, and pulls it out. When the sea is disturbed by a ripple, the old man sprinkles oil upon the water with his fingers and peers through the fatty mirror. In a good day he catches thirty, forty, and more lobsters. But every one has become impoverished during these years, and the demand for lobsters is as low as for Ford's automobiles.

Fishing with nets, being professional, is considered unworthy of a free artist. A superficial and false attitude! Fishing with a net is a high art. One must know the time and place for each kind of fish. One must know how to spread the net in a semicircle, sometimes a circle, even in a spiral, depending upon the configuration of the bottom and a dozen other conditions. One must lower the net noiselessly into the water, unrolling it rapidly from a moving boat. And finally — as the last act — the fish must be driven into the net. Today this is done as it was done ten thousand and more years ago, by means of stones cast from the boat. By this barrage the fish are first driven into the circle, and then into the net itself. A different quantity of stone is required for this at different times of the year and under different conditions of sea. From time to time the supply must be replenished on the shore. But in the boat there are two permanent stones on long strings. One must know how to throw them with force, and immediately retrieve them from the water. The stone should fall close to the net. But woe to the fisher, if it plunks into the net itself and becomes entangled! Then Charolambos chastises one with an annihilating look — and justly. Out of politeness and a sense of social discipline, Charolambos admits that I am generally not bad at casting stones. But I need only compare my work with his, and pride departs immediately. Charolambos sees the net after it is already invisible to me, and he knows where it is when it is no longer visible to him either. He feels it not only in front of him, but behind his back. His extremities are always in contact with that net through some mysterious fluids. Pulling the net up is stiff work, and Charolambos wears a wide woolen scarf tightly wound around his belly, even during the hot July days. One must row without either overpassing or lagging behind the curve of the net, and that is my job. I was not quick at learning to note the almost imperceptible motions of the hand by means of which the master directs his assistant.

Often after casting fifteen kilos of stone into the water, Charolambos pulls out the net with a lonely little fish the size of my thumb. Sometimes the entire net lives and quivers with captured fish. How explain this difference? "Deniz," replies Charolambos, shrugging his shoulders. Deniz means "sea," and this word resounds like "destiny."

Charolambos and I converse in a new language which has grown up slowly out of Turkish, Greek, Russian, and French words—all violently distorted and seldom used according to their honest connotation. We construct phrases after the manner of two- or three-year-old children. However, I firmly call out in Turkish the names of the more common operations. Chance observers have concluded from this that I command the Turkish language freely, and the papers have even announced that I translate American authors into Turkish—a slight exaggeration!

Sometimes it happens that no sooner have we got the nets lowered than we hear a sudden splash and a snort behind our backs. "Dolphin!" yells Charolambos in alarm. Danger! The dolphin bides his time until the fishermen drive the fish into the net with stones, and then he tears them out one by one, along with big chunks of the net itself by way of seasoning. "Shoot, M'sieu!" yells Charolambos. And I shoot from a revolver. A young dolphin will be scared by this and flee. But the old pirates cherish a complete contempt for that automatic popgun. Merely out of politeness they swim a little way off after the shot and give a snort and bide their time. More than once were we compelled to pull up our empty net in a hurry and change the fishing ground.

The dolphin is not the only enemy. The little black gardener from the north shore is very expert at cleaning out other people's nets if they are left overnight without surveillance. Toward evening, he pulls out in his skiff as if to fish, but in reality to find a point of vantage, whence he can well observe all those who are bringing out their nets for the night. There are people who steal nets (Charolambos and I have lost not a few during these years), but this is risky and bothersome. The net must be altered lest it be recognized; it must be tended, patched, and painted from time to time with pitch. The little gardener leaves all these wearisome cares to the owners of the nets; he contents himself with the fish and the lobsters. Charolambos and he cross glances in passing, sharper than a knife. We resort to subterfuge; pulling away some distance, we go through the pantomime of casting a net, and then rounding the little island full of rabbits, we secretly lower our net into the water. In about one case out of three we succeed in fooling the enemy.

The chief fish here are barbonnel and rouget. The chief fisher of rouget is the old man Kochu. He knows his fish, and sometimes it seems as though the fish know him. When rouget abounds, Kochu deals a quick strategic blow to his possible rivals. Going out earlier than anybody else, he works the watery field not from one end to the other, but after the fashion of a chessboard, as a knight jumps, or in some even more fancy figure. No one knows except Kochu where the net has already passed and where it has not. Having blocked off in this manner a large section of the sea, Kochu then fills in at leisure the unutilized squares. A great art! Kochu has succeeded in learning the sea because Kochu is old. But even Kochu's father worked until last year with another old fellow, a former barber. In a decrepit skiff they laid nets for lobsters, and they themselves, corroded to the bones with sea salt, resembled two aged lobsters. Both of them are now resting in the Prinkipo cemetery, which holds more people than the little village.

However, it should not be inferred that we restricted ourselves to nets. No, we used all the methods of fishing that promised booty. With hook and line we caught big fish weighing up to ten kilos. While I would be pulling up some invisible monster, now following me obediently and now frantically balking, Charolambos would watch me with unmoving eyes, eyes without a shadow of respect left in them. Not without reason did he fear that I would lose the precious prey. . . . At every awkward move of mine, he would growl savagely and menacingly. And when the fish finally became visible in the water, so beautiful in its transparency, Charolambos would whisper in admonition, "Buyuk, M'sieu" (a big one). To which I would reply panting, "Buyuk, Charolambos." At the boatside we catch up the prey in a small net. And now the beautiful monster, played over by all the colors of the rainbow, shakes the boat with its last blows of resistance and despair. In our joy, we eat an orange apiece, and in a language comprehensible to no one but us, and which we ourselves only half understand, share the sensations of the adventure.

This morning the fishing was poor. The season is over, the fish have gone to deep water. Toward the end of August they will return, but then Charolambos will be fishing without me. He is now downstairs nailing up cases of books, of the utility of which he is obviously not entirely convinced. Through the open window can be seen the small steamer which brings the functionaries from Stamboul to their summer homes. Empty shelves yawn in the library. Only in the upper corner over the arch of the window does the old life go on as usual. Swallows have built a nest there, and directly above the British "blue books" have hatched a brood which has no interest in French visas.

For better or worse, the chapter called "Prinkipo" is ended.

Trotsky, in France, in 1933.

Natalia, at extreme left, and Trotsky, with cane, leaving the ship that brought them to Norway in June 1935.

17

I Stake My Life!

The rest of Trotsky's life was spent in France (July 1933-June 1935), Norway (June 1935-December 1936), and Mexico (January 1937-August 1940). His major activity in those places was building the Fourth International.

The French government soon showed its hostility to such activity by ordering Trotsky to leave the country, an order that could not be carried out for more than a year because no country would accept him. Norway finally granted him a visa in mid-1935 after the Norwegian Labor Party took over the government.

The Kremlin was even more active than the imperialists in efforts to prevent the formation of the Fourth International. Thousands of Oppositionists in the Soviet Union were victimized, jailed, and sent to concentration camps. A reign of terror was directed against anyone suspected of dissenting, including staunch anti-"Trotskyists" and finally Stalinists too.

The climax came in the Moscow trials which startled the world: the trial in August 1936 of Zinoviev, Kamenev, and fourteen other defendants; the trial in January 1937 of Pyatakov, Radek, and fifteen others; and the trial in March 1938 of Bukharin, Rykov, Rakovsky, and eighteen others. The defendants were accused of plotting to overthrow the Soviet government, in collaboration with the fascist powers, in order to restore capitalism in Russia—and they confessed to this and other crimes. In addition, they all testified that they had done this on the orders of Trotsky.

The principal defendants were almost all executed immediately along with countless others who refused to "confess." Stalin was determined to eliminate all those identified with the Bolshevik tradition who might serve as a reminder of the past or a symbol for opposition in the future. And, he hoped, he would totally and permanently discredit and isolate Trotsky and the projected Fourth International.

Trotsky, the chief defendant although in absentia, began to answer the charges and expose the frame-ups in August 1936, at the start of the first trial. But after a few days the Norwegian government, responding to pressure from the Kremlin, effectively silenced him for four months by interning him and denying him the right to speak to or write for the press. At the end of the year Trotsky was hastily shipped off to Mexico, whose government had just granted him asylum.

Here, in January 1937, he began an untiring campaign to refute the charges against himself and the other victims and to explain to the puzzled world the mechanism of the frame-ups and their political motivation. His position was confirmed by all later revelations, including those by Khrushchev at the Twentieth Congress of the Soviet Communist Party in 1956.

The Moscow trials produced great concern and turmoil among radicals and intellectuals in the United States. An American Committee for the Defense of Leon Trotsky organized a mass meeting at the Hippodrome in New York City on February 9, 1937, and Trotsky was invited to speak there. The Roosevelt administration refused to let Trotsky cross the border from Mexico, so arrangements were made for him to address the meeting by telephone. Audible wire connections were not completed, however, and the audience of 6,600 listened instead to a reading of the speech from the manuscript that had been sent from Mexico for advance distribution to the press.

Trotsky, asking for the establishment of an impartial commission of inquiry into the Moscow trials, pledged to abide by its findings — even to surrender to the GPU — if found guilty on any point.

This text of "I Stake My Life!" is from Pioneer Publishers' 1937 pamphlet of the same title.

My first word is one of apology for my impossible English. My second word is one of thanks to the committee which has made it possible for me to address your meeting. The theme of my address is the Moscow trials. I do not intend for an instant to overstep the limits of this theme, which even in itself is much too vast. I will appeal not to the passions, not to your nerves, but to reason. I do not doubt that *reason* will be found on the side of *truth.*

The Zinoviev-Kamenev trial has provoked in public opinion, terror, agitation, indignation, distrust, or at least, perplexity. The trial of Pyatakov[1]-Radek has once more enhanced these sentiments. Such is the incontestable fact. A doubt of justice signifies, in this case, a suspicion of frame-up. Can one find a more humiliating suspicion against a government which appears under the banner of socialism? Where do the interests of the Soviet government itself lie? In dispelling these suspicions. What is the duty of the true friends of the Soviet Union? To say firmly to the Soviet government: it is necessary at all costs to dispel the distrust of the Western world for Soviet justice.

To answer to this demand: "We have our justice, the rest does not concern us much," is to occupy oneself, not with the socialist enlightenment of the masses, but with the policies of inflated prestige, in the style of Hitler or Mussolini.[2]

Even the "friends of the USSR," who are convinced in their own hearts of the justice of the Moscow trials (and how many are there? What a pity that one cannot take a census of consciences!), even these unshakeable friends of the bureaucracy are duty-bound to demand with us the creation of an authorized commission of inquiry. The Moscow authorities must present to such a commission all the necessary testimonies. There can evidently be no lack of them, since it was on the basis of those given that 49 persons were shot in the "Kirov" trials,[3] without counting the 150 who were shot without trial.

Let us recall that by way of guarantees for the justice of the Moscow verdicts before world public opinion, two lawyers present themselves: Pritt from London and Rosenmark from Paris, not to mention the American journalist Duranty.[4] But who gives guarantee for these guarantees? The two lawyers Pritt and Rosenmark acknowledge gratefully that the Soviet government placed at their disposal all the necessary explanations. Let us add that the "king's counsellor" Pritt was invited to Moscow at a fortunate time, since the date of the trial was carefully concealed from the entire world until the last moment. The Soviet government did not thus count on humiliating the dignity of its justice by having recourse behind the scenes to the assistance of foreign lawyers and journalists. But when the Socialist and Trade Union Internationals demanded the opportunity to send their lawyers to Moscow, they were treated — no more and no less — as defenders of assassins and of the Gestapo! You know, of course, that I am not a partisan of the Second International or of the Trade Union International. But is it not clear that their moral authority is incom-

parably above the authority of lawyers with supple spines?
Have we not the right to say: the Moscow government forgets
its "prestige" before authorities and experts, whose approba-
tion is assured to them in advance; it is cheerfully willing to
make the "king's counsellor" Pritt a counsellor of the GPU.
But, on the other hand, it has up to now brutally rejected
every examination which would carry with it guarantees of
objectivity and impartiality. Such is the incontestable and deadly fact! Perhaps, however, this conclusion is inaccurate? There
is nothing easier than to refute it: let the Moscow government
present to an international commission of inquiry serious,
precise, and concrete explanations regarding all the obscure
spots of the Kirov trials. And apart from these obscure spots
there is — alas! — nothing! That is precisely why Moscow resorts
to all kinds of measures to force me, the principal accused, to
keep my silence. Under Moscow's terrible economic pressure
the Norwegian government placed me under lock and key.
What good fortune that the magnanimous hospitality of Mexico permitted myself and my wife to meet the new trial, not
under imprisonment, but in freedom! But all the wheels to
force me once more into silence have again been set into motion. Why does Moscow so fear the voice of a single man?
Only because I know the truth, the whole truth. Only because
I have nothing to hide. Only because I am ready to appear
before a public and impartial commission of inquiry with documents, facts, and testimonies in my hands, and to disclose
the truth to the very end. *I declare: if this commission decides
that I am guilty in the slightest degree of the crimes which
Stalin imputes to me, I pledge in advance to place myself
voluntarily in the hands of the executioners of the GPU.* That,
I hope, is clear. Have you all heard? I make this declaration
before the entire world. I ask the press to publish my words
in the farthest corners of our planet. But if the commission
establishes — do you hear me? — that the Moscow trials are a
conscious and premeditated frame-up, constructed with the
bones and nerves of human beings, I will not ask my accusers
to place themselves voluntarily before a firing squad. No, the
eternal disgrace in the memory of human generations will be
sufficient for them! Do the accusers of the Kremlin hear me?
I throw my defiance in their faces. And I await their reply!

Through this declaration I reply in passing to the frequent
objections of superficial skeptics: "Why must we believe Trotsky
and not Stalin?" It is absurd to busy one's self with psychological divinations. It is not a question of personal confidence.

It is a question of *verification!* I propose a verification! I demand the verification!

Listeners and friends! Today you expect from me neither a refutation of the "proofs," which do not exist in this affair, nor a detailed analysis of the "confessions," those *unnatural,* artificial, inhuman monologues which carry in themselves their own refutation. I would need more time than the prosecutor for a concrete analysis of the trials, because it is more difficult to disentangle than to entangle. This work I will accomplish in the press and before the future commission. My task today is to unmask the *fundamental, original* viciousness of the Moscow trials, to show the motive forces of the frame-up, its true political aims, the psychology of its participants and of its victims.

The trial of Zinoviev-Kamenev was concentrated upon "terrorism." The trial of Pyatakov-Radek placed in the center of the stage, no longer terror, but the alliance of the Trotskyists with Germany and Japan for the preparation of war, the dismemberment of the USSR, the sabotage of industry, and the extermination of workers. How to explain this crying discrepancy? For, after the execution of the sixteen we were told that the depositions of Zinoviev, Kamenev, and the others were voluntary, sincere, and corresponded to the facts. Moreover, Zinoviev and Kamenev demanded the death penalty for themselves! Why then did they not say a word about the most important thing: the alliance of the Trotskyists with Germany and Japan and the plot to dismember the USSR? Could they have forgotten such "details" of the plot? Could they themselves, the leaders of the so-called *center,* not have known what was known by the accused in the last trial, people of a secondary category? The enigma is easily explained: the new amalgam [5] was constructed *after* the execution of the sixteen, during the course of the last five months, as an answer to unfavorable echoes in the world press.

The most feeble part of the trial of the sixteen is the accusation against Old Bolsheviks of an alliance with the secret police of Hitler, the Gestapo. Neither Zinoviev, nor Kamenev, nor Smirnov, nor in general any one of the accused with political names, confessed to this liaison; they stopped short before this extreme of self-abasement! It follows that I, through obscure, unknown intermediaries such as Olberg, Berman, Fritz David [6] and others, had entered into an alliance with the Gestapo for such grand purposes as the obtaining of a Honduran passport for Olberg. The whole thing was too foolish. No one wanted to believe it. The whole trial was discredited. It was

necessary to correct the gross error of the stage managers at
all costs. It was necessary to fill up the hole. Yagoda was replaced by Yezhov.[7] A new trial was placed on the order of
the day. Stalin decided to answer his critics in this way: "You
don't believe that Trotsky is capable of entering into alliance
with the Gestapo for the sake of an Olberg and a passport
from Honduras? Very well, I will show you that the purpose
of his alliance with Hitler was to provoke war and partition
out the world." However, for this second, more grandiose production, Stalin lacked the principal actors: he had shot them.
In the principal roles of the principal presentation he could
place only secondary actors! It is not superfluous to note that
Stalin attached much value to Pyatakov and Radek as col-
laborators. But he had no other people with well-known names,
who, if only because of their distant pasts, could pass as "Trotskyists." That is why fate descended sternly upon Radek and
Pyatakov. The version about my meetings with the rotten trash
of the Gestapo through unknown, occasional intermediaries
was dropped. The matter was suddenly raised to the heights
of the world stage! It was no longer a question of a Honduran
passport, but of the parcelling of the USSR and even the defeat of the United States of America. With the aid of a gigantic
elevator the plot ascends during a period of five months from
the dirty police dregs to the heights on which are decided the
destinies of nations. Zinoviev, Kamenev, Smirnov, Mrachkovsky went to their graves without knowing of these grandiose
schemes, alliances, and perspectives. Such is the *fundamental
falsehood* of the last amalgam!

In order to hide, even if only slightly, the glaring contradiction between the two trials, Pyatakov and Radek testified,
under the dictation of the GPU, that they had formed
a *"parallel"* center, in view of Trotsky's lack of confidence
in Zinoviev and Kamenev. It is difficult to imagine a more
stupid and deceitful explanation! I really did not have confidence in Zinoviev and Kamenev after their capitulation, and
I have had no connection with them since 1927. But I had
still less confidence in Radek and Pyatakov! Already in 1929
Radek delivered into the hands of the GPU the Oppositionist
Blumkin,[8] who was shot silently and without trial. Here is
what I wrote then in the Russian *Bulletin of the Opposition*
which appears abroad: "After having lost the last remnants
of his moral equilibrium, Radek does not stop at anything."
It is outrageous to be forced to cite such harsh statements about
the unfortunate victims of Stalin. But it would be criminal
to hide the truth out of sentimental considerations. . . . Radek

and Pyatakov themselves regarded Zinoviev and Kamenev as their superiors, and in this self-appreciation they were not mistaken. But more than that. At the time of the trial of the sixteen, the prosecutor named Smirnov as the "leader of the Trotskyites in the USSR." The accused Mrachkovsky, as a proof of his proximity to me, declared that I was accessible only through his intermediation, and the prosecutor in his turn emphasized this fact. How then was it possible that not only Zinoviev and Kamenev, but Smirnov, the "leader of the Trotskyists in the USSR," and Mrachkovsky as well, knew nothing of the plans about which I had instructed Radek, openly branded by me as a traitor? Such is the primary falsehood of the last trial. It appears by itself in broad daylight. We know its source. We see the strings off stage. We see the brutal hand which pulls them.

Radek and Pyatakov confessed to frightful crimes. But their crimes, from the point of view of the accused and not of the accusers, *do not make sense.* With the aid of terror, sabotage and alliance with the imperialists, they would have liked to reestablish capitalism in the Soviet Union. Why? Throughout their entire lives they struggled against capitalism. Perhaps they were guided by personal motives: the lust for power? the thirst for gain? Under any other regime Pyatakov and Radek could not hope to occupy higher positions than those which they occupied before their arrest. Perhaps they were so stupidly sacrificing themselves out of friendship for me? An absurd hypothesis! By their actions, speeches, and articles during the last eight years, Radek and Pyatakov demonstrated that they were my bitter enemies.

Terror? But is it possible that the Oppositionists, after all the revolutionary experience in Russia, could not have|foreseen that this would only serve as a pretext for the extermination of the best fighters? No, they knew that, they foresaw it, they stated it hundreds of times. No, terror was not necessary for us. On the other hand it was absolutely necessary for the ruling clique. On the fourth of March, 1929, eight years ago, I wrote: "Only one thing is left for Stalin: to attempt to draw a line of blood between the official party and the Opposition. He absolutely must *connect the Opposition with attempts at assassination, the preparation of armed insurrection, etc.*" Remember: Bonapartism [9] has never existed in history without police fabrication of plots!

The Opposition would have to be composed of cretins to think that an alliance with Hitler or the Mikado, [10] both of whom are doomed to defeat in the next war, that such an absurd, inconceivable, senseless alliance could yield to revolutionary Marxists anything but disgrace and ruin. On the other hand, such an alliance — of the Trotskyists with Hitler — was most necessary for Stalin. Voltaire says: "If God did not exist, it would be necessary to invent him." The GPU says: "If the alliance does not exist, it is necessary to fabricate it."

At the heart of the Moscow trials is an absurdity. According to the official version, the Trotskyists had been organizing the most monstrous plot since 1931. However, all of them, as if by command, spoke and wrote in one way but acted in another. In spite of the hundreds of persons implicated in the plot, over a period of five years, not a trace of it was revealed: no splits, no denunciations, no confiscated letters, until the hour of the general confessions arrived! Then a new miracle came to pass. People who had organized assassinations, prepared war, divided the Soviet Union, these hardened criminals suddenly confessed in August 1936 not under the pressure of proofs — no, because there were no proofs — but for certain mysterious reasons, which hypocritical psychologists declare are peculiar attributes of the "Russian soul." Just think: yesterday they carried out railroad-wrecking and poisoning of workers — by unseen order of Trotsky. Today they are Trotsky's accusers and heap upon him their pseudocrimes. Yesterday they dreamed only of killing Stalin. Today they all sing hymns of praise to him. What is it: a madhouse? No, the Messieurs Duranty tell us, it is not a madhouse, but the "Russian soul." You lie, gentlemen, about the Russian soul. You lie about the human soul in general.

The miracle consists not only in the simultaneity and the universality of the confessions. The miracle, above all, is that, according to the general confessions, the conspirators did something which was fatal precisely to their own political interests, but extremely useful to the leading clique. Once more the conspirators before the tribunal said just what the most servile agents of Stalin would have said. Normal people, following the dictates of their own will, would never have been able to conduct themselves as Zinoviev, Kamenev, Radek, Pyatakov, and the others did. Devotion to their ideas, political dignity, the simple instinct of self-preservation would force them to struggle for themselves, for their personalities, for their interests, for their lives. The only reasonable and fitting question is this: *Who led these people into a state in which all human reflexes are destroyed, and how did he do it?* There is a very simple principle in jurisprudence, which holds the key to many secrets: *id fecit cui prodest*; he who benefits by it, he is the guilty one. The entire conduct of the accused has been dictated from beginning to end, not by their own ideas and interests, but by the interests of the ruling clique. And the pseudoplot, and the confessions, the theatrical judgment and the entirely real executions, all were arranged by one and the same hand. Whose? Cui prodest? Who benefits? The hand of Stalin! The rest is deceit, falsehood, and idle babbling about the "Russian soul"! In the trials there did not figure fighters, nor conspirators, but puppets in the hands of the GPU. They play assigned roles. The aim of the disgraceful performance: to eliminate the whole Opposition, to poison the very source of critical thought, to definitively ensconce the totalitarian regime of Stalin.

We repeat: The accusation is a premeditated frame-up. This frame-up must inevitably appear in each of the defendant's confessions, if they are examined alongside the facts. The prosecutor Vyshinsky[11] knows this very well. That is why he did not address a single concrete question to the accused, which would have embarrassed them considerably. The names, documents, dates, places, means of transportation, circumstances of the meetings — around these decisive facts Vyshinsky has placed a cloak of shame, or to be more exact, a shameless cloak. Vyshinsky dealt with the accused, not in the language of the jurist, but in the conventional language of the past master of frame-up, in the jargon of the thief. The insinuating character of Vyshinsky's questions — along with the complete absence of material proofs — this represents the *second crushing evidence against Stalin.*

But I do not intend to limit myself to these negative proofs. Oh, no! Vyshinsky has not demonstrated and cannot demonstrate that the *subjective confessions* were genuine, that is to say, in harmony with the *objective facts.* I undertake a much more difficult task: to demonstrate that each one of the confessions is false, that is, contradicts reality. Of what do my proofs consist? I will give you a couple of examples. I would need at least an hour to lay before you the two principal episodes: the pseudotrip of the accused Holtzman[12] to see me in Copenhagen, to receive terrorist instructions, and the pseudovoyage of accused Pyatakov to see me in Oslo, to get instructions about the dismemberment of the Soviet Union. I have at my disposal a complete arsenal of proofs that Holtzman did not come to see me in Copenhagen, and that Pyatakov did not come to see me in Oslo. Now I mention only the simplest proofs, all that the limitations of time permit.

Unlike the other defendants, Holtzman indicated the date:

November 23-25, 1932 (the secret is simple: through the news-papers it was known when I arrived in Copenhagen) and the following concrete details: Holtzman came to visit me through my son, Leon Sedov,[13] with whom he, Holtzman, had met in the Hotel Bristol. Concerning the Hotel Bristol, Holtzman had a previous agreement with Sedov in Berlin. When he came to Copenhagen, Holtzman actually met Sedov in the lobby of this hotel. From there they both came to see me. At the time of Holtzman's rendezvous with me, Sedov, according to Holtzman's words, frequently walked in and out of the room. What vivid details. We sigh in relief: at last we have, not just confused confessions, but also something which looks like a fact. The sad part of it, however, dear listeners, is that my son was not in Copenhagen, neither in November 1932 nor at any other time in his life. I beg you to keep this well in mind! In November 1932, my son was in Berlin, that is, in Germany and not in Denmark, and made vain efforts to leave in order to meet me and his mother in Copenhagen: don't forget that the Weimar democracy[14] was already gasp-ing out its last breath, and the Berlin police were becoming stricter and stricter. All the circumstances of my son's pro-cedure regarding his departure are established by precise evi-dence. Our daily telephonic communications with my son from Copenhagen to Berlin can be established by the telephone office in Copenhagen. Dozens of witnesses, who at that time surrounded my wife and myself in Copenhagen, knew that we awaited our son impatiently, but in vain. At the same time, all of my son's friends in Berlin know that he attempted in vain to obtain a visa. Thanks precisely to these incessant ef-forts and obstacles, the fact that the meeting never materialized remains in the memories of dozens of people. They all live abroad and have already given their written depositions. Does that suffice? I should hope so! Pritt and Rosenmark, perhaps, say "No"? Because they are indulgent only with the GPU! Good: I will meet them halfway. I have still more immediate, still more direct, and still more indisputable proofs. Actually, our meeting with our son took place after we left Denmark, in France, en route to Turkey. That meeting was made pos-sible only thanks to the personal intervention of the French premier, at that time, M. Herriot.[15] In the French Ministry of Foreign Affairs my wife's telegram to Herriot, dated the first of December, has been preserved, as well as Herriot's telegraphic instruction to the French consulate in Berlin, on December 3, to give my son a visa immediately. For a time I feared that the agents of the GPU in Paris would seize those

documents. Fortunately they have not succeeded. The two telegrams were luckily found some weeks ago in the Ministry
of Foreign Affairs. Do you understand me clearly? I now have
copies of both telegrams at hand. I do not cite their texts,
numbers, and dates in order not to lose any time: I will give
them to the press tomorrow.* On my son's passport there
is a visa granted by the French consulate on December 3.
On the morning of the fourth my son left Berlin. On his passport there are seals received at the frontier on the same day.
The passport has been preserved in its entirety. Citizens of
New York, do you hear my voice from Mexico City? I want
you to hear every one of my words, despite my frightful English! Our meeting with our son took place in Paris, in the
Gare de Nord, in a second-class train, which took us from
Dunkerque, in the presence of dozens of friends who accompanied us and received us. I hope that is enough! Neither
the GPU nor Pritt can ignore it. They are gripped in an iron
vise. Holtzman could not see my son in Copenhagen because
my son was in Berlin. My son could not have gone in and
out during the course of the meeting. Who then will believe
the fact of the meeting itself? Who will place any credence in
the whole confession of Holtzman?

But that isn't all. According to Holtzman's words, his meeting with my son took place, as you have already heard, in
the hall of the Hotel Bristol. Magnificent. . . . But it so happens that the Hotel Bristol in Copenhagen was razed to its
very foundations in 1917! In 1932 this hotel existed only
as a fond memory. The hotel was rebuilt only in 1936, precisely during the days when Holtzman was making his un-

---

* The telegrams (originals in French) read as follows:
Copenhagen   PK120   38W I   23   50   Northern
Mr. E. Herriot, President of the Council, Paris:
Crossing France and desiring to meet my son Leon Sedov study-
ing Berlin I wish your kind intervention that he be permitted to
meet me while in transit best wishes

Natalia Sedova Trotsky

MINISTRY OF FOREIGN AFFAIRS
Paris, December 3, 1932
To the French Consul, Berlin:
Mme. Trotsky who is returning home from Denmark would be
glad if she could meet with her son, Leon Sedov, at present study-
ing in Berlin while passing through French territory.
I thus authorize you to vise the passport of Mr. Sedov for a five
day stay in France with the further assurance that he be allowed to
return to Germany at the expiration of this sojourn.

Diplomatic Service

fortunate declarations. The obliging Pritt presents us with the hypothesis of a probable "slip of the pen": the Russian stenographer, you see, must have heard the word Bristol incorrectly, and moreover, none of the reporting journalists and editors corrected the error. Good! But how about my son? Also a stenographer's slip of the pen? There Pritt, following Vyshinsky, maintains an eloquent silence. In reality the GPU, through its agents in Berlin, knew of my son's efforts and assumed that he met me in Copenhagen. There is the source of the "slip of the pen"! Holtzman apparently knew the Hotel Bristol through memories of his emigration long ago, and that is why he named it. From that flows the second "slip of the pen"! Two slips combine to make a catastrophe: of Holtzman's confessions there remains only a cloud of coal dust, as of the Hotel Bristol at the moment of its destruction. And meanwhile—don't forget this!—this is the most important confession in the trial of the sixteen: of all the old revolutionaries, only Holtzman had met with me and received terrorist instructions!

Let us pass to the second episode. Pyatakov came to see me by airplane from Berlin to Oslo in the middle of December 1935. Of the thirteen precise questions which I addressed to the Moscow tribunal while Pyatakov was yet alive, not a single one was answered. Each one of these questions destroys Pyatakov's mythical voyage. Meanwhile my Norwegian host, Konrad Knudsen, a parliamentary deputy, and my former secretary, Erwin Wolf,[16] have already stated in the press that I had no Russian visitor in December 1935, and that I made no journeys without them. Don't these depositions satisfy you? Here is another one: the authorities of the Oslo aerodrome have officially established, on the basis of these records, that during the course of December 1935, not a single foreign airplane landed at their airport! Perhaps a slip of the pen has also crept into the records of the aerodrome? Master Pritt, enough of your slips of the pen, kindly invent something more intelligent! But your imagination will avail you nothing here: I have at my disposal dozens of direct and indirect testimonies which expose the depositions of the unfortunate Pyatakov, who was forced by the GPU to fly to see me in an imaginary airplane, just as the Holy Inquisition forced witches to go to their rendezvous with the devil on a broomstick. The technique has changed, but the essence is the same.

In the Hippodrome there are undoubtedly competent jurists. I beg them to direct their attention to the fact that neither Holtz-

man nor Pyatakov gave the slightest indication of my address, that is to say, of the time and the meeting place. Neither
one nor the other told of the precise passport or the precise
name under which he traveled abroad. The prosecutor did not
even question them about their passports. The reason is clear:
their names would not be found in the lists of travelers abroad.
Pyatakov could not have avoided sleeping over in Norway,
because the December days are very short. However, he did
not name any hotel. The prosecutor did not even question
him about the hotel. Why? Because the ghost of the Hotel
Bristol hovers over Vyshinsky's head! The prosecutor is not
a prosecutor, but Pyatakov's inquisitor and inspirer, just as
Pyatakov is only the unfortunate victim of the GPU.

I could now present an enormous amount of testimony and
documents which would demolish at their very foundations
the confessions of a whole series of defendants: Smirnov, Mrachkovsky, Dreitzer, [17] Radek, Vladimir Romm, Olberg, in short,
of all those who tried in the slightest degree to give facts, circumstances of time and place. Such a job, however, can be
done successfully only before a commission of inquiry, with
the participation of jurists having the necessary time for a
detailed examination of documents and for hearing the depositions of witnesses.

But already what has been said by me permits, I hope, a
forecast of the future development of the investigation. On
the one hand, an accusation which is fantastic to its very core;
the entire old generation of Bolsheviks is accused of an abom-
inable treason, devoid of sense or purpose. To establish this
accusation the prosecutor does not have at his command any
material proofs, in spite of the thousands and thousands of
arrests and searchings. *The complete absence of evidence is
the most terrible evidence against Stalin!* The executions are
based exclusively on forced confessions. And when facts
are mentioned in these confessions, they crumble to dust at
the first contact with critical examination.

The GPU is not only guilty of frame-up. It is guilty of con-
cocting a rotten, gross, foolish frame-up. Impunity is deprav-
ing. The absence of control paralyzes criticism. The falsifiers
carry out their work no matter how. They rely on the sum-
total effect of confessions and . . . executions. If one carefully
compares the fantastic nature of the accusation in its entirety
with the manifest falsehood of the factual depositions, what
is left of all these monotonous confessions? The suffocating
odor of the inquisitorial tribunal, and nothing more!

But there is another kind of evidence which seems to me

no less important. In the year of my deportation and the eight years of my emigration I wrote to close and distant friends about two thousand letters, dedicated to the most vital questions of current politics. The letters received by me and the copies of my replies exist. Thanks to their continuity, these letters reveal, above all, the profound contradictions, anachronisms, and direct absurdities of the accusation, not only insofar as myself and my son are concerned, but also as regards the other accused. However, the importance of these letters extends beyond that fact. All of my theoretical and political activity during these years is reflected without a gap in these letters. The letters supplement my books and articles. The examination of my correspondence, it seems to me, is of decisive importance for the characterization of the political and moral personality—not only of myself, but also of my correspondents. Vyshinsky has not been able to present a single letter to the tribunal. I will present to the commission or to a tribunal thousands of letters, addressed, moreover, to the people who are closest to me and from whom I had nothing to hide, particularly to my son, Leon. This correspondence alone by its internal force of conviction nips the Stalinist amalgam in the bud. The prosecutor with his subterfuges and his insults and the accused with their confessional monologues are left suspended in thin air. Such is the significance of my correspondence. Such is the content of my archives. I do not ask anybody's confidence. I make an appeal to reason, to logic, to criticism. I present facts and documents. I demand a verification!

Among you, dear listeners, there must be not a few people who freely say: "The confessions of the accused are false, that is clear; but how was Stalin able to obtain such confessions; therein lies the secret!" In reality the secret is not so profound. The Inquisition, with a much more simple technique, extorted all sorts of confessions from its victims. That is why the democratic penal law renounced the methods of the Middle Ages, because they led not to the establishment of the truth, but to a simple confirmation of the accusations dictated by the inquiring judge. The GPU trials have a thoroughly inquisitorial character: that is the simple secret of the confessions!

The whole political atmosphere of the Soviet Union is impregnated with the spirit of the Inquisition. Have you read Andre Gide's[18] little book, *Return from the USSR?* Gide is a friend of the Soviet Union, but not a lackey of the bureaucracy. Moreover, this artist has eyes. A little episode in Gide's book is of incalculable aid in understanding the Moscow trials. At the end of his trip Gide wished to send a telegram to Stalin, but not having received the inquisitorial education, he referred to Stalin with the simple democratic word "you." They refused to accept the telegram! The representatives of authority explained to Gide: "When writing to Stalin one must say: 'leader of the workers' or 'chieftain of the people,' not the simple democratic word 'you.'" Gide tried to argue: "Isn't Stalin above such flattery?" It was no use. They still refused to accept his telegram without the Byzantine flattery. At the very end Gide declared: "I submit in this wearisome battle, but disclaim all responsibility. . . ." Thus a universally recognized writer and honored guest was worn out in a few minutes and forced to sign not the telegram which he himself wanted to send, but that which was dictated to him by petty inquisitors. Let him who has a particle of imagination picture to himself, not a well-known traveler but an unfortunate Soviet citizen, an Oppositionist, isolated and persecuted, a pariah, who is constrained to write, not telegrams of salutation to Stalin, but dozens and scores of confessions of his crimes. Perhaps in this world there are many heroes who are capable of bearing all kinds of tortures, physical or moral, which are inflicted on themselves, their wives, their children. I do not know. . . . My personal observations inform me that the capacities of the human nervous system are limited. Through the GPU Stalin can trap his victim in an abyss of black despair, humiliation, infamy, in such a manner that he takes upon himself the most monstrous crimes, with the prospect of imminent death or a feeble ray of hope for the future as the sole outcome. If, indeed, he does not contemplate suicide, which Tomsky preferred! Joffe earlier found the same way out, as well as two members of my military secretariat, Glazman and Boutov, Zinoviev's secretary, Bogdan, my daughter Zinaida,[19] and many dozens of others. Suicide or moral prostration: there is no other choice! But do not forget that in the prisons of the GPU even suicide is often an inaccessible luxury!

The Moscow trials do not dishonor the revolution, because they are the progeny of reaction. The Moscow trials do not dishonor the old generation of Bolsheviks; they only demonstrate that even Bolsheviks are made of flesh and blood, and that they do not resist endlessly when over their heads swings the pendulum of death. The Moscow trials dishonor the political regime which has conceived them: the regime of Bonapartism, without honor and without conscience! All of the executed died with curses on their lips for this regime.

Let him who wishes weep bitter tears because history moves ahead so perplexingly: two steps forward, one step back. But tears are of no avail. It is necessary, according to Spinoza's advice, not to laugh, not to weep, but to understand!

Who are the principal defendants? Old Bolsheviks, builders of the party, of the Soviet state, of the Red Army, of the Communist International. Who is the accuser against them? *Vyshinsky,* bourgeois lawyer, who called himself a Menshevik after the October Revolution and joined the Bolsheviks after their definitive victory. Who wrote the disgusting libels about the accused in *Pravda? Zaslavsky,* former pillar of a banking journal, whom Lenin treated in his articles only as a "rascal." The former editor of *Pravda,* Bukharin, is arrested. The pillar of *Pravda* is now *Koltzov,* bourgeois feuilletonist, who remained throughout the civil war in the camp of the Whites. *Sokolnikov,*[20] a participant in the October Revolution and the civil war, is condemned as a traitor. *Rakovsky* awaits accusation. Sokolnikov and Rakovsky were ambassadors to London. Their place is now occupied by *Maisky,* Right Menshevik, who during the civil war was a minister of the White government in Kolchak's[21] territory. *Troyanovsky,* Soviet ambassador to Washington, treats the Trotskyists as counterrevolutionaries. He himself during the first years of the October Revolution was a member of the Central Committee of the Mensheviks and joined the Bolsheviks only after they began to distribute attractive posts. Before becoming ambassador, Sokolnikov was people's commissar of finance. Who occupies that post today? *Grinko,* who in common with the White Guards struggled in the Committee of Welfare during 1917-18 against the Soviets. One of the best Soviet diplomatists was Joffe, first ambassador to Germany, who was forced to suicide by the persecutions. Who replaced him in Berlin? First the repented Oppositionist Krestinski, then *Khinchuk,* former Menshevik, a participant in the counterrevolutionary Committee of Welfare, and finally *Suritz,* who also went through 1917 on the other side of the barricades. I could prolong this list indefinitely.

These sweeping alterations in personnel, especially striking in the provinces, have profound social causes. What are they? It is time, my listeners, it is high time, to recognize, finally, that a new aristocracy has been formed in the Soviet Union. The October Revolution proceeded under the banner of equality. The bureaucracy is the embodiment of monstrous inequality. The revolution destroyed the nobility. The bureaucracy creates a new gentry. The revolution destroyed titles and decorations.

The new aristocracy produces marshals and generals. The new aristocracy absorbs an enormous part of the national income. Its position before the people is deceitful and false. Its leaders are forced to hide the reality, to deceive the masses, to cloak themselves, calling black white. The whole policy of the new aristocracy is a frame-up. The new constitution is nothing but a frame-up.

Fear of criticism is fear of the masses. The bureaucracy is afraid of the people. The lava of the revolution is not yet cold. The bureaucracy cannot crush the discontented and the critics by bloody repressions only because they demand a cutting down of privileges. That is why the false accusations against the Opposition are not occasional acts but a *system,* which flows from the present situation of the ruling caste.

Let us recall how the Thermidorians of the French Revolution acted toward the Jacobins. The historian Aulard writes: "The enemies did not satisfy themselves with the assassination of Robespierre[22] and his friends; they calumniated them, representing them in the eyes of France as royalists, as people who had sold out to foreign countries." Stalin has invented nothing. He has simply replaced royalists with fascists.

When the Stalinists call us "traitors," there is in that accusation not only hatred but also a certain sort of sincerity. They think that we betray the interests of the holy caste of generals and marshals, the only ones capable of "constructing socialism," but who in fact compromise the very idea of socialism. For our part, we consider the Stalinists as traitors to the interests of the Soviet masses and of the world proletariat. It is absurd to explain such a furious struggle by personal motives. It is a question not only of different programs, but also of different social interests, which clash in an increasingly hostile fashion.

"And what is your general diagnosis?" you will ask me. "What is your prognosis?" I said before: My speech is devoted only to the Moscow trials. The social diagnosis and prognosis form the content of my new book: *The Revolution Betrayed: What Is the Soviet Union and Where Is It Going?* But in two words I will tell you what I think.

The fundamental acquisitions of the October Revolution, the new forms of property which permit the development of the productive forces, are not yet destroyed, but they have already come into irreconcilable conflict with the political despotism. Socialism is impossible without the independent activity of the masses and the flourishing of the human personality. Stalinism tramples on both. An open revolutionary conflict between the people and the new despotism is inevitable. Stalin's regime is doomed. Will the capitalist counterrevolution or workers' democracy replace it? History has not yet decided this question. The decision depends also upon the activity of the world proletariat.

If we admit for a moment that fascism will triumph in Spain, and thereby also in France, the Soviet country, surrounded by a fascist ring, would be doomed to further degeneration, which must extend from the political superstructure to the economic foundations. In other words, the debacle of the European proletariat would probably signify the crushing of the Soviet Union.

If on the contrary the toiling masses of Spain overcome fascism, if the working class of France definitely chooses the path of its liberation, then the oppressed masses of the Soviet Union will straighten their backbones and raise their heads! Then will the last hour of Stalin's despotism strike. But the triumph of Soviet democracy will not occur by itself. It depends also upon you. The masses need your help. The first aid is to tell them the truth.

The question is: to aid the demoralized bureaucracy against the people, or the progressive forces of the people against the bureaucracy. The Moscow trials are a signal. Woe to them who do not heed! The Reichstag trial[23] surely had a great importance. But it concerned only vile fascism, this embodiment of all the vices of darkness and barbarism. The Moscow trials are perpetrated under the banner of socialism. We will not concede this banner to the masters of falsehood! If our generation happens to be too weak to establish socialism over the earth, we will hand the spotless banner down to our children. The struggle which is in the offing transcends by far the importance of individuals, factions, and parties. It is the struggle for the future of all mankind. It will be severe. It will be lengthy. Whoever seeks physical comfort and spiritual calm, let him step aside. In time of reaction it is more convenient to lean on the bureaucracy than on the truth. But all those for whom the word *socialism* is not a hollow sound but the content of their moral life—forward! Neither threats, nor persecutions, nor violations can stop us! Be it even over our bleaching bones, the truth will triumph! We will blaze the trail for it. It will conquer! Under all the severe blows of fate, I shall be happy, as in the best days of my youth, if together with you I can contribute to its victory! Because, my friends, the highest human happiness is not the exploitation of the present but the preparation of the future.

18

The Founding of the Fourth International

An impartial commission of inquiry, headed by the philosopher and educator John Dewey, was created soon after. It held thirteen hearings open to the press in Trotsky's home in Coyoacan, Mexico, in April 1937. Five months later, the commission concluded its deliberations with the verdict: Not guilty. (The full text of the commission's interrogation of Trotsky appears in the book, The Case of Leon Trotsky. *It contains one of Trotsky's greatest speeches, made at the close of the hearings. It is omitted here because it is over one hundred pages long and is available in that book.)*

Having done everything he could about the trials, Trotsky now returned to his work for the Fourth International, which he believed it was necessary to create as a distinct revolutionary party before World War II began. Early in 1938 his son and closest collaborator, Leon Sedov, was poisoned in Paris, and later that year his former secretary, Rudolf Klement, in charge of preparing the founding conference of the Fourth International, was found murdered in the Seine River, both undoubtedly victims of Stalin's secret police.

But the founding conference of the Fourth International was held in France in September 1938, five years after Trotsky had asserted the need for it. Twenty-one delegates from eleven countries participated in the conference. Trotsky could not attend but he wrote the main resolution adopted by the conference, "The Death Agony of Capitalism and the Tasks of the Fourth International," known also as the "Transitional Program," and actively engaged in the internal discussion that preceded it.

A month later, he presented his evaluation of the conference in a recording made on October 18 to be played at a New York mass meeting ten days later celebrating the founding of the Fourth International and the tenth anniversary of the American Trotskyist movement.

The text was first printed in Socialist Appeal, *November 5, 1938.*

I hope that this time my voice will reach you and that I will be permitted in this way to participate in your double celebration. Both events: the tenth anniversary of our American organization as well as the foundation congress of the Fourth International deserve the attention of the workers incomparably more than the warlike gestures of the totalitarian chiefs, the diplomatic intrigues, or the pacifist congresses.

Both events will enter history as important milestones. No one has now the right to doubt that.

It is necessary to remark that the birth of the American group of Bolshevik-Leninists, thanks to the courageous initiative of Comrades Cannon, Shachtman, and Abern,[1] didn't stand alone. It approximately coincided with the beginning of the systematic international work of the Left Opposition. It is true that the Left Opposition arose in Russia in 1923, but regular work on an international scale began with the Sixth Congress of the Comintern.

Without a personal meeting we reached an agreement with the American pioneers of the Fourth International, before all, on the criticism of the program of the Communist International. Then, in 1928, began that collective work which after ten years led to the elaboration of our own program recently adopted by our international conference. We have the right to say that the work of this decade was not only persistent and patient, but also honest. The Bolshevik-Leninists, the international pioneers, our comrades across the world, searched the way of the revolution as genuine Marxists, not in their feelings and wishes, but in the analysis of the objective march of events. Above all were we guided by the preoccupation not to deceive others nor ourselves. We searched seriously and honestly. And some important things were found by us. The events confirmed our analysis as well as our prognosis. Nobody can deny it. Now it is necessary that we remain true to ourselves and to our program. It is not easy to do so. The tasks are tremendous, the enemies — innumerable. We have the right to spend our time and our attention on the jubilee celebration only insofar as from the lessons of the past we can prepare ourselves for the future.

Dear friends, we are not a party as other parties. Our ambition is not only to have more members, more papers, more money in the treasury, more deputies. All that is necessary, but only as a means. Our aim is the full material and spiritual liberation of the toilers and exploited through the socialist revolution. Nobody will prepare it and nobody will guide it but ourselves. The old Internationals — the Second, the Third, that of Amsterdam, we will add to them also the London Bureau[2] — are rotten through and through.

The great events which rush upon mankind will not leave of these outlived organizations one stone upon another. Only the Fourth International looks with confidence at the future. It is the World Party of Socialist Revolution! There never was a greater task on the earth. Upon every one of us rests a tremendous historical responsibility.

Our party demands each of us, totally and completely. Let the philistines hunt their own individuality in empty space. For a revolutionary to give himself entirely to the party signifies finding himself.

Yes, our party takes each one of us wholly. But in return it gives to every one of us the highest happiness: the consciousness that one participates in the building of a better future, that one carries on his shoulders a particle of the fate of mankind, and that one's life will not have been lived in vain.

The fidelity to the cause of the toilers requires from us the highest devotion to our international party. The party, of course, can also be mistaken. By common effort we will correct its mistakes. In its ranks can penetrate unworthy elements. By common effort we will eliminate them. New thousands who will enter its ranks tomorrow will probably be deprived of necessary education. By common effort we will elevate their revolutionary level. But we will never forget that our party is now the greatest lever of history. Separated from this lever, everyone of us is nothing. With this lever in hand, we are all.

We aren't a party as other parties. It is not in vain that the imperialist reaction persecutes us madly, following furiously at our heels. The assassins at its services are the agents of the Moscow Bonapartistic clique. Our young International already knows many victims. In the Soviet Union they number by thousands. In Spain by dozens. In other countries by units. With gratitude and love we remember them all in these moments. Their spirits continue to fight in our ranks.

The hangmen think in their obtuseness and cynicism that it is possible to frighten us. They err! Under blows we become stronger. The bestial politics of Stalin are only politics of despair. It is possible to kill individual soldiers of our army, but not to frighten them. Friends, we will repeat again in this day of celebration . . . *it is not possible to frighten us.*

Ten years were necessary for the Kremlin clique in order to strangle the Bolshevik Party and to transform the first workers' state into a sinister caricature. Ten years were necessary for the Third International in order to stamp into the mire

their own program and to transform themselves into a stinking
cadaver. Ten years! Only ten years! Permit me to finish with
a prediction: During the next ten years the program of the
Fourth International will become the guide of millions and
these revolutionary millions will know how to storm earth and
heaven.

*Long live the Socialist Workers Party of the United States!
Long live the Fourth International!*

19

On the Eve of World War II

World War II came a year later. That Trotsky understood its character better than any other political figure in the world is demonstrated in the interview he gave to a group of American scholars (the Committee on Cultural Relations with Latin America, headed by Professor Hubert Herring) at his home on July 23, 1939. Here Trotsky predicted among other things the Stalin-Hitler pact that was to surprise the world a month later and the imminent emergence of the United States as "the most powerful imperialism and militarism in the world."

Trotsky spoke in English and the interview was taken down in shorthand by one of his secretaries, who later made a transcript that was presented to the group but not printed until September 8, 1969, in Intercontinental Press. *An editorial note accompanying the text of the interview explained: "The secretary evidently transcribed Trotsky's remarks without attempting to rectify his English, thus preserving some awkward choices in words and sentence structure. We have left these as they stand in the original, but have corrected some typographical errors in the copy that came into our possession. We have added a few clarifications, placing them within brackets."*

I welcome you, ladies and gentlemen, to our house, and I thank you very much for your visit, and I will try to answer your questions as well as I can. My English is as bad this year as it was a year ago. I promised Mr. Herring two years ago to improve my English on the condition that the people in Washington give me a visa for the United States, but it seems that they are not interested in my English.

**Trotsky at his desk
in Coyoacan, Mexico.**

Permit me to answer your questions sitting. There are eleven or twelve very important questions. They cover almost the whole world situation. It is not easy to answer them clearly, because they concern the activities of all the governments, and I don't believe that the governments themselves see very clearly what they want, especially at this time when we have a situation of a world impasse. The capitalistic system is in a state of impasse. From my side, I do not see any normal, legal, peaceful outcome from this impasse. The outcome can only be created by a tremendous historic explosion. Historic explosions are of two kinds—wars and revolutions. I believe we will have both. The programs of the present governments, the good ones as well as the bad ones—if we suppose that there are good governments also—the programs of different parties, pacifist programs and reformist programs, seem now, at least to a man who observes them from the side, as child's play on the sloping side of a volcano before an eruption. This is the general picture of the world today.

You created a World's Fair. I can judge it only from the outside for the same reason for which my English is so bad, but from what I have learned about the fair from the papers, it is a tremendous human creation from the point of view of the "World of Tomorrow." I believe this characterization is a bit one-sided. Only from a technical point of view can your World's Fair be named "World of Tomorrow," because if you wish to consider the real world of tomorrow we should see a hundred military airplanes over the World's Fair, with bombs, some hundreds of bombs, and the result of this activity would be the world of tomorrow. This grandiose human creative power from one side, and this terrible backwardness in the field which is the most important for us, the social field—technical genius, and, permit me the word, social idiocy—this is the world of today.

Question: How do you estimate the real military strength of Soviet Russia today?

Answer: The military strength of Soviet Russia, better to say the military status of Soviet Russia, is contradictory. On one side we have a population of 170 million awakened by the greatest revolution in history, with fresh energy, with great dynamics, with a more or less developed war industry. On the other side we have a political regime paralyzing all of the forces of the new society. What would be the balance of these contradictory forces I cannot foretell. I believe nobody can foretell, because there are moral factors which can be measured only by the events themselves. One thing I am sure: the political regime will not survive the war. The social regime, which is the nationalized property of production, is incomparably more powerful than the political regime, which has a despotic character. The new forms of property are of tremendous importance from the point of view of historic progress. The inner life of the Soviet Union, as the inner life of the army of the Soviet Union, is characterized by the contradictions between the political regime and the necessity for the development of the new society, economic, cultural, etc. Every social contradiction takes its sharpest form in the army, because the army is the armed power of society. The representatives of the political regime, or the bureaucracy, are afraid of the prospect of a war, because they know better than we that they will not survive a war as a regime.

Q: What was the real reason for the execution of Tukhachevsky and the generals?[1]

A: This question is connected with the first. The new society has its methods of social crystallization, or selection of different human beings for different functions. They have a new selection for the economics, a selection for the army and navy, a selection also for the power [administration], and these selections are very different. The bureaucracy became during the last ten years a tremendous brake on the Soviet society. It is a parasitic caste which is interested in their power, in their privileges, and in their incomes, and they subordinate all other questions today to their material interests as a caste. On the other side [hand], the creative functions of the society, economic, cultural, the army and navy—which is also in a certain sense a creative function—have their own selection of individuals, of inventors, of administrators, etc., and we see in every branch, in every section of social life, that one selection is directed against the other.

The army needs capable, honest men, just as the economists and scientists, independent men with open minds. Every man and woman with an independent mind comes into conflict with the bureaucracy, and the bureaucracy must decapitate the one section for [at the expense of] the other in order to preserve themselves. This is the obvious historical explanation of the dramatic Moscow trials, the famous frame-ups, etc. The American press is more interested for its side of the happenings [i.e., is more interested in certain aspects it can turn to account], but we can give them a more objective, scientific, social explanation. It was a clash between two kinds of selections in different strata of society. A man who is a good general, like Tukhachevsky, needs independent aides, other generals around him, and he appreciates every man according to his intrinsic value. The bureaucracy needs docile people, Byzantine people, slaves, and these two types come into conflict in every state. In view of the fact that the bureaucracy has in hand [holds] all of the power, it is the heads of the army that fall, and not the heads of the bureaucracy.

Q: How do you explain the dropping of Litvinov² as minister of foreign affairs?

A: On general lines it is explained by the considerations I developed some minutes ago. Personally Litvinov was a capable man — is a capable man. He is not an independent political figure; he never was. But he is intelligent; he knows several different languages; he has visited several different countries; he knows Europe very well. Because of his travels, his knowledge of different countries, he troubles and embarrasses the Politbureau [Political Bureau], which is the creation of Stalin. In the bureaucracy nobody knows foreign languages, nobody has lived in Europe, and nobody knows foreign politics. When Litvinov presented his views to the Politbureau they felt a bit unpleasant [annoyed]. This is one individual reason more for his being dropped, but I believe it was also a hint from the Kremlin to Hitler that we are ready to change our politics, to realize our objective, our aim, that we presented to you and Hitler some years ago, because the objective of Stalin in international politics is a settlement with Hitler.

We had a very interesting article by Krivitsky³ in the *Saturday Evening Post.* He observed these proceedings from a special point of view — his own. He was in the military espionage service, and he had very delicate missions from Moscow. What he says is very interesting as a confirmation of a general point of view which we expressed many times before this revelation. The Moscow bureaucracy do not wish war. They are afraid of a war because they will not survive. They wish peace at any price. The country which is now threatening the Soviet Union is Germany, and her allies, Italy and Japan. An agreement with Hitler signifies no war. An alliance with Chamberlain⁴ signifies military help during the war, but no more, because the hopes that an alliance between England, France, and the Soviet Union would avoid a war are childish. You remember that Europe was divided in two camps before the Great War, and those two camps produced the war. Then Woodrow Wilson proposed the League of Nations,⁵ with the argument that only collective security can avoid wars. Now after the collapse of the League of Nations they begin to say that the division of Europe in two camps, by the creation of an alliance between England, France, and Russia, will avoid a war. It is childish. It can signify only mutual help during the war. It is a repetition of the whole experience of twenty-five years ago on a new historic scale. It is better to have an alliance if war is inevitable, but the Kremlin wishes to avoid the war. It can be reached only by an agreement with Hitler. The whole policy of the Kremlin is directed to an agreement with Hitler. Stalin says that if you don't wish to come to an agreement with me, then I will be forced to conclude an agreement with England.

Q: What vitality has the stop-Hitler bloc? What course will Soviet Russia take in making an alliance with Britain and France? Do you consider it likely that Stalin may come to an understanding with Hitler?

A: It depends not from [on] Stalin, but from [on] Hitler. Stalin has proclaimed that he is ready to conclude an agreement with Hitler. Hitler until the last time [i. e., up to now] rejected his proposition. Possibly he will accept it. Hitler wishes to create for Germany a world-dominating position. The rational [rationalizing] formulas are only a mask, as for the French, British, and American empires democracy is only a mask. The real interest for Britain is India; for Germany, to seize India; for France, it is to not lose the colonies; for Italy, to seize new colonies. The colonies do not have democracy. If Great Britain, for example, fights for democracy, it would do well to start by giving India democracy. The very democratic English people do not give them democracy because they can exploit India only by dictatorial means. Germany wishes to crush France and Great Britain. Moscow is absolutely ready to give Hitler a free hand, because they know very well that if he is engaged in this destruction Russia will be free for years from attacks from Germany. I am sure they would furnish raw materials to Germany during the war under the condition that Russia stand aside. Stalin does not wish a military alliance with Hitler, but an agreement to remain neutral in the war. But Hitler is afraid the Soviet Union can become powerful enough to conquer, in one way or another, Rumania, Poland, and the Balkan states, during the time Germany would be engaged in a world war, and so approach directly the German frontier. That is why Hitler wished to have a preventive war with the Soviet Union, to crush the Soviet Union, and after that begin his war for world domination. Between these two possibilities, two variants, the Germans vacillate. What will be the final decision, I cannot foretell. I am not sure if Hitler himself knows today. Stalin does not know, because he hesitates and continues the discussions with Britain, and at the same time concludes economic and commercial agreements with Germany. He has, as the Germans say, two irons in the fire.

Q: How do you interpret the underlying purposes of the Chamberlain government?

A: I believe the underlying factors are panic and headlessness. It is not an individual characteristic of Mr. Chamberlain. I do not believe he has any worse head than any other person, but the situation of Great Britain is very difficult, the same as that of France. England was a leading world power in the past — in the nineteenth century — but no more. But she has the greatest world empire. France, with her stagnating population and more or less backward economic structure, has a second colonial empire. This is the situation. It is very difficult to be inventive as a British prime minister in this situation. Only the old formula of "wait and see." This was good when Great Britain was the strongest power in the world and they had enough power to reach their aims. No more now. The war can only crush and disrupt the British empire and the French empire. They can gain nothing by the war — only lose. That is why Mr. Chamberlain was so friendly to Hitler during the Munich period. 6 He believed that the question was about central Europe and the Danube, but now he understands that it is the question of world domination. Great Britain and France cannot avoid a war, and now they do everything they can in a feverish tempo to avoid the war threatened by the situation created by the rearmament of Germany. That war is inevitable.

Q: How do you analyze the movements in France? Is French nationalism strong enough to offset the unity of capitalistic interests between France and Germany?

A: I believe that every capitalistic government at the beginning of the war will have the tremendous majority of the people behind it. But I believe also that not one of the existing governments will have its own people behind it at the end of the war. This is why they are all afraid of the war which they cannot escape.

Q: Do you still believe that a socialist revolution in a single country is impossible without world participation?

A: I believe there is some misunderstanding in the formulation of this question. I never affirmed that a socialist revolution is impossible in a single country. We had a socialist revolution in the Soviet Union. I participated in it. The socialist revolution signifies the seizure of power by a revolutionary class, by the proletariat. Of course it cannot be accomplished

simultaneously in all countries. Some historic time is given for
every country by its conditions. A socialist revolution is not
only possible but inevitable in every country. What I affirm is
that it is impossible to construct a socialist society in the environment of a capitalistic world. It is a different question,
absolutely different.

*Q: Does not the great economic progress made by the Soviet
Union in the last five years demonstrate the practicability of
building a socialistic state in a capitalistic world?*

A: I would prefer to read it "of building a socialistic society,"
not a socialistic state, because the conquest of power signifies
the creation of the socialistic state. The socialistic state is only
instrumental for the creation of the socialistic society, because
the socialistic society signifies the abolition of the state as a
very barbaric instrument. Every state is a barbaric survival.
The question signifies if the economic progress during the last
five years does not prove the possibility of building a socialistic society in a capitalistic world.

Not in my mind, I do not believe, because the economic
progress is not identical with socialism. America, [the] United
States, had in its history more grandiose economic progress
on a capitalistic basis. Socialism signifies the progressive equality and the progressive abolition of the state. The state is an
instrument of submission. Equality involves abolition of the
state. During the five years, parallel with the indisputable economic progress, we had in the Soviet Union a terrible growth
of inequality, and a terrible reinforcement of the state. What
do the Moscow trials signify from the point of view of equality
and the abolition of the state? I doubt if there exists now any
man who believes there was justice in these trials. We had in
Moscow a purge, during the last few years, of a hundred
thousand people, the extermination of the old guard of the
Bolshevist party, generals, the best officers, the best diplomats,
etc. The state is not abolished. The state exists, and what is the
state? It is the subjugation of the populace to the state machine,
to the new power, the new caste, the new leader — the bureaucracy is a new privileged caste. It is not socialism and this
caste is not withering. They refuse to die. They prefer to kill
others. Even the best elements of the army, the instrument of
their own defense.

I do not say that there must be established immediately an
absolute equality. That is not possible. But the general tendency should be from the base bourgeois inequality towards
equality, but we now have an absolutely opposite tendency.
If you will establish statistical diagrams, it will prove that the

highest stratum of the Soviet society is living as [like] the highest bourgeoisie in America and Europe, the middle class as [like] the middle bourgeoisie, and the workers worse than in a large country such as the United States. From the economic point of view the revolution signifies for Russia a progress. Yes, it is absolutely indisputable. But it is not socialism. It is very far from socialism. It becomes now further and further from socialism.

Q: What is your analysis of the situation in Japan? Will Japan force Britain into a war in order to save her own face?

A: I do not believe that Britain will be surprised in a war with Japan, but Britain cannot avoid a war, and when the war begins Japan will of course use the European situation for her own purposes. Britain will have a war with Japan. It is not a question of saving face, but of saving lives.

Q: If Germany seizes Danzig, what will Chamberlain do? 7

A: If Germany seizes Danzig within the next month, it signifies that Germany wants a war, because Germany knows the situation. If Germany wishes war, a war there will be. If Germany feels she is strong enough, she will provoke a war, and Chamberlain will enter the war.

Q: What is your judgment as to the probable course of events in Spain?

A: I believe that the Spanish problem is only a small part of the European problem. Until the defeat it was a great problem. If the Spanish bourgeois republicans, with their Socialist allies, with their Communist allies, or with their Anarchist allies, did not succeed [had not succeeded] in stifling the Spanish revolution — because it was not the victory of Franco, it was the defeat of the People's Front — then they could hope that the victory of the Spanish proletariat could provoke a great revolutionary movement in France, and we observed the beginning of it in June, 1936, in the sit-down strikes in France, and in this condition Europe could avoid a war, but Moscow succeeded in killing the Spanish revolution and to help Franco in his victory. 8 It signifies now that Spain ceases to be an independent factor. Of course, in the Socialist press of Mr. Norman Thomas, and in the even less intelligent press of Mr. Browder, 9 you can find they observe that Franco will not dominate Spain, that he will fall down. It was almost the same as the victory of Hitler in June 1933. At that time, as now, I am [was] of the opposite opinion. The strength of Franco is not in Franco himself, but in the complete bankruptcies of the Second and Third Internationals, in the leadership of the Spanish revolution.

For the workers and peasants of Spain the defeat is not only a military accident, but it is a tremendous historic tragedy. It is the breakdown of their organizations, of their historic ideal, of their trade unions, of their happiness, all of their hopes that they have cultivated for decades, even for centuries. Can a reasonable human being imagine that this class, during one, two, or three years, can create new organizations, a new militant mind [spirit] and overcome, in this form, Franco? I do not believe it. Spain is now, more than all [other] countries, remote from revolution. Of course, if the war begins, and I am sure that it will begin, the tempo of the revolutionary movement would be accelerated in all countries. We will have a war. We had the experience in the last world war. Now all nations are poorer. The means of destruction are incomparably more effective. The old generation has the old experience in their blood. The new generation will learn from experience and from the older generation. I am sure that a consequence of a new war would be revolution, and in this case Spain would also be involved in the revolution, not on their own initiative, but on the initiative of others.

Q: What would be your advice to the United States as to its course in international affairs?

A: I must say that I do not feel competent to give advice to the Washington government because of the same political reason for which the Washington government finds it is not necessary to give me a visa. We are in a different social position from the Washington government. I could give advice to a government which had the same objectives as my own, not to a capitalistic government, and the government of the United States, in spite of the New Deal, 10 is, in my opinion, an imperialistic and capitalistic government. I can only say what a revolutionary government should do — a genuine workers' government in the United States. I believe the first thing would be to expropriate the Sixty Families. 11 It would be a very good measure, not only from the national point of view, but from the point of view of settling world affairs — it would be a good example to the other nations. To nationalize the banks; to give, by radical social measures, work to the ten or twelve millions unemployed; to give material aid to the farmers to facilitate free cultivation. I believe that it would signify the rise of the national income of the United States from $67 billions to $200 or $300 billions a year in the next years, because the following years we cannot foresee the tremendous rise of the material power of this powerful nation, and of course such a nation could be the genuine dictator of the world, but a very good one, and I am sure that in this case the fascist countries of Hitler and Mussolini, and all their poor and miserable people, would, in the last analysis, disappear from the historic scene if the United States, as the economic power, would find the political power to reorganize their present very sick economic structure.

I do not see any other outcome, any other solution. We have, during the last six or seven years, observed the New Deal politics. The New Deal provoked great hopes. I didn't share their hopes. I had, here in Mexico, a visit from some conservative senators, two years ago, and they asked me if we were still in favor of surgical revolutionary measures. I answered, I don't see any others but if the New Deal succeeds I am ready to abandon my revolutionary conception in favor of the New Deal conceptions. It did not succeed, and I dare to affirm that if Mr. Roosevelt [12] were elected for the third term the New Deal would not succeed in the third term. But this powerful economic body of the United States, the most powerful in the world, is in a state of decomposition. Nobody has indicated means how to stop this decomposition. A whole new structure must be made, and it cannot be realized as long as you have the Sixty Families. This is why I began with the advice to expropriate them.

Two years ago, when your Congress passed the neutrality laws, I had a discussion with some American politicians, and I expressed my astonishment about the fact that the most powerful nation in the world, with such creative power and technical genius, does not understand the world situation — that it is their wish to separate themselves from the world by a scrap of paper of the law of neutrality. If American capitalism survives, and it will survive for some time, we will have in the United States the most powerful imperialism and militarism in the world. We already see the beginning now. Of course, this armament is, as a fact, creating a new situation. Armaments are also an enterprise. To stop the armaments now without a war would cause the greatest social crisis in the world — ten millions of unemployed. The crisis would be enough to provoke a revolution, and the fear of this revolution is also a reason to continue the armaments, and the armaments become an independent factor of history. It is necessary to utilize them. Your ruling class had the slogan "Open Door to China," but what signifies it — only by battleships, in hope of preserving the freedom of the Pacific Ocean by a tremendous fleet. I don't see any other means of [defeating?] capitalistic Japan. Who is capable of doing this but the most powerful nation in the world? America will say we don't wish a German peace. Japan is supported by German arms. We do not wish an Italian, German, Japanese peace. We will impose our American peace because we are stronger. It signifies an explosion of American militarism and imperialism.

This is the dilemma, socialism or imperialism. Democracy does not answer this question. This is the advice I would give to the American government.

20

Testament

After the Moscow trials it was clear that Stalin would go to any lengths to have Trotsky killed. The Trotsky house in Coyoacan was guarded, but it was not impregnable. On May 24, 1940, a large band of men led by a well-known Mexican Stalinist, the artist David Alfaro Siqueiros, broke into the house and sprayed the bedrooms with machine-gun fire. Trotsky, Natalia, and their grandson escaped death by sheer luck; one of the guards, Robert Sheldon Harte of New York, was kidnaped and murdered. Precautions to strengthen security were taken, but the next killer used another method. Posing as a friend, a Stalinist agent calling himself "Frank Jacson" (Ramon Mercader) gained admittance to the house on August 20, 1940, and, as Trotsky sat reading an article the killer had asked him to look at, drove a pickax into his head. Trotsky died the next day.

Trotsky's testament, written February 27 and March 3, 1940, was not printed until 1958 when Harvard University Press published Trotsky's Diary in Exile, 1935, *in a translation by Elena Zarudnaya.*

My high (and still rising) blood pressure is deceiving those near me about my actual condition. I am active and able to work but the outcome is evidently near. These lines will be made public after my death.

I have no need to refute here once again the stupid and vile slander of Stalin and his agents: there is not a single spot on my revolutionary honor. I have never entered, either directly or indirectly, into any behind-the-scenes agreements or even negotiations with the enemies of the working class. Thousands of Stalin's opponents have fallen victims of similar false accusations. The new revolutionary generations will rehabilitate their political honor and deal with the Kremlin executioners according to their deserts.

I thank warmly the friends who remained loyal to me through the most difficult hours of my life. I do not name anyone in particular because I cannot name them all.

However, I consider myself justified in making an exception in the case of my companion, Natalia Ivanovna Sedova. In addition to the happiness of being a fighter for the cause of socialism, fate gave me the happiness of being her husband. During the almost forty years of our life together she remained an inexhaustible source of love, magnanimity, and tenderness. She underwent great sufferings, especially in the last period of our lives. But I find some comfort in the fact that she also knew days of happiness.

For forty-three years of my conscious life I have remained a revolutionist; for forty-two of them I have fought under the banner of Marxism. If I had to begin all over again I would of course try to avoid this or that mistake, but the main course of my life would remain unchanged. I shall die a proletarian revolutionist, a Marxist, a dialectical materialist, and, consequently, an irreconcilable atheist. My faith in the communist future of mankind is not less ardent, indeed it is firmer today, than it was in the days of my youth.

Natasha has just come up to the window from the courtyard and opened it wider so that the air may enter more freely into my room. I can see the bright green strip of grass beneath the wall, and the clear blue sky above the wall, and sunlight everywhere. Life is beautiful. Let the future generations cleanse it of all evil, oppression, and violence and enjoy it to the full.

L. Trotsky

February 27, 1940
Coyoacan.

All the possessions remaining after my death, all my literary rights (income from my books, articles, etc.) are to be placed at the disposal of my wife, Natalia Ivanovna Sedova. February 27, 1940. L. Trotsky.

In case we both die [*the rest of the page is blank*]

March 3, 1940

The nature of my illness (high and rising blood pressure) is such — as I understand it — that the end must come suddenly, most likely — again, this is my personal hypothesis — through a brain hemorrhage. This is the best possible end I can wish for. It is possible, however, that I am mistaken (I have no desire to read special books on this subject and the physicians naturally will not tell the truth). If the sclerosis should assume a protracted character and I should be threatened with a long-drawn-out invalidism (at present I feel, on the contrary, rather a surge of spiritual energy because of the high blood pressure, but this will not last long), then I reserve the right to determine for myself the time of my death. The "suicide" (if such a term is appropriate in this connection) will not in any respect be an expression of an outburst of despair or hopelessness. Natasha and I said more than once that one may arrive at such a physical condition that it would be better to cut short one's own life or, more correctly, the too slow process of dying. . . . But whatever may be the circumstances of my death I shall die with unshaken faith in the communist future. This faith in man and in his future gives me even now such power of resistance as cannot be given by any religion.

L. Tr

NOTES

CHAPTER 1

1. Constituent Assembly, to be elected by universal suffrage and establish constitutional government, was not convened until January 1918; by then, superseded by the Soviets, it was disbanded.

2. Okhrana, czarist secret police who hounded revolutionary movement.

3. January 9, 1905, "Bloody Sunday," day troops fired on mass protest march in St. Petersburg at czar's Winter Palace, marks start of 1905 revolution. **Commission of Senator Shidlovsky** was set up by czar to check into "unrest."

4. Union of Unions, combination of unions of professionals, in favor of imperial constitution.

5. Speransky, Russian minister of state in early part of 19th century. **Carbonari,** secret political association in Italy for a republic. **Articles 100 and 101** of czarist criminal code on which indictments were based.

6. Black Hundred gangs, extreme right-wing monarchists, chief organizers of pogroms against Jews and radicals.

7. Count Urusov, former deputy minister of internal affairs, revealed role of police in organizing pogroms.

CHAPTER 2

1. Principal contenders in World War I (1914-1918): Central Powers — Germany, Austria-Hungary, Turkey, Bulgaria vs. Allies — France, Russia, Great Britain, Italy, United States.

2. International Socialist congresses were held at Stuttgart, Germany, 1907; Copenhagen, Denmark, 1910; Basle, Switzerland, 1912.

3. International Socialist Bureau, executive committee of Second International, was established in 1900.

4. Signers of the manifesto: For the German delegation, Georg Ledebour, Adolf Hoffman; French delegation, A. Bourderon, A. Merrheim; Italian delegation, G. E. Modigliani, Constantino Lazzari; Russian delegation, N. Lenin, Paul Axelrod, M. Bobrov; Polish delegation, St. Lapinski, A. Warski, Cz. Hanecki; Inter-Balkan Socialist Federation, in the name of the Rumanian delegation, C. Rakovsky, in the name of the Bulgarian delegation, Wassil Kolarov; Swedish and Norwegian delegation, Z. Hoglund, Ture Nerman; Dutch delegation, H. Roland-Holst; Swiss delegation, Robert Grimm, Charles Naine.

CHAPTER 3

1. Petrograd, new name for St. Petersburg adopted August 2, 1914, day after declaration of war between Germany and Russia, because St. Petersburg was too Germanic. Petrograd was renamed Leningrad in 1924.

2. Russo-Japanese war, beginning in 1904, precipitated 1905 revolution; ended in summer of 1905.

3. Cossacks, Russian cavalry, given land consigned to special areas and other benefits in exchange for military service, formed privileged caste.

4. Raymond Poincare (1860-1934), president of France, 1913-20; prime minister, 1912, 1922-24, 1926-29.

5. Gregory Rasputin (1871-1916), illiterate Siberian monk with religious influence over czar and czarina, was killed by members of czar's court.

6. Nicholas II (1868-1918), czar from 1894 to 1917, was executed during civil war.

7. Octobrists, monarchist party of big commercial, industrial, landowning bourgeoisie, named for support of Manifesto of October 1905. **Liberals,** mainly from party of Constitutional Democrats (known as Cadets from initials of party's name), progressive landlords, middle bourgeoisie, intelligentsia. **Alexander Kerensky** (1882-1970), lawyer, late-joiner of Social Revolutionaries, was minister of justice in first Provisional Government, till May; prime minister, July-October.

8. Hohenzollerns, ruling dynasty in Germany; **Hapsburgs,** in Austria-Hungary. Both overthrown by defeat in war and revolution in 1918.

9. Progressive Bloc of the Duma, grouping of liberal and conservative factions, was formed in the Duma (Russian parliament) in 1915.

10. Paul Miliukov (1859-1943), professor of history, head of Cadets, minister of foreign affairs till May; outstanding bourgeois opponent of Bolsheviks.

11. Social-patriotic shadows, socialists who supported the war in name of patriotism.

12. Duma of June 3 refers to subservient character of dumas following coup of June 3, 1907, by Stolypin, prime minister, which disfranchised bulk of population and instituted terror against revolutionary parties.

13. Alexander Guchkov (1862-1936), Moscow capitalist, head of Octobrists, minister of war till May. **Romanov camarilla,** clique around czar who was of the Romanov dynasty.

14. Quotation from article in **Neue Rheinische Zeitung** (Dec. 15, 1848), newspaper of which Marx was editor, published in Cologne, Germany.

15. Michael Alexandrovich, brother of Nicholas II, appointed regent but abdicated.

CHAPTER 4

1. William II (1859-1941), king of Prussia and German emperor, 1888-1918; overthrown by revolution.

CHAPTER 5

1. Khrustalev-Nosar, nominal president of 1905 Petrograd (St. Petersburg) Soviet, had been arrested Nov. 22.

2. Alexander Konovalov, Moscow industrialist, Cadet minister in first coalition, vice president of last coalition government.

3. Mensheviks, faction of Russian Social Democratic Workers' Party opposing Bolshevik faction in 1903, became independent reformist party and opposed October Revolution and Soviet government. As other opposition parties, were permitted to function until 1921, when all were banned. Mensheviks remained in Second International as emigre group.

4. Berkenheim, leader of cooperatives. **Prokopovich,** minister in government.

CHAPTER 6

1. Smolny Institute, headquarters of Soviet, formerly school for daughters of nobility.

2. Alexei Kaledin (1861-1918), general, leader of Don Cossacks, later led counterrevolutionary armies. **Mikhail Karaulov,** capitalist minister.

3. Junkers, students in military officers' school.

4. Social Revolutionaries, peasant socialist party formed in 1901 as fusion of Populist tendencies, opposed October Revolution. **Left Social Revolutionaries** supported revolution, joined Soviet government in December 1917 but left in March 1918 in opposition to Brest-Litovsk treaty. Like Mensheviks, SRs continued as emigre group after ban on opposition parties in 1921.

5. Central Executive Committee, elected in June at First All-Russian Congress of Soviets, was predominantly right-wing.

6. Kerensky's attack was put down; he escaped, ending up in United States. The other ministers were soon released.

7. Nikolai Avksentiev (1878-1943), leading Right SR, minister of interior Aug.-Sept. **Alexandra Mikhailovna Kollontai** (1872-1952), popular Bolshevik agitator. Her first post in Soviet government was commissar of social welfare; later, was first woman in the world to serve as ambassador.

8. Feodor Dan (1871-1947), Menshevik member of Central Executive Committee. His close associate, **Mikhail Lieber** (1880-1937), Menshevik leader of Jewish Bund, also on CEC.

9. Mikhail Tereshchenko (1888-1959), financier, Cadet minister of foreign affairs.

CHAPTER 7

1. Party of Popular Liberty, name assumed by Constitutional Democrats.

2. General P. N. Krasnov (1896-1947) collaborated with Kerensky in attack on Petrograd; later, organized White Army in south Russia.

3. Judson, military attache of American embassy in favor of recognition of Soviets, soon was recalled to Washington. **Dukhonin,** chief of staff of army, was instructed by Allies to continue war.

4. George Chicherin (1872-1936), released from jail January 1918, returned to Russia; succeeded Trotsky as commissar of foreign affairs, 1918-1930. **Petrov** was a member of British Socialist Party.

CHAPTER 8

1. **Iraklii Tseretelli** (1882-1959), prominent Menshevik. **V. M. Chernov** (1876-1952), founder of Social Revolutionaries. Both were ministers in coalition government.

2. **Marshal Ferdinand Foch** (1851-1929), commander-in-chief of French, then of all Allied, forces in World War I.

3. **Dutov,** Cossack leader of counterrevolutionary forces in Urals.

4. **Brest-Litovsk treaty,** signed March 1918; annulled in 1919 after defeat of Germany.

5. **Philipp Scheidemann** (1865-1939), leading right-wing German Social Democrat; in October 1918 joined capitalist government that crushed German revolution. **Eduard David** (1863-1930), German Social Democrat in government with Scheidemann. **Julius Martov** (1872-1923), a founder of Russian Social Democracy, leader of Mensheviks in 1903; in 1917 was Left Menshevik; emigrated to Europe in 1920, founded publication of Mensheviks in exile.

CHAPTER 9

1. **August Bebel** (1840-1913), cofounder with Wilhelm Liebknecht of the German Social Democracy, most influential section of Second International; author of **Women and Socialism.**

2. In 1847 the Communist League asked Karl Marx (1818-1883) and Frederick Engels (1820-1895) to formulate a program. This was the origin of **Communist Manifesto.**

3. **Markin** and **Fyodor Raskolnikov** (1892-1939) were Bolshevik leaders of the sailors at Kronstadt during the revolution.

4. **Boris Savinkov** (1879-1925), Social Revolutionary terrorist, and **Lebedev,** an SR, were deputies for military and naval affairs in Kerensky government.

5. **Entente,** World War I alliance of European powers: France, Great Britain, Belgium, Italy, and, formerly, Russia.

6. **General Skoropadsky,** Cossack leader, German puppet head of Ukraine government until November 1918.

7. **Anton Denikin** (1872-1947), commander of a White army in south Russia. **General Mikhail Alexeyev** (1857-1918), czar's commander-in-chief till June 1917; founder of counterrevolutionary armies in south.

CHAPTER 10

1. Congresses of Communist Party were held annually until 15th, held at end of 1927 after two-year interval; subsequently held at longer intervals, 24th in 1971.

2. **War Communism,** policy of complete state control of production and distribution imposed to meet demands of civil war under conditions of scarcity and economic disruption. It led to conflict between peasants and workers' state, as produce was requisitioned or confiscated, and to decline in production. **New Economic Policy (NEP)** was adopted at 10th Congress (1921), on initiative of Lenin, to

relieve discontent of peasantry and to stimulate production. It permitted limited capitalist relations, free trade in agriculture, to some extent in industry. Key industries remained nationalized and intent was to develop socialist sector of economy as well.

3. Mussolini established fascist regime in Italy in 1922. French occupied the Ruhr, mining and industrial region in Germany, in 1923, which led to strikes and prerevolutionary situation in Germany.

4. Peter A. Stolypin (1862-1911), czarist prime minister, carried out reactionary coup in 1907 after defeat of 1905 revolution.

5. Communist International (Comintern, Third International), was founded in March 1919 under Lenin's leadership. It was dissolved in 1943 by Stalin.

6. Nikolai Skrypnik (1872-1933), Ukrainian Old Bolshevik, became fervent Stalinist; in 1933, in conflict with Stalin, committed suicide.

7. RSFSR, Russian Socialist Federal Soviet Republic, name adopted early 1918 at Third All-Russian Congress of Soviets for loose federation of Soviet Republics; end of 1922 the Union of Soviet Socialist Republics (USSR) was formed.

8. In Russian, new stage translates as novy etap (translator).

9. March events in Germany occurred in 1921. The German Communist Party led an insurrection which was crushed.

10. Glavkocracy, i. e. the rule of glavki, central administrative boards of separate industries (translator).

11. "Better Less, but Better" (written in February 1923 and after a month's delay published in **Pravda**) was the second article by Lenin criticizing the **Workers' and Peasants' Inspection,** a Soviet bureau established to check on functioning of state apparatus. It was headed by Stalin until 1922 (when he became general secretary of the Communist Party) and it was understood that Lenin's criticism of "bureaucracy not only in our Soviet institutions, but in our party institutions" was aimed at Stalin.

12. Workers' Truth group was one of a number of groupings of semisyndicalist and ultraleft character.

13. This article, titled "Civility and Politeness as a Necessary Lubricant in Daily Relationships," is included in Trotsky's **Problems of Everyday Life and Other Writings on Culture and Science.**

14. Nestor Makhno (1884-1934) opposed Whites and Germans in the Ukraine, then headed anarcho-kulak bandit movement against the Soviets in first half of 1919; was routed in spring 1921.

15. Smenovekhite, "Change of Landmarks" group of civil servants, were professionals who supported Soviet government in confidence that it was bound to develop into bourgeois-democratic regime (translator).

16. Kronstadt rebellion, involving sailors of naval base at Kronstadt, was forcibly suppressed by Soviet government. It was regarded as serious demonstration of discontent and hastened the introduction of NEP. Articles by Trotsky on meaning of Kronstadt and his role in its repression are in **Writings of Leon Trotsky (1937-38).**

17. Democratic Centralism group, characterized as semisyndicalist and ultraleft.

18. Lenin "sounded the alarm" on the national question in a series of angry notes he wrote (beginning Dec. 30, 1922) which were apparently circulated in leading bodies at the time but not published until 1956 in support of Khrushchev's attack on Stalin at 20th Congress. The notes were precipitated by Stalin's manipulations in Georgian Communist Party. Lenin condemned Stalin's actions as display of Great Russian chauvinism and violation of the rights of national minorities.

19. Christian Rakovsky (1873-1942?), prominent Bolshevik, president of Ukrainian Soviet, 1919-23; later, Soviet diplomat. Early leader of Left Opposition, was expelled from party in 1927; exiled to Siberia he remained in Opposition till 1934, then capitulated. Sentenced to 20 years' imprisonment in third Moscow trial, date of death uncertain.

20. S. Petlyura, leader of Ukrainian nationalist movement based on sections of peasantry and town petty bourgeoisie which forcibly opposed Soviet power in the Ukraine during civil war (translator).

21. Peter the Great (1672-1725), czar, 1682-1725, associated with Westernization of Russia.

22. From the Russian version of the **International,** equivalent to "No saviors from on high deliver, No trust have we in prince or peer" (translator).

23. Ulyanov-Lenin, born Valdimir Ilyich Ulyanov (1870-1924), adopted pen name of Lenin on arrival in Germany after serving term in Siberia, 1893-1900.

24. Nikolai Muralov (1877-1937), Old Bolshevik, commander in civil war. Opposed Stalin, exiled 1927, executed after second Moscow trial.

25. Richard von Kuhlmann (1873-1948), German foreign secretary, headed German delegation at Brest-Litovsk. **Count Ottokar Czernin** (1872-1932), Austrian minister of foreign affairs at Brest-Litovsk.

CHAPTER 11

1. Bessarabia, formerly part of Russia, was seized by Rumania in 1918.

2. Second International (Socialist, Labor International), organized in 1889 as loose association of national parties uniting both revolutionary and reformist groups. It fell apart during World War I when its major sections supported their own imperialist governments but revived as reformist organization in 1923. It was preceded by First International (International Workingmen's Association), 1864-1876, under Marx's tutelage.

3. Little Entente, French-dominated alliance of Rumania, Czechoslovakia, Yugoslavia.

4. Georges Clemenceau (1841-1929) became premier of France and minister of war in 1917 after waging campaign against government for its irresolute war policy.

5. Gustav Stresemann (1878-1929), founder of German People's Party after World War I, chancellor and foreign minister in 1923.

6. James Ramsay MacDonald (1866-1937), prime minister of first British Labour government, Nov. 1923-Oct. 1924. He bolted Labour Party during second term as prime minister, 1929-31, to form "national unity" cabinet with Conservative Party, 1931-35.

7. Versailles treaty, World War I treaty signed June 1919, set up stringent retribution against Germany by victors.

8. Arthur Henderson (1863-1935), one-time secretary of British Labour Party and president of Second International.

9. David Lloyd George (1863-1945), British Liberal Party prime minister, 1916-1922.

10. Otto von Bismarck (1815-1898), leader of Prussian government from 1862, first chancellor of German empire, 1871-1890.

11. Noah Zhordania, head of Menshevik government in Georgia till 1921.

12. William Gladstone (1809-1898), leader of British Liberal Party, prime minister, 1868-74, 1880-85, 1886, 1892-94.

13. Stanley Baldwin (1867-1947), leader of British Conservative Party, prime minister, 1923, 1924-29, 1935-37.

14. The USSR was officially recognized by Germany, 1922; England and Italy, 1924; France, October 1924; United States, 1933.

15. Left Front, Radical Socialist (bourgeois party neither radical nor socialist) and Socialist coalition under Edouard Herriot.

16. Trotsky refers favorably to "influx of workers" into party but rapid increase in membership was used by Stalin faction to tighten its control. Trotsky wrote about this later in **The Revolution Betrayed.**

17. RKP, Rossiiskaia Kommunisticheskaia Partiia, Russian Communist Party (translator).

18. Kuomintang Party (People's Party), bourgeois-nationalist party which emerged in first Chinese revolution of 1911. It was admitted to the Comintern as a sympathizing party in 1926. Stalinist policy of complete subordination to Kuomintang was imposed on the Chinese Communist Party, resulting in defeat of second Chinese revolution, 1925-27.

19. Emancipation of Labor, first Russian Social Democratic group founded in 1883 by George Plekhanov (1856-1918).

20. Alexander III (1845-1894), czar of Russia, 1881-1894.

21. Peter Struve (1870-1944), leader of the "legal Marxists."

22. Sun Yat-sen (1866-1925), founder of the Kuomintang, headed Canton Nationalist government.

23. Karl Kautsky (1854-1938), after Engels, most respected figure in Second International until he abandoned internationalism during World War I, and opposed Russian Revolution.

CHAPTER 12

1. Trotsky regarded theses of Comintern's first four congresses as programmatic cornerstone of Left Opposition and Fourth International; documents listed are in **The First Five Years of the Communist International** by Leon Trotsky. Congresses were held annually (1919-22) until the Fifth. Sixth Congress was held in 1928; Trotsky's criticism of its draft program is contained in **The Third International After Lenin.**

2. Vyacheslav Molotov (1890-   ), Old Bolshevik, was supporter of Stalin from start to finish. Foreign minister, 1939-49, 1953-56. Was eliminated from leadership in 1957 by Khrushchev "de-Stalinization" program following Stalin's death (1953).

3. Anglo-Russian Trade-Union Unity Committee, made up of representatives of British Trades Union Congress **General Council** and Russian trade unions, was formed in May 1925. It served as a left cover for the British when a general strike was sold out in 1926.

The Left Opposition had demanded that the Russians bolt the committee, but they remained on it until the British members walked out in May 1927. **Albert Purcell** (1872-1935) and **George Hicks,** British members of General Council and Anglo-Russian Committee.

4. Amsterdam International, popular name for Social Democratic-dominated International Federation of Trade Unions (or Trade Union International), was revived in 1919 after its demise during World War I. Its headquarters were in Amsterdam.

5. Nikolai Bukharin (1888-1938), Old Bolshevik, headed right wing in bloc with Stalin. He succeeded Zinoviev as president of Comintern, 1926. Broke with Stalin in 1928 to lead the Right Opposition with Tomsky and Rykov. Expelled from the party in 1929, capitulated; executed after third Moscow trial.

6. Arthur Cook (1885-1931), secretary of British miners' federation, with Anglo-Russian Committee. **Mikhail Tomsky** (1886-1936), Old Bolshevik always in right wing of party; head of Soviet trade unions. Expelled in 1929, capitulated; committed suicide during first Moscow trial. **Benjamin,** biblical reference to Jacob's youngest son, the young favorite. **Chiang Kai-shek** (1887-   ), military leader of Kuomintang during 1925-27 revolution, hailed as revolutionary by Stalin regime up until moment he staged coup in April 1927 against Shanghai insurrection, perpetrating massacre of workers and Communists. **Wang Chin-wei** (1884-1944), leader of **Left Kuomintang** government at Wuhan which broke with Communists in July 1927 after coming to terms with Chiang. **Minority Movement,** left wing of British trade-union movement. **Feng Yu-hsiang** and **Tang Cheng-chih,** militarists who supported Left Kuomintang.

7. Kliment Voroshilov (1881-1969), early supporter of Stalin, replaced Trotsky as president of Revolutionary War Council and commissar of defense, 1925-40. President of USSR, 1953-60.

8. Eighth plenum (full and formal meeting of a committee) of the ECCI was held in May 1927.

9. Centrism, general term used by Trotsky for tendencies that oscillate between reformism and revolutionary socialism. Trotsky considered Stalinism a special type of centrism, "bureaucratic centrism," up until 1935. He then characterized Stalinism as crude opportunism and social patriotism on the international arena.

10. Karl Liebknecht (1971-1919), leader of the German Social Democrats who broke with their war policy and opposed World War I. He founded Spartakusbund with Rosa Luxemburg, leading November 1918 uprising with her. Both were assassinated in January 1919 by order of Social Democratic war minister Noske.

11. Gregory Zinoviev (1883-1936) and **Leon Kamenev** (1883-1936) were Old Bolsheviks, associates of Lenin. Zinoviev was first president of the Comintern. They were a political team, forming triumvirate with Stalin in power bloc against Trotsky which led the party following Lenin's illness and death until their break with Stalin in 1925. Despite their capitulation in 1928, and two successive times, both were victims of first Moscow trial.

12. Thermidorian road, historical analogy with period of reaction in French Revolution. The ninth of Thermidor was date radical Jacobins were overthrown by right wing. Here Trotsky speaks of Thermidor as capitalist restoration. He later revised his analogy, setting period of Thermidor as beginning in 1924. This is explained in essay "The Workers' State, Thermidor and Bonapartism," **Writings of Leon Trotsky (1934-35).**

CHAPTER 13

1. Emelyan Yaroslavsky (1878-1943), author of falsified Soviet history, fell out of favor when previous falsifications did not suit new Stalinist versions.

2. GPU, one of abbreviated names for Soviet political police department.

3. Wrangel officer, GPU agent sent into ranks of Left Opposition towards end of 1927, was said to be former officer in General Wrangel's counterrevolutionary army. GPU also claimed to find underground printing press, which was a mimeographing machine used to turn out **samizdat** Opposition material.

4. Ivar Smilga (1892-1938), **Karl Radek** (1885-1939), **Ivan Smirnov** (1881-1936), **Alexander Beloborodov** (1891-1938), **Sergei Mrachkovsky** (1883-1936); all victims of Moscow trials.

5. "Sealed train" carried Lenin and 29 other emigres from Switzerland through Germany to Russia in March 1917; Lenin negotiated conditions on how trip would be made.

6. Testament, letter of Dec. 25, 1922 and postscript of Jan. 4, 1923, written by Lenin shortly before last stroke leading to his death. Existence of this testament was officially denied until Khrushchev period. It is reproduced in Trotsky's **On the Suppressed Testament of Lenin.**

7. N. Ustrialov, Russian professor and economist who believed capitalism could be restored gradually and supported Stalin against Trotsky as step in this direction.

CHAPTER 14

1. First Five-Year Plan for industrialization and collectivization of agriculture, covering period 1928-32, was adopted after expulsion of Left Opposition, the first advocates of planning. Trotsky's analysis of bureaucratic and excessive manner in which plan was carried out, and effects thereof, is contained in **The Revolution Betrayed.** A worldwide economic crisis of capitalism was in its second year at time of interview.

2. Oliver Locker-Lampson and **Godfrey Locker-Lampson,** brothers, were British politicians. **Hamilton Fish** (1888-   ), Republican member of U. S. House of Representatives, extremely anti-Soviet, opposed U. S. recognition of USSR.

3. Alexis Rykov (1881-1938), president of Council of People's Commissars after Lenin's death; joined with Bukharin and Tomsky in right bloc. Executed after third Moscow trial.

4. Theodore Roosevelt (1858-1919), Republican, 26th president, 1901-09.

5. Herbert Hoover (1874-1964), Republican, 31st president, 1929-33.

6. Quotation from article contained in **The Third International After Lenin;** Pathfinder Press 1970 edition, p. 9.

7. Leonid Krassin (1870-1926), people's commissar for foreign trade, 1922-24.

8. Woodrow Wilson (1865-1924), Democrat, 28th president of U. S., 1913-21. Issued his **Fourteen Points** as basis for peace settlement in January 1918 t.ɔ meet propaganda of Bolsheviks who were conducting peace negotiations with Germany at Brest-Litovsk.

9. Lord George Curzon (1859-1925), British Conservative Party leader, succeeded Churchill as foreign minister, 1919-24.

10. Fabians, adherents of the Fabian Society organized in England, 1884, to spread socialistic principles gradually. Quotation is from **Europe and America;** Pathfinder Press 1971, p. 25.

CHAPTER 15

1. Wilhelm Liebknecht (1826-1900), founder with Bebel of the German Social Democracy; member of Reichstag, 1867-70, 1874-1900.

2. Doctor Stockmann, protagonist in Henrik Ibsen's play **Enemy of the People.**

3. Karl von Clausewitz (1780-1831), Prussian army officer, military theoretician best remembered for books on science of war.

4. One **dessiatine** equals 2.7 acres.

5. Passages from "Results and Prospects," essay. first published in 1906; reprinted in **The Permanent Revolution,** Pathfinder Press 1970 edition, p. 63, p. 71, p. 75, p. 102.

6. Napoleon Bonaparte I (1769-1821) seized power in coup d'etat in 1804 ending First Republic of France, proclaiming French empire and himself emperor. Overthrown, 1815.

7. Alexander Ilyich Ulyanov (1868-1887) volunteered to shoulder entire blame in assassination attempt. He told the judges: "There is no better way of dying than to lay down one's life for one's country. Such death does not fill honest and sincere men with any fear. I have had only one aim, to serve the unfortunate Russian people."

8. Jacobins, popular name for members of Society of the Friends of the Constitution who provided leadership of the French Revolution.

9. Webster's definition of **pogrom:** "An organized massacre of helpless people as originally of Jews in Russia." **Nagaika,** whip; **kolkhoz,** collective farm; **Gosplan,** State Planning Commission in charge of industrialization; **Piatiletka,** Five-Year Plan.

CHAPTER 17

1. Yuri Pyatakov (1890-1937) supported Left Opposition, 1923-28, was expelled from party, capitulated. Executed after second Moscow trial.

2. Adolf Hitler (1889-1945), head of National Socialist Party (Nazis), established fascist regime in Germany in 1933. Committed suicide with defeat in World War II. **Benito Mussolini** (1883-1945) organized Italian fascist movement in 1919 becoming dictator, 1922-43. Killed by Italian Partisans when attempting to flee Italy, 1945.

3. Sergei Kirov (1886-1934), Stalinist, member of Political Bureau, was assassinated in December 1934 as result of GPU bungling of a plot designed to implicate Trotsky. **Kirov trials,** preliminary to Moscow trials, were followed with terror against Trotskyists, Zinovievists, disgruntled Stalinists.

4. Walter Duranty (1884-1957), **New York Times** Moscow correspondent, denounced by Trotsky as apologist for Stalinism.

5. Amalgam, term used by Trotsky to designate Kremlin's practice of lumping together different, or opposing, political groups, accusing them of common crimes.

6. Valentine Olberg (1907-1936) joined Left Opposition in 1930, wanted to be Trotsky's secretary but was rejected as suspect, then expelled. **Konon Berman-Yurin** (1901-1936). **Fritz David** (1897-1936). All three were executed.

7. Henry Yagoda, head of GPU, 1934-36; after supervising first Moscow trial, was made a defendant in third and executed in 1938. **Nicholas Yezhov** replaced Yagoda as head of GPU, disappeared after third trial.

8. Jacob Blumkin (1899-1929), first Russian supporter of Left Opposition to visit Trotsky in exile, in 1929. Bringing back a letter to the Opposition from Trotsky, was betrayed to GPU and shot.

9. Bonapartism, term used to describe a dictatorship which rules in period of crisis, elevating itself to seeming independence of conflicting forces. Trotsky saw two types: bourgeois Bonapartism and Soviet Bonapartism. See "The Workers' State, Thermidor and Bonapartism," and "Bonapartism and Fascism" in **Writings of Leon Trotsky (1934-35).**

10. The Mikado, Japanese Emperor Hirohito who began reign 1926.

11. Andrei Vyshinsky (1883-1954), chief prosecutor of Moscow trials, succeeded Molotov as foreign minister, 1949-53.

12. Edouard Holtzman (1882-1936), around Left Opposition but not a member, was executed.

13. Leon Sedov (1906-1938) was active in Communist youth movement. He adhered to Left Opposition and accompanied parents in last exile as closest collaborator in fight; edited **Bulletin of the Opposition.** Lived in Germany, 1931-33, and, forced to leave, in Paris, 1933 until his death, under mysterious circumstances, attributed to the GPU.

14. Weimar was small town in Germany where German Republic was organized in 1919.

15. Edouard Herriot (1872-1957), leader of bourgeois Radical Socialist Party, premier of France, 1924-25 and in 1932.

16. Konrad Knudsen, member of the IWW (International Workers of the World, Wobblies) when in the U. S., returned to native Norway and was active in Labor Party. **Erwin Wolf,** Czech Trotskyist, was expelled from Norway when Trotsky was put under house arrest. He was killed by the GPU in the civil war in Spain.

17. Ephim Dreitzer (1894-1936), Left Oppositionist, member of Trotsky's volunteer bodyguard in 1927. Victim of first Moscow trial.

18. Andre Gide (1869-1951), French novelist, critic, and essayist, soon broke with Stalinism.

19. Adolf Joffe (1883-1927), veteran revolutionist, as supporter of Left Opposition was prevented from receiving medical treatment. **M. S. Glazman,** hounded because of adherence to Opposition, committed suicide 1924. **Gregory Boutov,** arrested for refusing to sign false charges against Trotsky, went on hunger strike and died in prison, 1928. **Zinaida Volkov,** Trotsky's oldest child, sick and prevented from returning to USSR, committed suicide in Germany in January 1933.

20. Gregory Sokolnikov (1888-1939), prominent Bolshevik agitator 1905 and 1917; not a member of Opposition but sentenced to prison in second Moscow trial.

21. Alexander Kolchak (1874-1920) commanded one of eastern counterrevolutionary fronts during civil war.

22. Maximilien Robespierre (1758-1794), leader of Left Jacobins and head of revolutionary government, 1793-94, was known as "the Incorruptible."

23. Reichstag trial of leading Communists, Ernst Torgler and Georgi Dimitrov, who were accused of setting fire to government building. The fire had been set by the Nazis in February 1933, shortly after Hitler became chancellor, and was pretext for crackdown on Communists and others.

CHAPTER 18

1. James P. Cannon (1890-   ), IWW organizer, leader of left wing in Socialist Party, founder of American Communist Party. He became a supporter of Trotsky and Left Opposition when a delegate to Comintern's Sixth Congress in Moscow in 1928. Expelled from the Communist Party, he led in formation of the Communist League of America (American Left Opposition) and the Socialist Workers Party and Fourth International. **Max Shachtman** (1903-   ), founder of CLA, SWP, and FI, editor of several books and pamphlets by Trotsky. After splitting from SWP in 1940 on question of defense of USSR, he organized the Workers Party, later retitled Independent Socialist League, which in 1958 he led into the SP. **Martin Abern** (1898-1949), founding member of American CP, and, later, the CLA, SWP, and FI. Along with Shachtman, split from the SWP and organized the WP.

2. London Bureau (or London-Amsterdam bloc), organized in 1932, loose association of centrist parties not affiliated to either Second or Third Internationals, but opposed to formation of Fourth International. Disintegrated during World War II.

CHAPTER 19

1. Mikhail Tukhachevsky (1893-1937), outstanding commander in civil war; he and group of Red Army generals were condemned in secret trial, June 1937, executed.

2. Maxim Litvinov (1876-1951), Old Bolshevik, people's commissar of foreign affairs, 1930-39; ambassador to U.S., 1941-43.

3. Walter Krivitsky (1899-1941), former chief of Soviet intelligence in Western Europe, wrote series of articles in **Saturday Evening Post** in April 1939.

4. Neville Chamberlain (1869-1940), British leader of Conservatives, prime minister in 1937; succeeded by Churchill coalition, 1940.

5. League of Nations was created by victors of World War I; called a "thieves' kitchen" by Lenin. The United States did not join up.

6. Munich was site of four-power conference of Britain, France, Italy, and Germany. The Munich pact of 1938 gave approval to German occupation of Czechoslovakia.

7. German army marched into Danzig, in north Poland, in September 1939, triggering World War II.

8. The Spanish revolution began in 1931 when monarchy was overthrown and Second Republic set up. In 1936 the People's Front (or Popular Front) assumed government. **Francisco Franco** (1892-   ) organized counterrevolutionary forces and civil war began in 1936, ending in 1939 when Franco captured Madrid and set up fascist regime. For Trotsky's analysis of the Popular Front and events in France and Spain, see **Whither France?** and **The Spanish Revolution, 1931-39.**

9. Norman Thomas (1884-1968), leader of American Socialist Party, its presidential candidate six times, 1928-48. **Earl Browder** (1891-   ) became general secretary of American Communist Party in 1930, its presidential candidate 1936, 1940; he was abruptly expelled from the CP in 1945.

10. New Deal, phrase from Roosevelt's presidential acceptance speech which became campaign slogan in 1932, and term subsequently ascribed to policies of his administrations.

11. Sixty Families, term originated by Ferdinand Lundberg, author of **America's Sixty Families** (1937), which lists sixty families who own bulk of wealth in U. S.

12. Franklin Delano Roosevelt (1882-1945), Democrat, 32nd president, 1932-45; reelected to fourth term in November 1944, was succeeded by Harry Truman.

INDEX

BOOKS AND PAMPHLETS BY LEON TROTSKY
PUBLISHED IN THE UNITED STATES
AND IN PRINT AS OF 1972

The Age of Permanent Revolution
The Case of Leon Trotsky
The Chinese Revolution: Problems and Perspectives
The Death Agony of Capitalism and the Tasks of the Fourth
    International
Europe and America
Fascism: What It Is and How to Fight It
The History of the Russian Revolution (3 volumes)
In Defense of Marxism
Lenin: Notes for a Biographer
Leon Trotsky Speaks
Literature and Revolution
Marxism in Our Time
Military Writings
My Life
1905
On Black Nationalism and Self-Determination
On Engels and Kautsky
On the Jewish Question
On the Labor Party in the U. S.
On Literature and Art
On the Paris Commune
On the Suppressed Testament of Lenin
On the Trade Unions
The Permanent Revolution/Results and Prospects
Problems of the Chinese Revolution
Problems of Civil War
The Revolution Betrayed
Stalin
The Stalin School of Falsification
Stalinism and Bolshevism
Stalin's Frame-up System and the Moscow Trials